MAVERICK MARKETER

MAVERICK MARKETER

Time to Get Creative

Bob Johnstone

Charleston, SC
www.PalmettoPublishing.com

Maverick Marketer

Cover Photo by Gerard Sheridan of
Doug & Jack Jorgensen's J/111 *Picosa* at the
2017 World Championship on San Francisco Bay

First Edition

Hardcover ISBN: 979-8-8229-0354-8
Paperback ISBN: 979-8-8229-0355-5
eBook ISBN: 979-8-8229-0356-2

Contents

Time to Get Creative

T he book's subtitle is a self-imposed call to action. It refers to those moments when we are called upon to focus energy and imagination to solve a problem or create a new product.

Those times can be triggered by personal, organizational, or market threats—or by frustration with the status quo.

A creative response to the 1990 luxury tax breathed new life into J/Boats Inc. Frustration with "state-of-the-art" powerboats led to the creation of MJM Yachts.

This is a story about those two companies; inventing *instant arepas,* the bread of Colombia; the path to becoming a Fortune 500 "Marketing Man of the Year"; and an entrepreneurial foray into "ecopsychology" with Naturescapes Inc.

Prologue

O f several reasons for this book, the time available to write was at the top of the list. I'm grateful to my son, Peter, who purchased MJM Yachts, LLC, in November 2019. For the first time in 17 years, I had another 14 hours, seven days a week, freed up for writing, making new friends, and other projects.

Others Insisted

Writing a story about my life was never high on my list. It took a nudge from Harry Rein, a former treasurer of the New York Yacht Club. He was the instigator. It took place on the MJM Yachts display at the 2015 Palm Beach International Boat Show; he urged, "Bob, you've got to tell your story."

A year later, at the 2016 Palm Beach show, I was still immersed in the business and hadn't done any writing. Harry didn't give up, insisting, "Bob, your story needs to be told. I'm not the only one who thinks so. Gary Jobson* and Jay Cross agree with me."

Those were persuasive seconds to the motion from respected sailing friends who are part of this story.

Several other factors convinced me to proceed.

* An asterisk identifies 40+ *inductees* in the National Sailing Hall of Fame (NSHOF).

^ A carat identifies 20+ *nominees* for induction in the National Sailing Hall of Fame.

A Love of Sailing

Sailors love stories about boats—and learning how specific boat designs were created. I've been blessed with a life involving a series of incredible situations involving boats. This would be an opportunity to share them.

Predestination? I filled up my first-grade notebooks with drawings of sailboats, each with an "RJ" on the mainsail.

I'd digested the initial five C. S. Forester Horatio Hornblower novels by age 11.

My young life revolved around the next sail. Starting at age 12, I'd go sailing alone for hours. I'd be at peace. It was me, God, and nature. I lived from summer to summer.

My drawings became more advanced by the time I was in high school. In mechanical drawing class, I drafted the design (shown) of a 52-foot yawl—most likely inspired by similar drawings in *Yachting Magazine*.

Many years later, as Reverend Mary's spouse at clergy retreats, I found myself being "Father Confessor" to priests. Imagine! After a life of prayer, these senior clerics would confess that their goal upon retirement from the priesthood was to do what I was doing now: to spend time cruising on a sailboat. It's always rewarding to get a high-level endorsement of one's mission in life.

Priests weren't the only ones. The late Pete Nicholas, chairman of Boston Scientific, a leading medical-supply manufacturer, confessed, "Bob, after this Fortune 500 rat race, I want to do what you're doing."

This love of sailing is revealed in my introduction to AMF Alcort's 1976 full-line brochure, *The Fun of Sailing*, with photography by Eric Schweikardt. Twenty thousand copies were printed.

Sailing Is Many Things

Sailing is solitude and peace. Quiet and motorless, it is the sound of waves and wind broken occasionally by a gull's cry.

Sailing is pride in the accomplishment of simple tasks, satisfaction from feeling one with your boat, leaping over waves or flowing as in a ballet with the subtleties of an offshore breeze.

Sailing appeals to all the senses; warm sand between the toes, the caress of sun rays on the back, a teasing dash of cold spray, a hot deck, the coolness of a new breeze; blowing hair, deep lungfuls of clean air, a working body and mind which builds ravenous appetites and thirsts; pliant curves of sails and clouds, the feel of every wood grain in a tiller's end; a soft touch of morning mist, buffeting of stormy winds; primeval perfumes of decay and marsh, aromas of varnished wood, fiberglass and sails, sunspark diamonds on the waves, a mirrored image on smooth water, the trickle of bright droplets from a slanted deck. It is a world of textures and colors that change in kaleidoscope fashion, a world where one's sensitivity is magnified a hundredfold.

There's a timelessness and total involvement about sailing, which takes you away from city streets, exhaust, concrete modular structures, world affairs, and business conflicts. Today's pressures and sense of urgency seem to evaporate when mixed by a sail in the wind.

There's something about the view from a small sailboat that puts life in a happier, more sensible perspective. And upon returning to shore, one is overcome by a growing realization of self-worth and confidence.

One of the nicest things about sailing is the people you meet and the friends you make. Sailing people are very special people who appreciate the simple things in life, and who take the rainy days with the sunny ones. Sailing seems to bring out the best in people of all ages. Cut-offs, moccasins, t-shirts, and holed sweaters predominate. There is little sham or pretense. Sailing creates a strong and lasting kinship with people who love the water. It's an elemental bond that transcends society's superficial boundaries.

Sailing is an exciting challenge. It is perhaps the only sport where a ten-year-old or a novice of either sex can compete in the same race as an Olympic gold medalist and win.

Sailboat racing is a combination of speed, strategy, and technique—all on a game board that changes constantly and often unpredictably. One learns that going fast in the wrong direction is a sure way to lose. Sailing teaches one to continually assess probabilities, the essence of good judgment—which is needed in our rapidly changing world. One never knows all there is to know about wind, sail shape, hull design, or steering techniques. The challenge of sailing will always remain. That little bit of mystery about sailing lifts it out of the rationalized scientific realm to a place alongside the arts.

Sailing is freedom from many things and freedom to be oneself. There is something there for all of us. It is what you want it to be.

Sailing is a lifestyle. When you're away from it, memories and stories live forever. The mind, in creative moments, builds fantasies of future trips and undiscovered places.

There's a sense of adventure about every sail because no day on the water ever seems like another. There's a little Magellan and Drake in us all, even in those little sails to nowhere and back. There is no sense of monotony or repetition. Amazingly, such oceans of adventure are only minutes away from home—on a lake, pond, river or bay—a piece of the watery earth you can call your own that somehow seems larger than any kingdom.

The mystique of sailing, that sense of freedom, its world of dreams, is somehow built into every sailboat. Maybe that's why owning a sailboat is like owning 75% of the earth—the part covered by water is yours.

A Marketing Text

As a Fortune 500 "Marketing Man of the Year" and the founder of two award-winning boat companies with more than 60 designs in both sail and power, I have learned lessons that might benefit others. This book is about innovation, marketing, entrepreneurship, and product management within the framework of a sailor's life.

While managing Quaker Oats subsidiaries in Colombia and Venezuela, I learned you can't get good at marketing when you're off on your own. The product management experience at Quaker's home office in Chicago allowed me to learn from the successes and failures of others.

Did Sailboat Racing Help?

Thinking back, did sailboat racing at a young age develop the cognitive skills that helped me later in life? If so, that would be a great message for US Sailing to broadcast to parents, yacht clubs, and community sailing programs.

A sailboat race is a highly complex challenge dealing with the interaction of the wind, the waves, the currents, and the actions of competitors. There are myriad choices and consequences in an intensely competitive environment.

In Saturday races against adults, at age 13, I was so nervous before going out to the boat that I had to use the head in the men's locker room. Then, before the start, my foot would tremble when braced against the leeward seat.

Sailboat racing is a "live fire" version of Harvard Business School's "Decision Tree" methodology. That exercise teaches timely decision-making by assigning probabilities to several possible outcomes without knowing all the facts.

In his September 2015 article in *SAILING*, Nick Hayes describes what goes on in "Sailing Mind: Unlimited Variables That Are Oddly Clear":

A sailor will often tell you that they sail to clear the mind. They don't worry or fret or think about work, traffic, or trouble when they are on the water. They just focus, like a laser, on sailing. How does it happen? The key is in the limitlessness of the cognitive experience...Our bodies and minds have measurable limits; we can only do so many things at a time and, studies show, we can only think so many thoughts at a time. Research psychologists would call the ability to see, grasp and act in this complex space a "cognitive structure." It's an intense mental workout; our brains are awake, sharp, alert, and, as some science suggests, becoming more fit with each active hour. Sailors experience it as the clear-minded state that is addicting and can become an all-consuming lifelong passion.

Like other spiritual endeavors—yoga, meditation, playing music, vigorous exercise—sailing has the power to occupy and swell into every cranny of our physical and cognitive selves. While sailing, we willingly max out our bodies and minds. There simply isn't room for worry or other unimportant things. Clear mind-edness while sailing has a Zen counterpart to breathing during Yoga class. In Yoga, the practice is deliberately focused inward and done by reducing stimuli. In sailing, however, mind-clearing comes from opening the brain and body to as much stimuli as we can handle. Like filling an infinitely stretchable water balloon with a firehose.

In his book, *Invent & Wander,* Amazon's Jeff Bezos says that to sustain the energy and dynamism of a day-one start-up enterprise, "High-velocity decisions need to be made with only about 70 percent of desired information available."

Auteur Style

I'm often asked, "How did J/Boats get started?" Or "How did you ever come up with MJM Yachts?" The story of these companies and their boat designs fascinate people.

Steve Jobs's approach was like ours, more personal than big-company design-by-committee. This "auteur" style is described in a *New York Times* article dated January 31, 2010, "Apple in His Eye."

"Auteur" is the word for an author or artist who creates a product out of their own experience and view of the world, then pursues a "vision" of what he or she thinks the market needs or will soon want.

This connection between the project leader and what's created is evident in J/Boats designs, the One-Design 14, JY15, Gunboat Catamarans, and MJM yachts. All have origins in the extensive boating experience of their creators.

We looked inward to ask ourselves, "What type of boat would I like to own that doesn't exist right now?" Or "How can we improve upon what's out there?"

If the market seemed small at the outset, the bet was: "When others realize what we've created, the market will grow."

Such visionary products reflect the taste and perspective of the creator rather than the "wisdom of the crowd." Not everyone's ideas are included. Things that aren't part of the author's vision are "edited" out, like standing headroom in a J/105. We tried to avoid succumbing to *featuritis* (incorporating all imaginable features).

Jobs said great products are "triumphs of taste" resulting from immersion in past and present culture: bringing the best from each era into the new design.

From the past, features of five of my favorite powerboats were combined to create the signature look of an MJM yacht.

From the present, in contrast to other production powerboats, MJM Yachts used state-of-the-art epoxy-composite construction derived from experience with Gunboat catamarans and J/125-type carbon-epoxy sailboats.

A Family History?

A narrative can add dimension to family history. But where would I start, and who would be included?

In the 1990s, Mary and I took a trip to Plymouth, Massachusetts, to see the Mayflower and honor one of Mary's notable ancestors, Governor William Bradford. Being a history major and with a sense of familial evenhandedness, I asked, "Why are we spending so much time with this guy? Shouldn't we pay equal homage to all our other ancestors since 1620?"

Going back that far would be an insurmountable challenge. The numbers add up so quickly: 2-4-8-16-32-64, etc. After 16 generations, barring intermarriages, I'd have 131,072 direct ancestors—equal to the population of Charleston, South Carolina.

A comprehensive family history could rival the *Encyclopedia Britannica* in size. Given my focus on innovation and family business, the scope of this book is limited to those family members directly involved.

CHAPTER 1

Beginnings

L egend has it that sailing and innovation have populated Johnstone family DNA since the early 1600s in the Caribbean.

Pierre LeGrand

The story starts with Pierre LeGrand, a French pirate called the "Scourge of the Mosquito Coast."

Alexandre Exquemelin's *Buccaneers of America* claims that Pierre, born in Dieppe, started the Golden Age of Piracy as early as 1602.

Initially, pirates didn't have large enough vessels to do battle with the richest prizes sailing the Caribbean, which were Spanish galleons. So how could they capture such a large, armed Spanish ship?

Time to Get Creative. LeGrand came up with an innovative tactic. At night, with no more than a dozen of his men in a longboat using padded oars, they could sneak up astern of a becalmed galleon, heave a rope ladder over the taffrail, then quickly climb aboard to overwhelm the crew.

To motivate his men to stick with the plan, LeGrand drilled a hole in the bottom of the longboat. Before boarding the galleon, he pulled the plug to sink it. His men had to capture the galleon.

His first mission was a success! LeGrand's men scrambled aboard a becalmed galleon, killed the sleeping watch, captured the officers at their dinner, seized the gun room, and rounded up the rest of the surprised crew.

Rather than return to Tortuga, LeGrand dumped most Spanish crew and officers on a nearby island, keeping only enough men to sail the captured galleon and its treasure back to France.

He then retired early as a wealthy gentleman farmer in the Normandy region. Allegedly, his descendants, my LeGrand forbearers, returned to settle in the Virginia Tidewater region.

We named our fourth child Peter LeGrand Johnstone in honor of Pierre LeGrand's legacy. Peter has lived up to the name as a collegiate All-American, US Youth Champion boardsailor, and boat-company entrepreneur.

Robert Johnston(e) (1827–1876)

Our family history reads like a novel. My great-grandfather, Robert Johnston, graduated from the University of Virginia in 1851. There's no record of his parents, his hometown, or who paid for his education.

My uncle, David Johnstone, claimed, "He was the illegitimate son of pirate Robert Johnston, captain of the ship *Le Brave*, who was hung as one of Jean Lafitte's associates on May 26, 1820, in New Orleans.

"For the education of his unborn son, Johnston left his treasure in trust to his beloved paramour." Never mind that this puts his date of birth about five years earlier than otherwise documented.

The story becomes more intriguing. This alleged son of a pirate from Selma, Alabama, was reputed to be either a Confederate officer or a Union spy.

His only known nautical connection is his survival in the shipwreck of the *Sheridan*, somewhere off the coast of Norfolk, Virginia.

Supposedly, the "e" was added to "Johnston" for dubious identity purposes when crossing Civil War battle lines.

Official records confirm he married Cornelia Anne Elizabeth LeGrand (1838–1922) of Selma on July 16, 1857, thus combining the LeGrand and Johnston pirate legends.

He later became a dentist with a creative mind, either inventing or making a handheld adding machine.

Robert LeGrand Johnstone (1870–1928)

The grandfather I never knew met my grandmother, Caroline MacLaren ("Grandma J"), of the Canadian MacLaren Paper Company, on a steamship voyage to Jamaica. He founded the Chicle Products Company to take advantage of a process he invented to make MO-JO brand chewing gum...which remained white after chewing.

There's an entertaining, nasty exchange of letters in my files between him and William Wrigley, each accusing the other of selling the public contaminated junk.

His gum factory, with five buildings, was behind our suburban home in Glen Ridge, New Jersey. As kids, we used to go out to a mound of raw chicle, whack off hunks, and chew it...our private gum supply.

He never got past the fifth grade yet became wealthy enough to purchase Elihu Island, off Stonington, Connecticut. Then, upon selling that island to a Glen Ridge neighbor, Clayton Freeman, he bought an adjacent forty-acre island called Salt Acres with a large Victorian home. Unfortunately, he kept the formula to make MO-JO Chewing Gum a secret. He would personally add the ingredients to mix batches.

After he died, Grandma J hired Arthur D. Little to figure it out. They never could. So MO-JO Gum went out of business, taking with it the family's source of future income.

But we did get a good family boat name from the brand: *Mojo*.

Robert LeGrand Johnstone Jr. (1909–1966)

Dad was born in Glen Ridge, New Jersey. Whether grief following his father's death contributed to his severe illness at the Hill School is unknown. He dropped from a strapping 190 pounds to 120 pounds with a combination of hepatitis, pneumonia, yellow jaundice, and appendicitis.

Sadly, he succumbed to peritonitis and heart failure at age 57, never having the joy of seeing the creation of J/Boats or MJM Yachts.

After graduating from the Hill School in 1928, he entered Princeton, where he graduated with honors in the Class of 1932 as an Electrical Engineer. That was during the middle of the Great Depression.

He was one of only two classmates who had a job. He earned $10 a week ($170, or $4.25 an hour, in 2022 dollars), slinging hash in an all-night diner in Newark, New Jersey.

After four years at a mortgage company, he managed a restaurant chain, then joined the Prudential Insurance Company of America in 1936.

Besides three years in World War II as a Lieutenant JG in the Navy's Bureau of Supplies & Accounts in Washington, DC, he stayed with Prudential, commuting daily from our home in Glen Ridge to Newark.

From 1954 to 1957, he was in charge of constructing, leasing space, and managing the new Prudential Building in Chicago. He was the "Mr. X" who, at age 46, secretly negotiated the air rights over the Illinois Central Railroad tracks to build the 41-story One Prudential Plaza—the city's tallest building at the time.

One of my roommates wrote an article about my father and the Chicago building in *Princeton Engineering* magazine. This reporting got the attention of Princeton President Harold Dodds. He offered Dad a job as the business manager of the university, responsible for the $52 million ($500 million in 2022 dollars) building expansion, which included the I. M. Pei–designed Woodrow Wilson School.

The only indication I have of him considering another job is a copy of a letter he sent in 1964 to the president of the College of the Virgin Islands, in which he expressed interest in the position of business manager there. Nothing ever came of that inquiry.

Dad fostered an intra-family competition among himself, Mom, me, and my three younger siblings: Bobette, Rodney, and John. He insisted we record every game score and play in every family combination from two to six players, whether it was aces, pounce, eights, hearts, rummy, chess, checkers, Chinese checkers, backgammon, Parcheesi, Scrabble, canasta, Monopoly, h-o-r-s-e, etc. Dad said, "It's to build up my armchair lead."

1926 Sears Bowl

Dad spent his teenage summers in Stonington, sailing from the family island. He and his sister, Helen, had a fifteen-foot Scamp keelboat named *Prodigal.* His two younger brothers, David and Paul, had another, named *Houqua.* The latter was named after the first fast American clipper, codesigned by Stonington Captain Nathaniel Palmer, also known as the first American to discover the Antarctic Continent.

Dad was good enough to win the Wadawanuck Country Club's junior championship. He crewed for John Streeter to reach the 1926 Sears finals at the Eastern Yacht Club in Marblehead, Massachusetts. The Sears Bowl, now "Sears Cup," is US Sailing's national junior championship. At the time, the event was conducted in a match-race format with windward-leeward courses.

Having won the semifinal match by four minutes, Wadawanuck was disqualified for not allowing sufficient room for the other boat at the weather starting mark. Under today's Racing Rules of Sailing, that other boat would be disqualified for "barging."

The eventual winner, Duxbury Yacht Club, was coached by 18-year-old C. Raymond Hunt*, who'd won the Sears for Duxbury in 1923 and 1925.

To illustrate how small the world of sailboat racing is: 26 years later, as a 17-year-old, I lost a tiebreaker for third place in the 1951 Sears Cup Finals at the Eastern Yacht Club, the same club where Dad had lost. The following year as an 18-year-old (the same age Ray Hunt had been), my job was to coach the Indian Harbor Yacht Club crew of Skip Purcell and twins Connie and Carrie Neher. They won the 1952 Sears Cup.

Ninety-one years after Ray Hunt had coached Duxbury to victory and 65 years after I'd done the same with Indian Harbor, I had the honor of presenting Ray Hunt for induction into the National Sailing Hall of Fame.

Start of Intercollegiate Sailing

Dad was in the same 1928 class at the Hill School as Alfred E. "Bill" Luders^, who went into his father's boatbuilding business instead of college.

Both Dad and Bill Luders were a year behind another famous yachtsman at Hill, Briggs Cunningham*.

The first intercollegiate championship for the May Challenge Cup was organized by Cunningham* and Arthur Knapp* of Princeton's Class of 1928. It was held that year at the Pequot Yacht Club in Southport, Connecticut, with Harvard, Yale, and Princeton racing new 8 Meters, one boat per college.

Arthur Knapp*, a Larchmont Yacht Club member familiar with Long Island Sound, won the first two races of the three-race series, giving Princeton the victory. For the following year, 1929, Knapp lobbied to expand the sport by including other colleges.

Commentary in *The New York Times* voiced the concern that going beyond the "Big Three" of Harvard, Yale, and Princeton might water down the quality of the sport. They needn't have worried. One of

Cornell's skippers was Rod Stephens*, who, with his brother, Olin*, later formed the design firm Sparkman & Stephens.

The 1929 event was held in Herreshoff S-Boats at the Seawanhaka Corinthian Yacht Club as a three-way team race with two boats per college. Dad, a freshman, crewed for Rufus Smith ('29) of Houston, Texas, in one of the Princeton boats.

The other Princeton skipper was Osmond A. "Ozzie" Willauer ('30), father of my friend and Princeton classmate, Peter Willauer ('56), who married Mary's Smith college roommate, Betty Isom. They founded the Hurricane Island Outward Bound School. We did some two-couple, premarital cruising together. I'll never forget going through Woods Hole at night, delivering a 36' yawl from Hyannisport to New London for an Off-Soundings regatta, with Peter at the shrouds with a searchlight, shouting, "Rocks!" as I threw the helm hard over to escape disaster.

After retiring from Outward Bound, Peter lived aboard the J/42 *Eight Bells* for eight years, making several Atlantic crossings. His younger brother, Brad Willauer, has campaigned his J/46, called *Breezin' Up*, in the Bermuda Race several times and has been the commodore of the Cruising Club of America.

My First Race

It was 1936. I was two years old. Our young family continued to summer at Salt Acres in Stonington.

My grandfather, Robert L. Johnstone (RLJ), had donated a beautiful silver serving bowl to the Wadawanuck Yacht Club as a perpetual parent-child race trophy. The deed of gift stated that the parent must hold the tiller on the first lap, and the child must hold it on the second. The parent couldn't touch the tiller during the child's turn.

Dad (RLJ Jr.), passionate about sailing, couldn't wait until I (RLJ III) could join him in this race so all three RLJ names could be on the trophy. Speak about silly things that motivate parents!

Instead of sticking to the Wadawanuck Yacht Club beach (pictured), he figured that, as a two-year-old, I could be trained by rote to respond to the words "push" and "pull" while holding the tiller of a sailboat. A practice session must have encouraged him to enter the race.

The story is that Dad built a big lead after the first lap and turned the tiller over to me. While I may have done OK in the practice session, my attention span wasn't yet attuned to the sport of yacht racing. After about thirty seconds, I exercised my First Amendment rights as a two-year-old, saying, "No!"

The boat spun in circles, and that was that.

Much later, at age 65, when I first qualified for the Maine Retired Skipper's Race in Castine, Maine, Steve White, owner of the Brooklin Boat Yard, invited me to drive his 55-foot sloop, *Vortex*, in the event. We won.

Celebrating at a local bar afterward, his psychiatrist wife, upon hearing the story of my first race, as a two-year-old, slapped her hand down on the bar, exclaiming, "That explains everything!"

"What do you mean?" I asked.

"You've been trying to make it up to your dad ever since!"

One takeaway from that early race is that I can take pride in knowing I may be the only sailor on the planet with 86 years of experience with a hand on the tiller in a sailboat race.

Thanks, Dad! Eventually, we did win the Robert L. Johnstone Parent-Child Trophy together in 1947 and again in 1953. I won it with Mom in 1951.

Sailing Instructor Mom

Mom, Elizabeth Van Liew Johnstone (1910–1987), from Bloomfield, New Jersey, taught me how to sail.

She met Dad in neighboring Glen Ridge in their youth, attended Dobbs School, and married Dad while he was a Princeton undergraduate. She never went to college.

Mom worked in an antiaircraft manufacturing plant during the early years of World War II. I loved her dearly and can remember anxiously awaiting her return home from work on weekday afternoons. Later, she had some success selling real estate and was an administrator at the Educational Testing Service in Princeton, New Jersey. She outlived three husbands. That's us, around the time I sailed my first race.

Mom's Van Liew nautical roots are better documented than Dad's. They trace back to Manhattan Island in 1623. Among the original Dutch settlers was their shipwright, Mom's ancestor from Bergen, Norway, named John. He later became John Bergen, progenitor of Bergen County, New Jersey.

Another ancestor was Dirk Benson—master of the open boat *Endraght*, which plied the Hudson River to Albany—who later ran the original Manhattan-Brooklyn ferry in the mid-1600s.

In summers at Salt Acres between 1933 and 1936, Mom raced with Dad and his brothers on the family's new, dark-hulled Fishers Island H23 #8 Ojai, designed and built by Sidney Herreshoff

H23s are 23 feet on the waterline and 34 feet overall. They are pretty boats, designed following the concept of a 30 square meter to be light and narrow. Fifteen were built starting in 1932.

Shown is a 1932 photo (courtesy of the Herreshoff Museum) of five H23s being commissioned at the Herreshoff yard in Bristol, including #8. Sadly, the boat became a total loss in the 1938 hurricane.

Built during the Depression, the H23 replaced a larger Fishers Island class. To cut costs, they were single planked, as opposed to Herreshoff's standard double-planked construction. They sold for $2,500 new, or $55,000 today...about the same as a J/70. A great buy!

The reader will later learn that J/Boats also responded to economic setbacks, coming out with lower-cost and better-performing designs to restore sales: the J/29 in 1983 and the J/105 in 1991. History does repeat itself!

Summer of '42

This was a time made famous by the movie of that name. It was wartime. Dad and his two brothers were away in the Navy: Dad in the Supply Corps in Washington, DC, Dave guarding the Panama Canal Zone, and Paul as the gunnery officer on the cruiser *USS Boise*.

Mom took the kids to Salt Acres in Stonington for the summer. One of her missions was to teach me how to sail.

The plan was to put me and a fellow eight-year-old, John Taylor, in one of the 15-foot family keelboats. These were similar to a Bullseye. Mom and Aunt Ginny would then get in the other boat and shout instructions to us over the water.

Mom dealt with many unique challenges during my youth…and not all with good outcomes. I remember when a nest of baby rabbits was plowed up in a field next to our house in Glen Ridge. She debated whether to warm them up in the oven or give them an eye-dropper of brandy. She decided on the latter. In less than a minute, they went rigid with rigor mortis!

On another occasion, to get rid of lice on my pet bantam chickens, she bathed them with turpentine. Killed the lice just fine…along with the chickens!

It was a wonder I survived to the age of eight to be subjected to her fast-track sailing instruction technique.

It was a great concept in theory. Mom rowed us out to our boat, then rowed to the second boat and got aboard. Maybe she forgot to tell us not to cast off the mooring until the instructors were underway. Or perhaps we were so excited we took off with overconfidence.

We sailed across the narrow Watch Hill channel toward Sandy Point, directly onto a sandbar. Mom and Aunt Ginny were late getting off the mooring, so they couldn't warn us about the shallow water. There we were, stuck!

So Mom had to sail back to the mooring, get into a dinghy, and row back out a quarter mile to rescue the aspiring mariners, towing us into deeper water.

The next day, mildly chagrined, undaunted, and intent on making amends to gain the respect due to a proper seaman, I rowed out to the boat we'd been sailing.

There was a sloppy pile of rope on the cockpit sole. This mess didn't fit my high standards of seamanship. So I pulled out my trusty new sailing knife and sliced off the tail of the mainsheet. Of course, the boat could no longer sail downwind with the mainsheet eased out.

Two weeks later, after the mainsheet had been replaced, I had been adequately chastised, and believing ourselves eminently qualified, this pair of eight-year-olds boldly ventured westward beyond established beginner boundaries, five miles down Fishers Island Sound.

We made it back home to the mooring just fine. But it didn't do much to calm Mom, who, in a proper snit, had called the Coast Guard.

Youth Sailing Years

The 1940s were the fun days of my youth! My friend John Taylor and I sailed almost every day. We did crazy things like engage the Chesebrough brothers in naval warfare, trying to torpedo each other with floating logs and tossing water bombs. It was wartime, after all. These naval battles were a great way to improve boat handling.

Another fun boat-handling exercise was the "pop-the-balloon game" played in the junior sailing program at the Wadawanuck Yacht Club. A balloon on a 25-foot length of string was towed behind the boat. The crew held a boat hook or broomstick with a pin taped to the end to pop the balloons trailing behind other boats. The last boat with a balloon still floating won.

We started racing in Long Island One-Designs, which were similar to small Star boats, with centerboards and no spinnakers.

Upon my arrival in Stonington for the summer, my first job was to get the orange-painted *Prodigal II* commissioned for launching. This mainly involved painting the bottom with antifouling and varnishing the mast and boom.

Juniors raced against one another on Wednesdays and against adults on Saturdays. That was the best instruction we could have had. There's nothing more gratifying than beating one's elders on Saturday and, at the same time, learning all their tactical tricks.

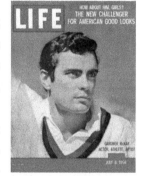

We didn't have "kiddie" boats like Optimist Prams and 420s. This trial by fire helped me follow Gardner McKay as the "Wad" Club's Junior Champion for the next five years, from 1947 to 1951.

However, success on the racecourse didn't qualify me to follow Gardner to Hollywood. Instead, I continued on my life's sailing track by twice winning Eastern Connecticut Yacht Racing Association (ECYRA) Midget and Junior Championships.

Gardner McKay became famous in Hollywood as Captain Adam Troy of the sailing ship *Tiki* in the TV serial *Adventures in Paradise*. He appeared on the cover of the July 6, 1959, issue of *Life*.

Jimmy Buffet^ built his lifestyle around Gardner's TV role, which he memorialized in the song "We Are the People Our Parents Warned Us About," with lyrics, "Hey, hey, Gardner McKay, take us on the leaky *Tiki*."

The closest we junior sailors got to such Pacific island adventures was to race a half dozen of our boats 15 miles west to the Harkness Estate beach on the Thames River, near New London. We had a cookout and camped overnight on the beach with sand fleas, then raced back to Stonington the next day.

I never forgot those sand fleas. For family adventures, sleeping on J/24 bunks is far preferred.

Garage-Built Lightning #3310

Dad thought building a nineteen-foot Lightning from a kit in our New Jersey garage would be a great family project. This experience may have helped my younger brother Rodney avoid a few mistakes later when he was 37 and building the J/24 prototype *Ragtime* in his Stonington garage.

To get the project started, Dad ordered a home-builder's kit from an official Lightning Class supplier on Long Island. The kit included a "wood frame set (to ensure designed shape), steel centerboard, mast, boom, spinnaker pole, and rudder." Dad sourced a brass mast hardware kit from Merriman. Added to the collected parts were nylon sails, several sheets of Masonite and canvas for the deck, a 20-foot length of white oak for the keel, and one-by-six mahogany planks for the hull.

Any competitive sailor today would have been horrified, saying, "Stop right there! Cancel the order. That boat will be a beast!"

It came in 30 percent over the Lightning Class minimum weight of 700 pounds. Dad's dream of owning a beautiful, varnished mahogany boat overrode what his Princeton engineering degree should have told him about specs for a race-winning sailboat.

Other than Mom mashing her thumb while hammering a mahogany bung over a brass screw, several other episodes became reminders of how not to build a competitive one-design sailboat.

The first was bending a long, 1.5-by-6-inch piece of oak as the keel over frames (ribs) of the boat, which was upside down on the garage floor. Oak is so stiff and unyielding that without steaming, it would be impossible to bend in a curve and secure over the center of each frame. The sharper curve near the transom would be tough.

Time to Get Creative. Dad planned on steaming the 20-foot length of oak, then bending it down over the frames. He put a car jack and an eight-foot four-by-four between the aft end of the oak keel board and a large panel under the ceiling above. After steaming the oak, he started cranking the car jack. The oak board was bending down nicely over frames amidships. As the pressure increased near the stern, and about the time Dad would have congratulated himself, *cr-a-a-a-ck*! The ceiling of the garage exploded upward.

On the second try, with the ceiling reinforced and the oak given more time in the steam box, the keel was bent close but not quite according to plans.

As a result, the deck became slightly hogged near the stern, and the boat became an inch or two longer, with a flatter run that was fast in heavy air.

The official measurer for the class, who sold the kit, had sufficient pity on us to sign the measurement certificate for #3310 *Prodigal III*.

The second episode occurred after launching. We put the boat on its mooring at the Wadawanuck Yacht Club in Stonington and were excited to soon be sailing.

Several days later, we attached the sails, then tried to lower the centerboard. Oops! It wouldn't go down. Squinting down the trunk, we could see that the slot in the keel was open at either end but squeezed shut in the middle. The wooden hull had swollen so much that the centerboard slot was closed.

The classic method of making a planked boat watertight was to caulk the bottom. This required a caulking iron and a mallet to pound strands of cotton moistened with blobs of Kuhls caulking compound between the planks. Being enthusiastic practitioners of this ancient art, we'd "overcaulked" the bottom.

How could we open the centerboard slot in the keel so the centerboard could drop down?

Time to Get Creative. Dad's solution was to tow *Prodigal III* to the boatyard and haul it out on an iron ships' railway. He would then get underneath the boat with a heavy-duty, handheld electric drill and go back and forth with the bit to grind open the slot.

It was a wet environment. He turned on the drill, hollered, and fell onto the rails, stunned by an electric shock.

This Princeton electrical engineer had the mind to twist while falling, banging the drill against the metal rail to electrically ground it. He lived to sail another day.

Prodigal III then had a wineglass-shaped oak keel. Maybe the pinched-in slot allowed the centerboard to twist slightly, allowing the boat to climb to weather.

The boat never did become watertight. It was the job of a crew member to constantly work a Step-On-It bilge pump.

On a summer visit, my Princeton roommate, John Hill Wilson, was assigned the job of foot pumper when racing. As we joked later, when he was a partner at Morgan Stanley and the chairman of the Environmental Defense Fund, "Pumping out the bilge water is what qualified him to become EDF chairman."

A heavier boat did not give me the speed to compensate for mistakes made on the racecourse. To win, I had to be smarter, playing wind shifts, finding wind streaks, and taking advantage of tidal currents.

That unwelcome discipline paid off later when I got my hands on the tiller of faster, minimum-weight boats. And it was an early lesson learned: heavy boats don't perform.

Lightning #4151 *Houqua*

The first Lightning my grandparents purchased for family use was #1924 *Mojo*, a Skaneateles-built boat. I crewed for my uncle and sailing mentor, David, the Massachusetts Institute of Technology Phi Beta Kappa grad, who was way ahead of his time in the science of boat prep. Before every Saturday race, we'd beach *Mojo*, pull it over on its side, and go over the entire hard, white, enameled bottom and centerboard with a rottenstone paste comparable to 1200-grit wet-dry sandpaper. Uncle Dave would get so excited when racing that he once swallowed a cigar stub. Later, he owned the first Hobie 14 and Windsurfer in Stonington.

Most likely, Uncle Dave persuaded Grandma J to upgrade our Lightning to give young Robbie a better shot at winning races. So *Mojo* was replaced with a minimum-weight, Saybrook-built #4151 *Houqua*. She was dark green, with a hard, red Woolsey Vinylast racing bottom. All the boats were wet-sailed off moorings.

While trying to figure out how to make the boat faster, I wondered about the ideal shape for the centerboard.

Time to Get Creative. A Lightning has a 130-pound, 5/16" steel plate for a centerboard. Class rules permitted "a streamlined or chamfered edge all round of not greater than one inch." The builder delivered the centerboard with a radiused leading edge and a knife-sharp trailing edge. I wondered about that.

To test a theory, I ran a dinner knife through water in our kitchen sink in both directions. With the sharp edge forward at the slightest angle, the blade wanted to leap sharply off to the side. With the radiused edge forward, nothing much happened. Might this trick help my boat sail better to windward? It was worth a try. So I rented a metal disc grinder, laid the centerboard on some blocks, and sent sparks flying to put a sharp edge on both sides. That knifed leading edge seemed to work.

In my last year with *Houqua*, I won the Wadawanuck Yacht Club and ECYRA junior championships, Lightning Fleet #183 season, and the ECYRA Lightning Districts. Bill Healy from Niantic, in his Lightning, *Holy Smoke*, was runner-up in the latter. One of his sons, Tim, now sails J/70s as a North sailmaker, and his son, Bill Jr., is an assistant sailing coach at Yale.

The neighboring village of Watch Hill also had a Lightning fleet. That's where I sailed against and got to know the late James M. "Ding" Schoonmaker*, who was instrumental in helping me get the North American Yacht Racing Union (NAYRU) board's approval for the inaugural 1973 United States Youth Championship.

1950 Sears Cup

In 1950, I won the ECYRA quarterfinals in Lightnings. We sailed the Sears semifinals on Quincy Adams 17s in Pine Orchard, Connecticut.

We would have qualified as one of the top three for the finals had we not blown a considerable lead by rounding the first weather mark to starboard, as we always did in Stonington.

I didn't know the rules. Unless otherwise specified, the first mark is rounded on the same side as the starting mark, which had been to port.

1951 Sears Cup

In 1951, I'd again won the ECYRA quarterfinals in Lightnings, then the mid-Atlantic semifinals at the Stamford Yacht Club in Rhodes 18s. Like my father 25 years earlier, I was headed to the national junior championship for the Sears Cup at the Eastern Yacht Club in Marblehead.

My crew were R. B. Jones and Gordon Frierson, with Dick Woolworth as the alternate. Regrettably, after the semifinals, my steady crew, cousin Holt Rose, had to return to Pasadena.

We were in contention to win in the last race. It was a light-air day. The fleet of 210s was not matched. Some had Orlon sails, others wrinkly nylon or blown-out Egyptian cotton. In a breeze, it didn't make much difference. Skill could overcome such variations, but not in the light air of the final race.

It was our turn to sail the "heavy" lemon of the fleet. We finished last, losing the tiebreaker for third to finish fourth in the regatta. Déjà vu all over again—like father, like son. Skunked at the Eastern Yacht Club in Marblehead!

1952 Sears Cup

Three's the charm! There was a silver lining to that 1951 black cloud. Since I'd dominated the Sears quarterfinals and districts in Lightnings that year, and since the Yacht Racing Association of Long Island Sound (YRALIS) Sears Cup quarterfinals, semifinals, and finals in 1952 would be in Lightnings, the Indian Harbor Yacht Club (IHYC) in Greenwich, Connecticut, hired me as their "coach."

While this frequently happens today, it was rare for a yacht club to hire a teenager solely as a coach without beginner sailing instruction duties.

Job number one was to get the IHYC Lightning #3577 *Indian Belle* up to speed. The centerboard got the sharp, leading-edge treatment and a new suit of Ulmer sails.

My IHYC team breezed through to win the 1952 Sears Cup, with Skip Purcell as skipper and the Neher twins, Connie and Carrie, as crew.

Woody Harris was the "heavy air" alternate. Woody's son, Joe Harris, is currently in the 2021–2022 Globe40 doublehanded race around the world in his *GryphonSolo2*.

Despite my success in Lightnings, I couldn't imagine being competitive with top sailors I'd read about in the *Lightning Yearbook*: the likes of Dick Bertram, Karl Smither, and Walt Swindeman. Nobody encouraged me to attend the Lightning North American Championship, even though I was winning just about all events locally.

I didn't forget that 20 years later. The founding concept of the 1973 US Youth Championship was to scour the country for 150 or so youth, as I'd once been, and invite them for a chance to compete against one another at the highest level.

The US Youth Championship is a very successful program and perhaps my most gratifying achievement in the sport. We will pick up on that story later.

CHAPTER 2

College Years

S ailing was my obsession among the three sports of my youth, the others being tennis and riflery. During summers in Stonington, when not working at a part-time job, we played tennis in the morning at the Wadawanuck Yacht Club. Then maybe we'd cool off with a swim, have lunch at the snack bar, and sail in the afternoon when the sea breeze normally fills in.

Tennis

I bring this up because, like sailboat racing, tennis is a sport that may have contributed to my performance on the racecourse and later in business.

Timothy Gallwey seemed to think so. In his popular book *The Inner Game of Tennis*, he wrote, "Tennis is primarily a mental game." It requires quick decision-making, critical thinking, and coordination.

Pro Keegan Barkley agreed, saying that, among the seven types of intelligence described by Harvard psychologist Howard Gardner in his *Frames of Mind: The Theory of Multiple Intelligences* (1983), tennis develops and improves "logical-mathematical intelligence":

> Having strong problem-solving skills is essential to be a good tennis player. Many situations can arise during a match where being able to come up with efficient solutions would make the difference between winning or losing a match. Besides, tennis can teach players to plan and execute different strategies, as well as to make spur-of-the-moment decisions. In a tennis point, players need to anticipate

their opponent's actions and adjust to them constantly. Further-more, the game requires players to have a good judgment of angles, heights, speed, and, to a certain degree, geometry and physics.

Having won the Wadawanuck Yacht Club men's tennis championship and been on the Loomis School team, I joined the Princeton freshman team (pictured). They attracted top tennis talent from around the country. I wasn't one of them.

My team ranking was pretty far down the ladder. Usually, only the top four to six ranked players get to play in a match.

Imagine my surprise when the coach asked me to be ready to leave on the team bus for a Saturday match in New York City against Columbia. Was he serious?

When I asked him if I was going to play, he was honest, saying, "Probably not."

Ranking no higher than ninth, I confessed, "Coach, I'm sorry, but I'm loaded down with studies right now. While I'm happy to support the team, warming the bench in an out-of-town match and being unlikely to play doesn't seem like a good move for me now."

Without trying to persuade me otherwise (which was telling of his opinion of my game), he answered, "If that's the way it's going to be, then you are off the team!"

My improbable collegiate tennis career thus ended.

What was likely behind my poor-team-player attitude was the lingering thought, "Wouldn't I really be having more fun as a member of the Princeton freshman sailing team?"

I didn't completely give up tennis. Eight years later, with Quaker Oats in Cali, Colombia, there was no place to sail. So I took up tennis again and won the 1960 Club Campestre Open Men's Singles. That six-inch-tall silver cup is still one of my most cherished trophies.

Later, in Venezuela, I spearheaded the construction of a tennis court at Club Guataparo de Valencia.

Then afterward in Wilmette, Illinois, during the winter, I played some indoor tennis.

Ten years later, in 1976, when I was working for AMF Alcort, we built a tennis court in our backyard at 145 Rimmon Road in Woodbridge, Connecticut.

Intercollegiate Sailing

Yes, sailing was my favorite sport. As commodore of the Nautical Club at Loomis School, I competed in a couple of interscholastic regattas. After that brief stint on the Princeton tennis team, I joined the sailing team and did well enough to earn my freshman 1956 black numeral sweater.

A late classmate and friend, the Delaware governor and presidential candidate Pete du Pont, crewed for me in several regattas. In our junior year, we were on the Princeton crew that finished second in the Mac-Millan Cup, which was sailed in Naval Academy yawls. In 1955, the team placed third in the Morss Trophy for the National Dinghy Championship. I wasn't active in dinghies at the time due to a load of studies, junior papers, and a challenging senior thesis.

However, my postgraduate allegiance to Princeton sailing and its storied history was strong enough to rekindle a commitment to help them reclaim past glories.

My current role is senior alumni advisor to the Princeton sailing team. In the past year of 2021–2022, following weekly Zoom sessions, we relocated the team's venue from the Raritan Yacht Club in Perth Amboy, New Jersey, to the Anchor Yacht Club on the Delaware River in Bristol, Pennsylvania, thirty minutes closer to campus. A new fleet of 12 Zim 420Es was purchased, and a sailing coach was hired.

Fishers Island

In 1953, at the end of my first year, Princeton sailing teammates allowed me to "take care" of one of the new Tech sailing dinghies for the summer. I car-topped it to my job as harbormaster and sailing instructor at the Hay Harbor Club on Fishers Island, New York. Multiple du Pont families from Wilmington, Delaware, summered on the island. So I can probably thank Pete for the job.

The highlight of that Fishers Island summer, in retrospect, though not fully appreciated at the time, was sitting in a rowboat and seeing a cute girl walking down the Hay Harbor Club dock. She had two youngsters in tow who were coming for sailing lessons.

This was my future wife, Mary McAvoy, from Washington, DC. Mary had just graduated from Mount Vernon Seminary and was on her way into Smith College's class of 1957.

She was an au pair for the Gerry family children during July. The two older Gerrys took sailing lessons from me on the club's small catboats.

We greeted each other. But it wasn't until a few days later, when she returned to the dock, that we first chatted.

Mary asked, "Could I take one of the boats out sailing with the two kids?"

I replied, "Sure. Could I ask what your sailing experience has been?"

"I've had my own Cape Cod sailing dinghy since age ten on Little Cranberry Island in Maine. Last summer, I had a job in Padnarum on Buzzards Bay and taught a youngster how to sail."

"OK, that works," I said, and ferried them to one of the club's small catboats.

Mary was more adventurous than I'd anticipated. I watched the little boat sail around that tiny harbor several times. About half an hour later, they started to sail out of the narrow channel into the sound.

Uh-oh! One of my jobs as harbormaster was "safety." An important rule was that only qualified adults could take a boat out of the harbor into that treacherous stretch of water called "the Race." Tides can flow up to five knots as water races in and out of Long Island Sound in the narrowed, almost funnel-like gap between Gull Island and Fishers Island.

So I picked up the megaphone and hollered over to Mary, gesturing with a sweeping motion of my arm, "Hey! Come back!"

Looking a bit miffed, she sailed toward me to ask, "What's the problem?"

"I'm sorry, but I can only allow qualified adults to sail a boat out of the harbor."

Looking exasperated, she said, "Well! Don't you think I'm a qualified adult?"

Time to Get Creative. But I blew it! My least creative response ever was, "I certainly do not!"

That did it. It wasn't long before the competition moved in. I saw Mary being driven around in a shiny-new, baby-blue Chevy convertible by Bill Ridgeway, my former Short Hills, New Jersey, neighbor.

Next thing I know, she's sailing with the future director of the National Gallery of Art, Carter Brown, in his parents' magnificent, Olin Stephens-designed 72-foot yawl, *Bolero*. As a working stiff living in a rundown employee shack on Hay Harbor Club grounds, I didn't stand a chance.

However, about a month later, there was a glimmer of hope. The relationship thawed in new surroundings. In August, Mary had a similar job in Watch Hill, Rhode Island. Maybe her prospects there were not as dashing as they were on Fishers Island.

So she accepted an invitation, later that month, to spend a weekend at our family cottage on Wamphassuc Point in Stonington.

I'm not sure that Dad's routine of rousting everyone out of bed went over that well. At about seven o'clock each morning, he'd put on a Dixieland band record by Firehouse Five Plus Two at full volume and holler up the stairwell, "Last one in the water washes all the dishes!" We'd all go running down the dock to jump in.

At this point, Mary and I still hadn't even done anything so serious as kissing.

But in retrospect, God was clearly in charge and had someone very special in store for me: that caring young lady on the Hay Harbor Club dock who, wonderfully, came with a family summer home on a Maine island and a shared love of sailing. Time would tell.

Captain of *Yawl Cat*

The following summer of 1954 was a time for a new adventure, other than being a yacht-club sailing instructor. I put a classified ad in *Yachting Magazine*, seeking employment as captain on a large cruising or racing yacht. Two good job offers resulted: captain of Sumner A. "Huey" Long's^ early *Ondine*, a 50-foot racing sloop on Long Island Sound, or captain with a mate on the classic, flush-decked, 55' *Yawl Cat*, based in Charlevoix, Michigan.

Yawl Cat was built by Herreshoff during the height of the Great Depression using the same half model that Captain Nat used for George

F. Baker Jr.'s (Citibank founder and namesake of Harvard Business School) *Ventura* in 1922.

Taking my friend and Princeton classmate Bill Knight along as mate made the *Yawl Cat* job more appealing, with a chance to see some spectacular new cruising grounds. Bill was related to Admiral Austin Melvin Knight, author of the classic text *Modern Seamanship*.

I'd already spent a summer on Long Island Sound, after all. This job would be an exciting challenge. I'd be responsible for running the ship and doing all the meal planning, shopping, cooking, barkeeping, maintenance, and sailing for Otto Frenzel, chairman of the Merchants National Bank of Indianapolis, and his family.

Mom supplied me with a dozen family recipes to enhance my cooking credentials. It was a great summer of cruising the North Channel, McGregor Bay, Bay Finn, and Georgian Bay. We dipped a stainless cup over the side for drinks of cold, fresh water and picked blueberries off the side of surrounding hills.

Chris-Craft

One memorable stay in the North Channel might have led to an early start in the marine industry.

Between visits from members of the Frenzel family, Bill and I were alone on *Yawl Cat*, anchored at Harbor Island.

At one point, Chris-Craft's latest, a 57' Constellation motor yacht, pulled in and dropped anchor close by. We could see that the family aboard included two cute girls and a younger boy.

After exchanging a few greetings and where-are-you-headed-for questions across the water, the father, likely trying to make life interesting for the girls, shouted an invitation, "Hey, come on over."

So Bill and I dove in and swam over to climb aboard for "afternoon tea."

It turns out it was Harsen Smith, chairman of Chris-Craft, with his wife, his son Harsen Jr., his daughter Barbara, and her school friend.

Harsen was the grandson of Christopher Columbus Smith, who founded the company in 1894.

That year we met, in 1954, Chris-Craft was producing 139 models, with 5,000 employees in 12 factories.

Five years later, he was on the cover of the May 1959 *TIME* and was described as "the man who perhaps more than any other put the U.S. family afloat. His vision was to turn motorboats from a pure luxury item into an affordable expense for middle-class families, to make them attractive for outings by an entire family instead of simply sports enthusiasts."

One thing led to another in the absence of *Yawl Cat*'s owners. Bill and I may have cooked them dinner aboard, or maybe it was the reverse on the Chris-Craft. The next day, we took the entire Smith family for a sail on *Yawl Cat*.

Looking back at that time, it never occurred to me to get a job in the marine industry. As a sailor, the thought of contacting the chairman of a powerboat company for a job never entered my mind.

But it is amusing to speculate how my path in the marine industry might have evolved had I joined Chris-Craft instead of Quaker Oats. We were to share a common goal of popularizing America's family-boating culture. Ironically, Harsen Smith passed away at age 94 on December 7, 2002, five days before I signed the MJM Yachts licensing agreement with Boston BoatWorks to build the MJM 34z, my first powerboat creation.

It seemed that the baton was being passed to carry on the mission of promoting the shared adventure of family powerboating.

That memorable stay in the North Channel might have led to an early start in the marine industry.

70-mph White Squall

The most unforgettable, frightening day aboard *Yawl Cat* was when we headed South on Lake Michigan from Harbor Springs to Charlevoix, a short reach on a windy, cloudy day under jib and mizzen. We cruised with the owner's daughter, his ex-Marine son-in-law, and their friends. All seemed well until a long, cigar-shaped tube of white surrounded by black stretched across the western horizon.

"Bill, this looks like a white squall. Go forward and be ready to drop the jib. And one of you guys get on the mizzen halyard winch. Gals, please get belowdecks."

The lee shore of Michigan was not that far away. That white horizontal tube we saw was the tops of waves being blown into the air by the force of a 70 mph blast of wind.

It hit, slamming the boat down to about 45 degrees. The jib was blown up the rig and wouldn't drop. The flaying jib sheet tore its block out of the deck to mutilate the varnished, mahogany-topped metal safety rail.

My mouth filled up with water when I tried to shout commands. I was frantically praying to God for help to get these people and the boat through safely. My prayers were answered in about five minutes, which seemed like an hour.

The line squall passed. It was still blowing 45 knots with huge seas. I activated engine-room blowers to start the motor safely and headed the last several miles to Charlevoix's Round Lake entry channel.

The Google Map satellite photo shows the 100'-wide channel from Lake Michigan with a breakwater on either side. There's about a 20-degree turn toward a drawbridge about a quarter mile from the turn.

You can't see the drawbridge until after entering the channel. The sea was running so high that breakwaters on either side of the channel could only be seen in troughs. The passage could be dicey.

We could not put *Yawl Cat* in reverse while surging in on those waves. She had an offset prop. If put into hard reverse, the props would pull the stern to port, with the boat sideways in the channel.

I slowed the boat as much as possible to keep steerage, repeatedly giving three horn blasts. We hoped to see the bridge going up when we got halfway down the channel. No such luck. There was no one in the bridge-control house or visible in the Coast Guard station we were passing.

Spectators had gathered, some concerned and a few waiting for the impending disaster. Not good!

Time to Get Creative. "OK, crew, let's get ready to save the rig," I barked. "Pull out the anchor chain; run it outboard of the port shrouds and back along the deck. If that bridge doesn't open in the last hundred yards, I'll run the boat up against the pilings to port. Then throw the chain over the pilings to stop the boat."

We were halfway down that final quarter-mile leg, repeatedly sounding the three blasts of the horn when a man came running out of the adjacent bar, as we were very visible now.

He hurried into the control room and threw himself on the levers. The bridge began to rise ever so slowly—too slowly.

What were the chances of making it through without taking the mast down? I decided to risk it, lining up the mast where the opening should appear.

We slid through with inches on either side of the upper shrouds. Whew! Thank God! I couldn't smile for a week.

With curiosity and outrage, the marine and I walked back to the Coast Guard station. There was nobody outside. We opened the door to the main building. About eight of them were sitting on the floor playing some card game.

Astounded, I asked, "What was the wind velocity in that squall that just went through?"

The reply was a puzzled, "What squall?"

Afraid of our violent response beyond any imaginable form of road rage, we silently turned, steamed, and left.

That was the same 1954 summer when Hurricane Carol swept through Stonington to destroy our family Lightnings, *Prodigal III* and *Houqua*.

CHAPTER 3

Military Service

I t was hard to ignore guns, the military, and war in the 1940s and early
1950s. I still remember Friday, September 1, 1939, when Nazi Germany bombed Poland. I was five years old. The family had been staying in the farmer's cottage on Salt Acres in Stonington for the summer.

Dad came across the causeway toward the cottage, driving our Buick convertible from his Prudential job in Newark for the weekend. He repeatedly honked the horn to signal the start of World War II in Europe.

Dad, at age 30, felt obliged to do his duty, enlisted in the New Jersey State Guard, and was appointed captain. Later, he was accepted as an officer in the Navy Supply Corps and stationed in Washington, DC.

As much as I hate to admit it now, it was thrilling for a 7-year-old to be close to the real thing. Dad took me to a shooting range to fire live ammunition at a target, first with a .45-caliber pistol, then with a Thompson submachine gun. Once, he took me on maneuvers with his New Jersey State Guard unit and gave me a pistol to shoot blanks as an "enemy" approached silently through the woods. I remember him warning me, "Don't aim at his head, or the blanks will put his eyes out."

We were no longer cowboys and Indians. The outside game was war: Americans versus Germans. We'd divide into teams armed with replica machine guns, M1 rifles, and .45 pistols. The woods and fields behind our house were dotted with trenches for mock battles.

Mom and Dad gave me a Winchester 52 "Bull Gun" for Christmas 1947 when I was 13. This was the premier .22-caliber, small-bore target rifle with a heavy barrel weighing 13 lbs. Shooting became my winter

32

sport. I joined the local rifle club at the police station in Glen Ridge. They had a 50-foot shooting range. By age 15, I was competing in local events and had earned the highest ranking in the National Rifle Association (NRA): "Expert Rifleman."

At the Loomis School, I led its rifle team as captain to two undefeated seasons. Later, at Princeton, entering the annual championship among all service ROTCs, I won the event four years straight.

Color-blind?

In the mid-1950s, all college students either signed up for the Reserve Officers' Training Corps or were subject to being drafted upon graduation. While at Loomis, I applied for the Navy ROTC full-scholarship program, which included a living allowance at my college of choice.

Both my uncles and my father had been in the US Navy. I maintained an up-to-date record of *Janes Fighting Ships*. When one was sunk, I crossed it off. When launched, it was added. I was Navy all the way

I aced the Navy aptitude test to be ranked second in New England. That meant I could attend Princeton with a full scholarship to help with the family finances. It wasn't to be. The next step was a physical examination. In a blinding ice storm, I traveled by bus from the Loomis School in Windsor, Connecticut, to Springfield, Massachusetts.

The first command was, "Strip to skivvies for height and weight." Next was, "What number do you see here?" as a booklet with colored pages was thrust in front of me. "Read the numbers you see on these pages, son."

"Well, that looks like a **6.** That's a **12**. This one might be a **7**." I got about half of them right.

The Navy medic then says, "That's it. Get dressed. You're finished!"

What? I was being washed out for failing to identify half the numbers in the American Optical HRR Color Blindness Test. This was a shock! I could pick out distant red nun buoys and green can buoys on the water quicker than anyone.

When rejected, my response should have been, *Time to Get Creative.* But, back in prep school, I'd not yet learned to challenge authority or question a situation counter to experience. In later years, I would ask questions or seek other sources of information until doubts were resolved. In this instance, that shortcoming cost my family the price of a Princeton education. For me, it meant spending military time in the dust of Fort Sill, Oklahoma, instead of on the bridge of a ship at sea.

Years later, an eye doctor would answer my lingering doubts. "The only color-blindness test recognized in a court of law is the Farnsworth D15 test, wherein you line up subtly shaded colored discs in red-to-green order," he told me. "Farnsworth was a US Navy commander who developed this test to screen sailors. I have one you can try. Here it is."

While the doctor was out of the room, I tried it. When he returned, I asked, "How did I do?"

He started turning the small oval discs over, as some numbers were on the backside. Then he said, "You cheated; they are perfectly aligned!"

"No, Doc. I didn't cheat. How was I to know there were numbers underneath?"

Navy to Air Force to Army

I blamed my alleged color blindness on the ice storm on the way to Springfield. So for the regular Navy ROTC program at Princeton, I took the same American Optical test again. The Navy failed me again.

A friend helped, "Hey Bob, join Air Force ROTC. They just use strands of colored wool." So I joined Air Force ROTC to become a pilot...or so I thought.

Halfway through sophomore year, our flight physicals were scheduled at McGuire Air Force Base near Trenton. Uh-oh! I learned the Air Force flight physical used the dreaded American Optical Color Blindness Test.

So I got a copy and memorized it. After I passed that, they slid a bead down a ruler between my eyes to test "convergence." Damn!

I couldn't cross my eyes. I'd always been able to do that. So I went out into the car and practiced crossing my eyes for about 30 minutes, then went back into the examining room and pleaded for them to test me again. They did, and I failed again.

No flight school, and maybe not graduating as a commissioned officer? This wasn't fair. So I went to the university's dean and successfully pleaded my case for not spending more time in Air Force ROTC during the spring term.

Entering junior year that fall, I saw my friend Jerry Rodts in an Army uniform. He'd been in Air Force ROTC. "Redman, how'd you get that uniform?"

He said, "The Army will take anyone. Just go down and sign up."

Rather than let my three semesters of Air Force ROTC go to waste and graduating as an airman basic, I did likewise.

Army Camp: A Father's Perspective

After our junior year in college, it was a requirement that Army ROTC cadets spend a month of summer training living in tents, firing 105 mm howitzers, and participating in other drills at the US Army Field Artillery School in Fort Sill, Oklahoma.

Me being at an army camp brought back WWII memories for my father. This precipitated a pair of heartfelt letters from him, segments of which are worth repeating because they provide insight into my parents' relationship and are the only letters I remember ever receiving from him.

7:00 AM Saturday, July 16, 1955

Dear Bob,

…It seems like yesterday, I was slithering around on my stomach for 5 miles at a clip (probably 500 yds), riding the light tanks all day with crash helmets and winding up so black and blue you couldn't move, shooting water-cooled machine guns, BARS and '03 Springfields to the point you didn't much care if you hit anything or not.

The worst, however, was trying to sleep in the lousy pup tents in the mud with your feet sticking out in the rain.

The most satisfying…was that I got my first real opportunity to command a group of other men, to build an esprit de corps. Winning camp competitions…has done more toward helping me in business than any other single thing.

That Mary of yours is great. That your mother and I have never come up with one criticism of her is amazing. Even our own children can't pass that one

What I've taken four pages to say is, "I am very proud of you, what you are doing, your outlook on life, your feelings toward Mary and Mary herself…and sincerely wish you will be as happy as your Mother and I over the years. God bless you both!"

Love, Dad

Short CIA Career

My boat captain, expert rifleman, and leadership credentials had not gone unnoticed. The CIA was always on the prowl for recruits in Ivy League colleges, as was the case with General Mark Milley, who became chairman of the Joint Chiefs of Staff years later. I graduated as a second lieutenant.

In the Princeton ROTC program, I had been a battalion commander and was honored as a Distinguished Military Graduate. If I'd accepted the offer of a regular Army commission, it would have been equivalent to a West Point degree.

The CIA probably figured sailing and sniper skills qualified me as the ideal field agent…someone to secretly sail a fishing smack to an isolated Baltic shore to terminate bad guys.

Their recruiting process started in the spring of my senior year at Princeton. Through the university's placement office, I received an inquiry as to whether I'd be willing go to New York for an aptitude test.

It turned out to be in a dark, stuffy Greenwich Village basement with overhead steam pipes. I was asked, "How would you like to jump from a plane at night into Yugoslavia to organize guerrilla bands to unseat a repressive Communist regime?" Not wanting to be rejected at this early stage, I put down something noncommittal, like "sounds interesting" or "could be exciting."

My answers warranted an invite from a "Toy Company" to visit Washington, DC, for further applicant tests and interviews. The address was not too subtle. It was one of those "temporary" World War II US Navy buildings along the Lincoln Memorial Reflecting Pool.

After registering, I was directed to walk down the hall and enter the first door on the left. I got there and looked into a dimly lit, narrow office. At the far end was an unshaven, scruffy-looking, Eastern European type. I said, "Good morning."

He just stared at me, not responding for the longest time, just staring. Then he gruffly asked, "How many languages do you speak?"

Not very cordial! I was thinking, *This isn't starting well*, so I stammered, "Well, er, three. English, three years of high school Spanish, and a year of German in college." Another long silence.

I couldn't stand it any longer, so I blurted out, "Er, ah, how many languages do you speak?"

With lowered eyelids and a scowl, he replied suspiciously, "What's behind that question?"

"Oh, I, er, nothing…just trying to have a friendly conversation." I can't remember exactly how that interview ended, but I'm fairly certain it ended badly.

Next, I was directed further down the hall to a psychiatrist, who, if anything, was a bit on the effeminate side. The only line of questioning I remember started with, "I see you are engaged to be married next month."

"Yes, that's true."

Not very subtly, he blurted out, "How many times have you had sex?" At least I recall him using that word. I understood it as "intercourse." Otherwise, defining the heavy petting of the 1950s age of innocence as "sex" might have resulted in an unacceptably high frequency.

I was thinking, *This is outrageous*, and stammered in an offended way, "Well, er, never!"

That must have done it. I was washed up. No James Bond, the streetwise, man-of-the-world, undercover agent, was I! I boarded the train back to Princeton with my tail between my legs.

Meanwhile, spooks were asking innumerable questions of friends everywhere we'd lived—Connecticut, New Jersey, and Illinois. I was getting concerned calls: "Bob, you're not in any trouble, are you?"

Then, a surprise of surprises! I got invited back to Toy Company Headquarters in Washington to meet the CIA's personnel director. They must have been looking for deceptive ingenue types with wicked skills who wouldn't stand out as CIA agents.

The CIA director of personnel greeted me in his large office. "Johnstone, you've passed with flying colors. After graduation next month from Princeton, we'd like you to start with the CIA."

I asked a few questions about salary and what would happen with my US Army military commitment. The salary mentioned was acceptable, and the director assured me, "Don't worry about the Army. We'll take care of those guys."

This was exciting and an honor. But I still had lingering doubts. Did I want to remain secretive about what I was doing…coming home at night not being able to share stories about what went on in the office that day? That would be unnatural and challenging to keep bottled up most of the time.

As a history major, a second concern haunted me. Eighteen months earlier, Senator Eugene McCarthy had been censured by the Senate, on December 2, 1954, by a 67–22 vote, for his over-the-top bullying of witnesses and red-baiting campaigns. That still left 22 senators who could be a problem. The country was far from complacent about communism.

So I decided to bring up the subject of Mary's father…to be sure that wouldn't become a problem. I thought, *It's better to get it out on the table now if it's going to be an issue.* So I said, "Director, I'm honored by the offer and am prepared to accept. Before doing so, however, I would like to get your assurance on one matter. I'm sure your background checks have been thorough. Based on all the phone calls I've gotten from friends, the agency must know everything about me by now. But I have to be sure. I don't want any information to surface in the future to sidetrack my career path."

"Sure, I understand. Go ahead. What's on your mind?"

"My employment application form declared for 'marital status' that I'm engaged to Mary B. McAvoy, daughter of Frances Chisolm Land of Washington, DC, and Clifford Thomas McAvoy of New York City."

"OK, we got that information. No problem."

"Did your security check pick up on the background of my fiancée's father, Clifford McAvoy? Are they aware that he had been Deputy Commissioner of Welfare under Mayor LaGuardia, chairman of the Committee for Socialist Unity, and a candidate for mayor of New York on the American Labor Party ticket?"

The CIA director's reaction bordered on the apoplectic, almost *SNL* comical. He practically fell out of his chair, turning white, stammering, "Ah…ah…no! I am not aware of that. This changes things. We're… we're going to…er…have to retract the offer. The background security check did not pick up on that. I'm sorry. Thank you for bringing it to our attention."

I guess he figured his job was at risk if it was discovered that such info got past his security-clearance process. At that moment, my career in the United States Central Intelligence Agency ended…ten minutes at most after having been offered the job.

In some ways, that was a relief.

This Is the Army, Lieutenant

My efforts to serve the country were not being met with great enthusiasm. First, it was the navy, then the Air Force, then the CIA. Next, it was the Army. My interface there had its moments, too.

About 60 days before being commissioned as a second lieutenant, the Army ROTC offered me, as a graduating senior, the choice of either (a) six months of active duty, with seven years of reserve duty and two weeks of annual summer training camp or (b) two years active duty, with three years of reserve duty with weekly meetings and two weeks of summer camp. The ROTC colonel continuously lobbied me to accept the regular Army commission or at least go the two-year route. But Quaker Oats had already offered me an international job upon completing military service, and I was anxious to get on with my life after getting married, which would be four days after graduation. So I signed up for the six-month program.

Two weeks later, I got a brown envelope from the US Department of the Army with orders to "Report to Fort Sill Oklahoma on 7 July for two years active duty." What?

I hustled down to the ROTC office on campus and complained, "There's been a mistake. Please change this to the six months I signed up for."

The staff sergeant at the desk threw up his hands and said, "Sorry, we can't do it. The colonel says you are going in for two years, not six months."

"You've got to be kidding. Is he in his office?" I was pointed to the door. I knocked and was invited in.

"Colonel, there's been a big mistake here. I put in for six months, and these orders came back as two years. I would appreciate your correcting the error."

"Sorry, son, but don't think we can do that. Orders are orders. You're going to have to live with it."

"I beg your pardon, *sir*! This is outrageous. How do you have the right to trample on the choice we were all given by the US Army?"

Furrowing his brow to look seriously concerned, he said, "You may think that now, but I believe we've acted in your best interest."

I was steaming, afraid to express in words what I was thinking for fear of getting kicked out of the ROTC and Princeton for disrespect. He'd probably been given some ultimatum of coming up with a minimum quota of Princeton graduates for the two-year program...whether those rebellious students liked it or not.

I walked out, closed (maybe slamming) his office door, exasperated, and returned to the sergeant's desk.

Time to Get Creative. I was already scheming and about to test what I heard about sergeants running the Army.

"Sarge, this is hard to believe! Tell me, what happens to these orders? How are they processed after they leave Princeton?"

He replied, "Well, from here, they are mailed to an Army facility on Staten Island. There's a big room full of sergeants at desks. They sort the incoming signed order requests or confirmations into six-month or two-year piles. Then those individual orders are assigned to officer-training sections at various Army centers. Princeton graduates attend Fort Still, where you had your training last summer."

"So, Sarge, do you have any friends up there?"

"Well, yeah. Sure, several. Why?"

It was time to beg. "Do you think you could do a favor for this future officer, who's otherwise starting his military career being trampled upon by this midlevel brass? Could you somehow get them to move my orders from the two-year pile back to the six-month pile, where my initial request should have gone in the first place?"

With just the slightest hint of a conspiratorial smirk, he said, "Can't promise anything but will see what I can do."

My military career and our schedule after marriage, coming up on June 16, 1956, were up for grabs.

CHAPTER 4

Mary McAvoy

J unior year at Princeton became a roller coaster for my love life. I'd had infrequent correspondence with Mary throughout my sophomore year and during my 1954 summer job as captain of the *Yawl Cat* on the Great Lakes. Mary was on a summer trip abroad. Her letters told of the great times she'd been having with some of my Princeton friends on the continent and ocean voyages over and back.

By September, I was beginning to feel like a fifth wheel and that our relationship was going nowhere. I wrote, "Dear Mary, I'm glad you are having such a good time. Please let me know when you are ready to focus a bit more on what the two of us can have fun doing together. Until then, my letters will be less frequent. Good luck!"

About sixty days later, at Cap & Gown Club, during the Harvard football game weekend party: Surprise! There's Mary! She'd been invited down from Smith by Lew Gustafson ('55), as his date. She met him on one of those ocean voyages that summer.

I was a "dateless" wallflower that weekend, seated on the sideline, watching other couples dance. Needless to say, my eyes were on Mary, probably trying to catch her eye in return. She didn't appear to be having much fun getting her feet stomped on by a clumsy Gustafson, who was three sheets to the wind.

Time to Get Creative. I tapped Gustafson on the shoulder to cut in. "May I have this next dance?" It turned into several dances. We had a great time reminiscing and making up for the lost time. I wondered at the time where that fun encounter might lead us.

The answer came a week later. I was in my dorm room after classes, on the third floor of Lockhart Hall, thinking nice things about Mary, when, believe it or not...the phone rang. It was Mary! What a coincidence! God had to be in charge.

She said, "Would you like to come up to Smith and be my date for the December House Party Weekend?"

Needless to say, after practically falling out of my chair at this sudden elevation to number-one status, I accepted.

I took the long train ride to Northampton and fell in love again. We shared our first kiss. It was a rushed clinch and kiss in front of Parsons House as the house mother was hollering for everyone to get inside for the 11:00 p.m. curfew.

That kiss took one and a half years to happen! But it only took a few more weekends, including an ice-skating party in Stonington, before we got engaged, seated on a railroad-tie bench in front of the large

stone fireplace at my family's cottage on Wamphassuc Point in June. That odd bench has remained with us for the 18 moves we've made in 66 years of marriage.

You can see Mary's reaction upon being presented with a huge box, then found inside a small jewelry box with an 1871 Tiffany-setting diamond engagement ring. That ring was passed down from Mom and my great-grandmother.

Sadly, that centerpiece of our original ceremony was stolen years later from our home in Cali, Colombia, by someone masquerading as a Quaker employee. He talked our maid into believing he was coming to fix some cracks in the house. The insurance paid for an even lovelier Colombian Muzo emerald ring set off with a pair of diamonds.

Another cherished family artifact that moved with us to Colombia, Venezuela, Wilmette, and Woodbridge, Connecticut, was Mary's grandmother's Steinway "O" model baby grand piano, which dated to the early 1900s. When moving back to Wilmette after eight years in the tropics, we had it totally reconditioned with new strings and hammer felts, then painted in a glossy black.

It was too large for our Newport condo. So we replaced it with a new upright Steinway. Mary's perfect-pitch ear not only gave her the ability to readily pick up a language, but she could sit down at the piano and play nonstop for several hours—every show tune, George Shearing piano piece, or popular song requested.

This made her a favorite after-dinner entertainer at Princeton's Cap & Gown Club during her weekends in from Smith. It also gave rise to Mary's career fantasy at one point, playing at a piano bar. Piano music continues to be an ongoing joy in our lives.

Francis Drake

Mary aced the premarital sailing compatibility test. This was a two-day delivery from Manchester, Massachusetts, to Stonington on the 30-square-meter *Ajax* with me and owner Francis Vivian "V" Drake.

Imagine three people staying overnight in the cramped, 7-foot wide quarters of that needle of a boat!

It went so well, I recall thanking V by saying, "Mary and I decided to name our second son 'Francis Drake' after you."

He was a crusty Brit, an authority on airpower, and a contributor to *Reader's Digest*. His good-natured, haughty response was, "Why not the first?"

Of course, a name like Francis Drake Johnstone was a good seafaring name to perpetuate the family's fanciful, galleon-snatching buccaneer DNA. According to the Spanish, *El Draque* was Queen Elizabeth's pirate, who seized the treasure galleon *Nuestra Senora de la Concepcion* to return home to England as the richest pirate ever.

Living up to the name, our son, Drake, perpetuated the legacy of making others wealthy. He was named by *The Wall Street Journal* as the number-one fixed-line telecommunications analyst in its 2002 "Best on the Street" survey and as number four in the software sector in the 2004 edition.

Doubling Up DNA

What was I getting myself into? I had fallen in love with a wonderful, caring young woman. I was about to embark on a life voyage as a loyal, responsible, newly minted family man, properly pursuing a military and business career to survive an unknown future, come what may. Thinking back as a historian and having only a hint of what might be in store for us made me wonder. By linking into another ancestral world, what would I burden any future offspring with? The prospects were interesting, adventurous, and foreseeably challenging.

Mary's DNA on the paternal side had a heavy dose of law and order. Her paternal great-grandfather, "Big Tom" McAvoy, was an Irish-born Tammany Hall product who became a New York City police commissioner. He was a huge, imposing man who retired with a nice contract to build the American League Park for the New York Highlanders in 1903, later known as the New York Yankees. It was built by 500 workers to hold 16,000 fans for $200,000 ($6 million in 2022).

Her grandfather, John V. McAvoy, was associate justice in the New York courts, and her father, Clifford, was a champion of the common man in the struggle with the corporate establishment.

What about the women? My grandmother, Caroline MacLaren Johnstone, counseled me, "Before you marry a girl, be sure to check out her mother...for that's who she's likely to become."

This photo of Mary's mother, "Willy," at the wheel of a sailboat indicates that I needn't have worried. It didn't hurt the blossoming relationship that the Boardman side of Mary's family were sailors with coastal cottages on the Cape and nearby Sutton Island, Maine.

Mayflower

Mary is a *Mayflower* descendant of Governor William Bradford of the Plymouth Colony, a courageous leader who took on the challenges of the church, a dangerous ocean voyage, and risk of setting up a colony in an unknown land.

Since this book is about innovation, yacht design, and seaworthiness, it's worth pointing out an interesting 17th-century design feature of the *Mayflower*...but not one that J/Boats is likely to adopt: a raised poop deck.

Believe it or not, there may not have been a Plymouth Colony, a Thanksgiving feast, or a Mary without it. It got the pilgrims to America's shores safely.

To quote friend, author, and all-American sailor Nathaniel Philbrick's description from his award-winning history, *Mayflower*:

Mystic Seaport Museum Photo

In 1957, the crew members of the *Mayflower II*—a replica of the original vessel, built in Brixton, England—became the first mariners of the modern era to experience what it was like to ride out a gale in a Jacobean-era ship. Over the course of the first few weeks of the passage, they had discovered that the *Mayflower II's* boxy hull shape took some getting used to. At times, the motion in the high aft poop cabin became so violent that Captain Alan Villiers—one of the most experienced blue-water sailors in the world—feared that he might be flung out of his bunk. What this ship would do in survival conditions was a matter of deep concern to Villiers and his men.

He needn't have worried. Toward the end of the voyage, a storm set in, forcing Villiers to do as Master Jones had done 337 years before. As the motion of the ship in the giant waves became intolerable, he decided he had no option but to lie ahull. The sails were furled, and everything on deck was tied down. Then with considerable trepidation, Villiers ordered that the helm be secured to leeward. "This was the crucial test," Villiers wrote. "Would she lie that way, more or less quietly, with the windage of the high poop keeping her shoulder to the sea? Or would she just wallow hopelessly in the great troughs, threatening to roll her masts out? We didn't know. No one had tried the maneuver in a ship like that for maybe two centuries."

As soon as the ship's bow swung into the wind, a remarkable change came over the *Mayflower II*. Even though she was under bare poles in a howling gale, her slab-like topsides functioned as a kind of wooden storm sail, magically steadying the ship's motion. Almost perfectly balanced, the *Mayflower II* sat like a contented duck amid the uproar of the storm. After being pounded unmercifully by the waves, the ship was finally at peace. "I reflected that the Pilgrim Fathers, who tossed through many such a wild night in Atlantic storms, at least knew tranquility in great gales," Villiers wrote.

South Carolina Rebel Roots

While possibly outside the purview of this book, there are compelling first-person accounts online documenting the amazing story of Mary's great-grandfather, Lieutenant Colonel Alexander Robert Chisolm (1824–1910), senior aide-de-camp to General P. G. T. Beauregard throughout the Civil War.

This Chisolm DNA may also explain Mary's courageous nature—her willingness to partner in pursuit of new product ideas that risked becoming lost causes.

It may also explain why so many people in Charleston claim to be Mary's fifth cousin and why this Yankee was cordially welcomed as a member of the Carolina Yacht Club, which looks out toward Fort Sumter.

Charleston ultimately became the birthplace of MJM Yachts, LLC, in 2002 and is our current home.

The New York Historical Society Museum Library has an extensive collection of his papers from 1861 to 1908 (MS 670.5) and is the source of his photo displayed in the Fort Sumter Museum in Charleston.

This story has a nautical twist. Chisolm's boats and knowledge of Low Country waterways around Charleston are why he was recruited to help the Confederacy.

With his boats, Chisolm played a central role in the bombardment of Fort Sumter on April 12, 1861. Then, a scant 90 days later, during a pause in the first Battle of Bull Run, he took an arduous 60-mile overnight horseback ride that arguably changed the course of the war, making Paul Revere's ride seem like a trot in the park. Both rides were at the outset of major wars on American soil.

Chisolm's military involvement started on December 20, 1860, after South Carolina seceded from the Union. South Carolina Governor Francis Pickens asked Chisolm to bring his boats and oarsmen to Charleston from his Coosaw Island rice plantation near Beaufort. Additionally, Pickens wanted Chisolm to supervise the construction of gun batteries on Morris Island, adjacent to the main ship channel at the entrance to Charleston Harbor, to prevent the Union from resupplying or reinforcing Fort Sumter. Chisolm agreed with the caveat that he would be granted a military commission as a lieutenant colonel.

He must have worked fast because on January 9, scarcely three weeks later, the unarmed supply steamer *Star of the West* started up the channel. A new 24-pounder had already been installed and manned by Citadel cadets. They put a shot across the ship's bow for it to stop. Thinking that adjacent Fort Moultrie was still a Union fort, the ship ran up a US Naval flag that the cadets read as an act of defiance. From the battery works Chisolm was erecting, they fired a seven-shell salvo, and two of them hit the ship. There were no injuries, but it was enough to make the ship beat a hasty retreat back toward New York.

One hundred fifty years later, on January 9, 2021, The Citadel proudly celebrated the anniversary of that episode, claiming it had been the start of the Civil War...although it was a one-sided, 10-minute incident against an unarmed ship.

Beauregard was appointed brigadier general by Jefferson Davis on February 22, 1861. He arrived in Charleston on March 2 to take command and receive Colonel Chisolm as his aide.

Six weeks later, Southern spies learned that a seven-ship Union fleet had left New York on April 6 and 7 under sealed orders. Nobody doubted they were headed to Charleston to reinforce Fort Sumter.

So on April 10, Jefferson Davis ordered Beauregard to open fire on Fort Sumter. He wasted no time. At 3:00 p.m. that same afternoon,

Beauregard had Captain Stephen Lee, Colonel James Chestnut, and Colonel Chisolm go to Sumter in one of Chisolm's boats to demand the fort's surrender.

Major Anderson's noncommittal reply was, "We'll abandon the Fort if directed...but we'll soon be starved out anyway."

Relationships were still very collegial at the time. As the aides were leaving, Anderson commented to Chisolm, "We're in a sorry state here and have already run out of tobacco and wine."

Beauregard was not pleased to get such a wishy-washy answer from Major Anderson. So he sent his aides back out again, late that evening, at 11:00 p.m. Another aide, Colonel Pryor, was sent along to ask Major Anderson, "What day would you be willing to evacuate if not attacked?"

Anderson came up with another cagey reply: "April 15 at noon if not otherwise instructed or relieved by that time." This would be five days later. Beauregard and Anderson knew each other from West Point, and Beauregard knew that Anderson, who was from Kentucky, agreed with him on the slavery issue...but not on states' rights. So Beauregard was not about to launch an all-out attack on his friend if he didn't have to.

Chisolm had even brought out a peace offering of a box of cigars and a case of claret. But Anderson, starting to feel the pressure, rejected the offer, saying, "Under the circumstances, Chisolm, I don't think that's appropriate."

Beauregard had his limits. If he waited until April 15, as Anderson was angling for, the Union fleet of seven ships would be upon them, reinforcing the fort, and might attack the city itself. He sent his emissaries out again four hours later, at 3:20 a.m. that same morning, April 12.

Three round trips in 12 hours had to have been grueling for Chisolm's rowers! Negotiating was over. This was an oddly named "courtesy call."

"We're here to give you fair warning; we will open fire in exactly one hour." Anderson still didn't capitulate. That was the start of two-sided hostilities. The Civil War had begun in earnest only a month after Lincoln's inauguration.

Battle of Bull Run

After Fort Sumter, an outraged Northern press and public clamored for a Union army victory. So Lincoln planned a massive quick strike to end the war before it went too far. He ordered General Irvin McDowell to march his 32,230-man army of raw recruits into Virginia and overwhelm Beauregard's smaller Confederate force of 21,900 troops near Bull Run, then immediately continue to take Richmond for a decisive victory.

The plan was to do this before the South got further organized at a planned Confederate Congress on July 20. A Grant or Sherman might have pulled it off, but McDowell was not the right man for the job.

Only 25 miles from Washington, General Beauregard had his outnumbered and outgunned Confederate army lined up behind Bull Run, a large creek running east-west near Manassas Junction.

Lincoln's plan was brilliant. But General McDowell lacked accurate maps, and logistics weren't his strong point. He wrongly assumed General Patterson's 18,000-man Union force near Harper's Ferry would keep General Joseph Johnston's 12,000-man Confederate Army of the Shenandoah pinned down in the valley 50 miles away. He overlooked that the two Confederate armies had a railroad line between them that could allow them, given warning and time, to concentrate their forces against him.

Furthermore, no one in American warfare had ever managed as many as 30,000 troops in battle or the logistics to sustain action. This was a challenge for even the best of generals, and McDowell was far from that. He was meticulous to the point of inaction. If an order were given, he'd soon come up with a reason to change it, creating utter chaos. By the time McDowell was ready to move, even the enemy knew when and where he was going.

McDowell lobbied Lincoln to postpone the attack to "better train all his raw volunteers." But Lincoln said, "No, the Confederates have the same problem we have, and we've got the advantage in numbers."

The Confederate espionage network in Washington reported that McDowell's army started moving out of Washington on July 16.

On the morning of July 18, the Confederates were ready and waiting behind Bull Run.

Longstreet's biography describes Colonel Chisolm and Brigadier General James Longstreet on horseback, looking down from a hill at the first advance of the Union army in the war. Longstreet turned to Chisolm and asked to borrow his "opera glasses" to get a better look.

Those mother-of-pearl Parisian opera glasses (pictured at right) are a family treasure. The leather case is pretty well beaten up, having bounced around on horseback with the Colonel throughout the war.

Hustling back to Beauregard, Chisolm understood his general's concern that his army was about to be crushed by the sheer, nearly two-to-one advantage of McDowell's approaching forces.

His earlier request of President Davis in Richmond to authorize General Johnston to send all or half of his twelve-thousand-man army to combine forces near Manassas had been denied.

At that time, Johnston's army could be 50+ miles away in the Shenandoah Valley. It could take several days to link up. That would be too late. The South would be defeated!

That morning, Beauregard belatedly received word that Richmond had finally authorized Johnston's support. But communications were so slow and confusing that Johnston didn't know Beauregard's disposition or exact location, nor vice versa.

Time to Get Creative. Colonel Chisolm rose to the occasion. He volunteered to ride west to find Johnston immediately, even if it meant riding 50 miles through the night to Winchester, where Johnston's Army of the Shenandoah was last reported to be.

All was not lost yet. There was a remote chance that McDowell's dithering would allow Chisolm's mission to work.

On that first day of battle, on June 18, Longstreet's troops held off Union advanced troops, which withdrew at noon after initial attempts at crossing Bull Run. If McDowell would procrastinate another day or so, Johnston and 6,000 or more of his troops might be able to get into the battle.

Chapter 8 in *Battle at Bull Run* by William C. Davis recounts from Chisolm Papers in the New York Historical Society the story of Chisolm's ride.

He took off on his horse, heading west along the Manassas Gap railroad bed toward Thoroughfare Gap and through the first range of mountains. He hoped that Johnston's army might be found near the rail line. That afternoon, the first 18 miles of hard riding were tough on his horse. As he approached the gap where it narrowed through the Bull Run Mountains, his horse was ready to collapse.

It was growing dark. Passing a farmhouse, Chisolm spied an unattended horse in a farmer's pasture.

Time to Get Creative...again. "Negotiations be damned," he reasoned. Time was critical. So Chisolm left his horse in the pasture and saddled up the farmer's. With a fresh mount, he rode another 15 miles. Fortunately, he found General Johnston and more than half of his men only 33 miles away at Piedmont Station.

The challenge was to move 8,900 men and equipment east to Manassas before the superior Union forces attacked. That could be a two-to-three-day march on foot, which would be too late. But Johnston's army could "take the train" to Manassas to reinforce Beauregard and better even up troop numbers with McDowell.

After briefing Johnston on the dire tactical situation Beauregard faced and the urgency of reinforcements, Chisolm grabbed a bite to eat and insisted on riding back to give Beauregard the good news that help was on the way.

The return trip, on a moonless night, was not easy. Chisolm remembered, "I couldn't see the reins in my hand." Fighting sleep, he carefully picked his way back through the gap, eventually arriving at the same farmer's field where he'd left his horse. He again swapped the farmer's horse for his now-rested steed. As he galloped off, he wondered whether that sleeping farmer would ever know the pivotal role he may have played in changing the course of the war.

Getting back into Confederate camps at daybreak on July 19, he spread the good news. He'd completed a 66-mile nighttime round trip on horseback. General Beauregard was elated. Chisolm had done the impossible!

Meanwhile, true to form, McDowell dawdled for two more days instead of pressing the attack on July 18 or 19 while opposing Confederate armies were still split 33 miles apart.

By the night of July 19 and the next day, July 20, Johnston's army was rolling into position by rail alongside Beauregard's forces. Union officers reported hearing train whistles and the rumbling of railroad cars along the tracks, which were only six miles away.

On July 21, McDowell's army, having blown a three-day opportunity, finally attacked, shelling Rebels across Bull Run. Union troops then crossed the river at Sudley Ford, hitting the Confederate left flank, and began to push some 4,500 rebels back across the Warrington turnpike and up Henry House Hill.

A crowd had come down from Washington, along with reporters and congressmen, to enjoy a picnic on a nearby hillside while watching the anticipated victory. They had already started celebrating that victory when the tide turned.

Johnston and Beauregard brought their combined numbers into play while the Union scrambled to coordinate piecemeal regimental attacks. By 4:00 p.m. that afternoon, with both sides having about 18,000 troops engaged, Beauregard ordered a massive counterattack across the entire line, with all the Confederates screaming the "rebel yell" for the first time in the war.

Facing these wild, crazed, screaming banshees, the Union line broke, running in panic back across Bull Run Creek, colliding with hundreds of startled Washington picnickers, which put everyone into a mad-dash retreat back to Washington.

The Northerners, expecting a quick, decisive victory, were shocked. Lincoln removed McDowell from command and replaced him with General George McClellan, who wasn't much better. McClellan procrastinated, spending an inordinate amount of time retraining and reorganizing the Army of the Potomac, further delaying hostilities.

Tragically, the war was prolonged another four years, until April 9, 1865, with the loss of 618,222 lives on both sides.

One can only speculate what might have happened had Chisolm not volunteered for that ride...or had General Ulysses Grant or Sherman been in command of superior Union forces to aggressively charge forward on June 18 and 19, when McDowell pulled back.

There's a possibility that Union forces would have overrun Beauregard to reach Richmond and end the war before it started in earnest.

Honeymoon Cruise

On June 16, 1956, four days after my Princeton graduation, Mary and I were married on a very hot day at Westmoreland Congregational Church in Washington, DC, with a small family bridal party reception at Mary's mother's house on Klingle Road.

We departed that same evening for Traverse City, Michigan, to commence our two-week North Channel honeymoon cruise on the 28-foot Hinckley 21 *Hizzoner.*

The North Channel is a long body of water that runs east-west and is only about 35 feet deep. So gale-force winds from the west build up huge waves.

Robert L. Johnstone

It was an adventurous "moon." At one point, we anchored in the Turnbull Islands, a remote group of small islands off Blind River, Ontario.

A strong westerly weather system kept us hunkered down for several days. It was blowing so hard that the Dyer dinghy, astern while at anchor, literally was lifted up in the air and turned upside down.

We were running low on food supplies, and the wind did seem to be moderating down to about twenty-five knots.

Time to Get Creative. I said, "Let's make a break for it."

We fitted a storm trysail for a beam reach across open water, south to Manitoulin Island, where there was a large bay protected by a high mountain on its western side.

Seas were still running high, and I was worried about the dinghy flipping over again as it crested a wave behind us. So all the way across, I was holding the tiller with one hand and the dinghy painter in the other, giving it a yank to pull the bow down so it wouldn't take off.

The only time Mary seemed alarmed was shortly after she went below to use the head. The boat dropped off the back side of a particularly large wave. I heard a yelp. Asked what happened when she came back up on deck, she said, "I went airborne!"

We survived to cruise back to Mackinac Island and Traverse City.

Fort Sill

After our honeymoon adventure, we drove back to Stonington to participate in my younger sister Bobette's wedding to a submariner, Naval Academy grad, and future Director of Naval Intelligence Al Burkhalter. Waiting for us was a familiar brown envelope from the US Army. *Change of Orders. Instead of 2 years of active duty starting July 17, report to Fort Sill for 6 months of active duty starting August 12.* The sergeants in Staten Island had done it!

With changed orders, we entered Fort Sill with the graduating class from West Point, who had elected artillery. We were offered married-officer housing off base in a neighborhood of single-story houses with carports called Sneed Acres.

The program started with 90 days of basic officer training with a lot of classroom work and the firing of 105-mm howitzers in the field. Essentially, we were being trained as forward observers, sited on the front lines, in an advantageous location, to identify targets through binoculars. We'd call in single rounds of artillery fire to bracket a target before "firing for effect," when a battery of six guns or more would open up on the target. The targets were generally a lot of beat-up old tanks, etc.

It was a game to win, to be the best among my fellow officers. I won the night-orienteering course in which we had to go through woods and streams with only a compass to arrive at the objective. Using my sailing background, I realized the key was to take an initial compass bearing, then look up to see a star or cloud configuration in that direction. Then I'd jog, avoiding stumps, trees, etc., in the direction of that object in the sky. The others would be walking or stumbling along while focused on the compass needle.

I loved gunnery and went through with perfect scores on all the tests except high-angle fire. But it was good enough to finish third in class, with a General's Commendation, ahead of all but one of the West Point graduates.

That commendation also came with an offer to remain at Fort Sill as a gunnery instructor for two years. This was an appealing honor, but for two years? I was tempted because a future career option was to become a history teacher. This could provide a good classroom experience.

But I'd learned not to trust people trying to make a career army man out of me. I asked, "If I said yes, how might those new orders be processed?"

They answered, "We send the request to the Pentagon, and they change your assignment from the six-month program to a two-year program. Then another branch of the army assigns you to Fort Sill."

"OK, so what are the chances of that not happening once I agree to the two years? If I don't get assigned to Fort Sill, where would I most likely be assigned?"

"The chances are only about 2 percent that our request would be denied. In that unlikely case, you'd most likely be posted to Korea."

Oh, no! Here we go again. No guarantees in the army. "Gentlemen, thank you for the honor of being selected as qualified to be a gunnery instructor here at Fort Sill. But I've got a wonderful wife and a nice job lined up with Quaker Oats International, and I just can't afford to take that 2 percent risk."

At that point, I was assigned as the Assistant S-3 of the Sixth Field Artillery Battalion stationed at Fort Sill. The Sixth was meant to be an active unit, ready to depart overseas on short notice.

Taking my job seriously even then, considering it was *Time to Get Creative*, I submitted to army headquarters a rewrite of fire-control procedures in the Forward Observer Manual to reduce the time lapse between identifying a target and "firing for effect" with a full battery of guns.

Another subject that intrigued me was the use of more timely artillery barrages to suppress dug-in enemy infantry yards in front of our advancing troops, so they could be on top of the enemy before they could recover from the shock of the barrage. There'd be less chance of one of our soldiers being killed by an errant shell from our artillery than of giving the enemy time to recover and start shooting at our advancing infantry with an accurate rifle and machine-gun fire.

Mary and I left Fort Sill in late January 1957 to enjoy a brief respite with family in Geneva before starting with Quaker Oats, at the world's largest cereal mill, in Cedar Rapids, Iowa.

For me, the two most memorable personalities with a Fort Sill artillery background I encountered over the years were football's Heisman Trophy winner, Billy Vessels, of the University of Oklahoma Sooner fame, and Commodore Henry A. "Harry" Anderson* of the New York Yacht Club.

Harry trained at Fort Sill before going overseas in World War II to serve in Patton's army. I felt a unique personal affinity for Harry. We were two sailors who were army officers in a club full of naval personnel. And due in part to Mary's and my love of the man, Harry requested of Mary, in her role as priest, to preside over his memorial service. Mary responded, "OK, Harry, I'll do it as long as I don't die before you do."

She fulfilled Harry's request in 2021, just before his 100th birthday.

CHAPTER 5

South America

O ne of my senior-year job interviews at Princeton was with Augustin S. "Gus" Hart, vice president of Quaker Oats International. This came about because I had been sufficiently impressed with Quaker people I'd met during Christmas parties at my parents' home in Geneva, Illinois. Dad was then managing the Prudential Building downtown. Two neighbors of his were Quaker's vice presidents of production, Jack D'Arcy, and personnel, Tom Bartel. I'm not sure in retrospect whether this was a subtle move by Dad to help me get a real job after college or not. If so, it worked.

During the interview on campus, Gus asked whether I liked visiting grocery stores. Thinking back on the interview, I realized this was a loaded question, and I had given him a wishy-washy answer along the lines of, "They're OK. I sometimes help out with the shopping."

Time to Get Creative. Before sending a letter of thanks for the interview, I decided to do a store check of several markets in Princeton and talk to store managers. I had to report the bad news to Gus. Quaker was not doing a very good job servicing the stores, and as a result, they were getting less shelf space than they probably deserved.

That undoubtedly sealed the deal! Gus didn't take much time to respond. Short-circuiting the normal employment dance, he said, "Would it be possible for you to come to New York and for me to meet your fiancée? We usually want to interview the wife of anyone we send overseas, as they can be a problem sometimes. Asking to meet the fiancée may be a first."

After I answered in the affirmative, he asked, "Where would you like to meet?"

"Mr. Hart, contrary to what you might imagine Princeton students doing lately"—he was Princeton '37—"this one hasn't spent any time in New York. So we'll meet you wherever you'd like."

He suggested, "How about under the clock at the Biltmore?" This struck me as very funny. How preppy can you get?

Several weeks later, Mary came down from Smith, and we met at a small, marble-top table. Contractors were making lots of noise repairing the ceiling. I later heard Gus didn't like soft violins playing in the background at dinner. Gus asked Mary leading questions like, "How do you like Washington, DC, in the summer?" A little too obviously, he was trying to assess Mary's staying power in the tropics.

When Mary answered, "I hate it; much too hot. We go to Maine in the summer," I was kicking her under the table and rolling my eyes to convey, "Wrong answer!"

But we got the job. The plan was to first put me through a one-year production training program in Cedar Rapids, Iowa, after getting out of the army.

Cedar Rapids

In February 1957, we'd finished our six-month army stint. Before reporting to my first job at the world's largest cereal mill in Cedar Rapids, Iowa, and after visiting my parents' home in Geneva, Illinois, Mary and I drove to Ishpeming, Michigan, for a week of skiing. There I received further affirmation of Quaker's worth as my future employer.

The ski hill in Ishpeming had a rope tow that only functioned on weekends. So there was nobody but the two of us during weekdays, herringboning up the hill, then skiing back down. On the second day, curiosity got the best of the 80-year-old caretaker of the facility, who had a small shack with a stove. He asked, "Son, what do you do for a living?"

I replied defensively, "Well, I just got out of the army, and we had a few days free before starting work at the Quaker Oats Company cereal mill in Cedar Rapids, Iowa. So we thought we'd have some fun here in snow country."

With surprising enthusiasm, he said, "Quaker Oats? Why let me tell you, young fella, you couldn't have picked a better company to work for. About 25 years ago, when I was in my fifties, I was taking six different kinds of pills and medicines every day. A friend told me to forget all those chemicals and just have a hot bowl of Quaker oatmeal every day, and I'd be fine. Look at me! I took his advice and feel fit as a fiddle at 80."

This wasn't the only testimonial to provide career reinforcement. One of my later favorites was the story of "Jungle Rudy," who lived in the jungle of Southeastern Venezuela. He would emerge every month to fill up his canoe with just two items: cases of beer and Quaker Oats!

Derecktor's Boat Yard?

As a 23-year-old, the question, "What will I do with the rest of my life?" continued to crop up. While making a positive contribution to world health at Quaker Oats was appealing, the draw of sailing was ever present. There wasn't much sailing on the Cedar River. I started out by having to learn every job in the world's largest cereal mill in Cedar Rapids, Iowa, starting with the dirty job as a mill sweeper at 6:00 a.m. This wasn't the management training I'd bargained for. I already knew how to work a broom.

Time to Get Creative? It won't surprise the reader that I'd stayed in touch with the sailing world through a subscription to *Yachting*...nor that I'd scan the classifieds. That's how I came across the information that Derecktor's Shipyard in Mamaroneck, New York, was looking for an assistant yard manager. I sent my sailing resume to the owner, Bob Derecktor^. He was sufficiently intrigued to call.

I explained my interest to him on the phone. "Sailing is my passion, and the Gulfstream 30 you make is a boat we could aspire to own someday. My greatest satisfaction would come from building similar craft and participating in the expansion of a successful boatyard." That answer passed the test, and I was invited to visit Derecktor's yard in Mamaroneck.

Using too much of our paltry salary, I flew into LaGuardia and took a train to Mamaroneck, expecting to be met at the station. But there was no such courtesy! Bob was a gruff, Germanic type who got right to his yard-worker frame of reference: "What is the best brush to use applying the final coat of varnish to a taffrail?"

My response was, "I don't know but could learn soon enough." He wasn't happy with my answer.

After a few other technical questions, he concluded, "The trouble is, Johnstone, you are too smooth and need roughing up a bit, and I'm too rough and could be a bit smoother."

Did I like this guy? Would this be a "fun" association? I was having my doubts. Sadly, the chemistry wasn't there. During the interview, a thought was gathering momentum: Sailing, to me, was my escape and joy. Did I want to "have to" deliver any boat as a job requirement, particularly if it wasn't a boat of my choice to sail?

I thanked him for taking the time to see me and agreed he was probably right. So it was back to Cedar Rapids and Quaker Oats. This flight of fancy came to naught. Sailing could come later. I had to support a family with a real job.

How's that for scratching the surface, for the second time, of what was to come 18 years later? I didn't pick up on Chris-Craft and walked away from Derecktor's.

"South American Getaway"

After another six months of visiting applicable Quaker plants and their engineering department in Chicago, on December 25, 1957, our first child, Stuart, was born. Two months later, we were winging our way to Cali, Colombia.

In retrospect, the title of this section is one of my favorite Burt Bacharach tunes, as sung by the Swingle Singers in the movie *Butch Cassidy and the Sundance Kid.* So I guess I was to become the Quaker Oats Kid at age 23, as production manager of Productos Quaker SA, responsible for 125 employees and staff...with only three years of high school Spanish and hoping for a better ending than Newman and Redford had in Bolivia.

This assignment in a small manufacturing company was tantamount to embarking on my own Harvard Business School case study. Within two years, I was promoted to the general manager (CEO). But at the outset, I was not that confident in my abilities to make the right business decisions and forecast outcomes.

I certainly didn't fancy myself a creative, risk-taking, adventurous entrepreneur. As a Depression baby graduating from Princeton in the 1950s, I was more the loyal employee, imbued with my parents' Depression-era need for security. I had signed up with a Fortune 500 corporation at the outset. I was sent down into South America to sink or swim. Resourcefulness was called for. There were no experts to bounce a problem off of or another department to shuffle responsibility to, saying, "This is your area; fix it!" There was no email or iPhone. Airmail and Telex were it. Overseas phone calls were exorbitantly expensive. A letter exchange could take two to four weeks.

Before departing from the States, I learned that my first major challenge would be balancing the high-speed, 3,600 RPM rotor assembly of a Daffin Hammer Mill. This was like balancing an auto tire, except this rotor was about 24" wide and swinging an  array of two-by-eight-inch, rectangular steel plates (hammers), which pulverized corn, wheat, soybeans, etc. into flour. Requests from Colombia to Quaker HQ were desperate. Even a local MIT grad couldn't figure it out.

Quaker was producing Ful-O-Pep poultry and animal feed mixes. When hammers wore down, the mill got out of balance and started jumping around, heating up the bearings, which then failed. They had to import one of these expensive mill rotor assemblies about every three weeks. In the States, it was easy: clamp the rotor onto a balancing machine and bring it up to speed to balance it statically and dynamically. It showed how much and where to place balancing weights on the rotor. Those expensive machines didn't exist in Colombia.

Time to Get Creative. I went to an elder Quaker engineer in the Chicago office and asked him what they did in the old days before we had these newfangled balancing machines.

He vaguely remembered some old process and pulled out a 1925 engineering textbook that outlined a primitive method: placing trial weights in various locations and marking the shaft at either end with a pencil to identify peak deflection.

My initial credentials in Cali were quickly established when I, admittedly to my own surprise, pulled it off. Not bad for a history major!

Unlike businesses in the US, where companies are loath to share information, I sought input for resolving labor management and other business problems from fellow American managers of local subsidiaries. These included Colgate-Palmolive, American Home Products, Container Corporation, and Corn Products Refining Company. We all sat on the US consul's business advisory board.

One of the more challenging problems was negotiating the company's first labor contract with a rough, Moscow-trained union organizer. This was precipitated by my initial moves to improve plant efficiency.

Of the total 135 workers, it was quite evident that about 30 of them were redundant and had been put to work doing useless tasks like trimming bushes with scissors.

The general manager was a Yale graduate who had been wounded in the Korean War. We kept him in the background so I could propose some reasonable-sounding benefit, saying, "Let's bring that up with the general manager to see if it's acceptable."

Of course, there were more benefits requested that were not acceptable than were. Eventually, with some reasonable new provisions, we got to a stalemate on the contract. I felt we'd gone as far as we could since our workforce was split on whether to accept the contract conditions or not, and the Communist was recommending the rejection of our offer.

Time to Get Creative. I decided to employ a combination shut-down-and-lockout strategy by closing the plant and backing up a large van to our loading docks to move office furniture, equipment, and files to rented space in a hotel downtown. I expressed great regret, saying, "We hate to do it; we love you all, but that labor agitator you're using forced us into it." The contract was signed within 48 hours.

For product development opportunities and marketing strategies, I leaned on J. Walter Thompson, Grey Advertising, and McCann Erickson managers, who had offices in South America. But there was a limit to what they knew and how much they could help me in our specific business areas.

Down there, you were it! So I had to come up with solutions by myself.

Lago de la Cocha

After eight months on the job, needing a break from that challenging labor negotiation, I was ready for our annual vacation (we had to stay local for this one). Mary, 10-month-old Stu, and I went to a Colombian-government-owned hotel on a large crater lake, 8,800 feet up, near the city of Pasto, almost on the equator. The Swiss-born proprietor was a sailor who had built his Snipe-like sailboat and was persuaded to lend it to us. Our first sail was on a beautiful, crisp day with a nice, moderate breeze.

Had the strands of DNA gotten twisted? Ten-month-old Stuart, a future collegiate Sailor of the Year, lay on the cockpit floor and screamed for the entire two hours. It must have been like cowboys breaking in a young colt. Any complaints he may have had later about being on a boat were worked out of his system before age one. That was it. No more prolonged outbursts, although the kid did have a temper streak that surfaced on occasion when sailing, making me wonder whether it was a latent reaction to some poor parenting at the time. It seemed possible, however, that we had a powerboater on our hands.

The next day, while fishing, Stu seemed happy holding the handle of an outboard underway. We landed a rainbow trout on just about every cast of our spinning gear. Normally, I'd string them on a wire hanging off the stern in cold water. At one point, they were coming in so fast a few were still flopping around in the boat. Stu picked one up and bit it like he would eat it raw, making it like a baby bear. That did inspire us to land on a wild section of shore, build a driftwood fire, and have chargrilled trout for lunch. The rest of the stay was fantastic. We caught more than 40 rainbow trout on spinning gear.

At such a high elevation, nights were cold. We were the only guests at the time. The chef-proprietor served us trout for every meal but never prepared it the same way. We played chess and shot darts from native blowguns at gourds lined up on the mantelpiece over a roaring fire. Hot-water bottles were put under a mountain of quilts to warm our beds.

The natives went out on the lake with jacklights on our last night to pull in the same number of trout we'd caught during the week, then packed them in paper and ice to take home.

Club Campestre

Cali was at 3,300 feet elevation in Valle del Cauca, 50 miles inland over the Andes Mountain range from the tropical port of Buenaventura. There was no place to sail on weekends at the time, although now, Calima Lake and the hydroelectric project have been completed with a resort 60 miles from Cali. It was the site of the inaugural Junior Pan Am Games in December 2021.

So how was I going to sail?

Time to Get Creative. The only convenient body of water was a small pond at the Club Campestre golf course. Model sailboats had to be the answer. Eight expatriate American manager friends were talked into importing Dumas model Star boats to build. This was before radio control. The plan was to sail them on the pond as they do in the Model Boat Basin in Central Park, turning them away from the shore with long sticks. Only one model got completed—mine. This fleet-building effort didn't bode well for a future in the marine industry.

The reader will eventually learn that it took another 60 years when this author had retired to a residential senior community in Charleston, South Carolina, to finally put together an active racing fleet of 22 DragonFlite 95 radio-controlled model sailboats as Commodore of the Bishop Gadsden Yacht Club.

Santa Marta

The northern coast of Colombia has a couple of amazing ports. My favorite is Cartagena. Walking through that old city, with its imposing forts and old walls, was like stepping back into the 17th century, imagining Spanish galleons in the harbor. The place made me think that the alleged swashbuckling-pirate DNA was real.

A clue to our future in the sport occurred in the port of Santa Marta, in eastern Colombia, on a beach in front of our hotel. This was the country's major banana port, and I was there to check on Quaker's distributor and shelf presence in the local markets. As Mary and I were sipping our Ron Viejo rum drinks on the balcony one evening, we studied local fishermen on the beach and their craft, similar to dugout canoes. The wind was blowing parallel to the beach. Two fishermen would paddle their boat to windward to launch their fishing nets, then raise a mast and sail, which seemed to be made of old grain sacks, to return downwind along the beach. One occupant had a wide paddle, and the sternman had a thinner one to use as the rudder steering the boat. It was a shame they had to work so hard paddling upwind.

Time to Get Creative, possibly after too many Ron Viejos. I told Mary, "I bet we could sail one of those boats to windward."

The next morning, a native boatman accepted our proposition, accompanied by a few pesos. With the sail raised, Mary knelt in the middle of the boat, holding the wide paddle down in the water, vertically against the hull, like a leeboard. I sat in the stern with the thin paddle and held the mainsheet controlling the gunnysack sail.

We sailed to windward up the beach, then back downwind to the surprised owner. He seemed pleased, but, yachting being the reactionary sport it is, the innovation never caught on—he probably chalked us up as a couple of gringos locos.

25-Year-Old CEO

As production manager, to better gauge my performance and that of my department heads, I became interested in financial controls and statements being sent to the parent company. This ultimately led General Manager Jack Hussey to rely on me to write the monthly and quarterly reports submitted to Quaker International headquarters on Wall Street.

In 1960, Quaker transferred Hussey to Brazil, Assistant Manager Pierson Oliver to Mexico, and Product Development Manager Art Ortiz to Venezuela.

I was tapped to be the new General Manager (CEO) for Colombia and Ecuador. I was 25 years old at the time. Talk about "fast track!" Could book learning at Harvard Business School be any better?

Our 1959 Christmas card shows the newly minted "Jefe" in a suit and polished shoes, with Senora Mary and the young family of Stuart, age 2, and Drake at 11 months, being guarded by our pet beagle, Banner.

ArepArina

Coming up with the instant version of Colombia's staple food was a major innovation that did catch on…and caused Quaker to make its largest investment in South America at the time.

In many respects, Quaker subsidiaries depended on Quaker research in the US to develop new products. Arepas, the bread of Colombia, are traditionally made with degerminated white corn, cooked overnight, ground into a mush, kneaded, formed into burger-shaped patties, and cooked on a grill to fulfill the family's needs for all three meals.

That purse of Juan Valdez's in Colombian coffee ads is called a *carriel*, which holds his arepas for the day.

Quaker had worked for seven years in their Barrington, Illinois, research lab to develop an instant product. Since Quaker is the largest manufacturer of corn grits in the US, they figured this would be right up their alley. When they believed they'd done their best, we were instructed to put up a pilot plant to produce the dry mix and launch it into a test market.

Because the mix was hygroscopic and infestation was a problem, distributing flour products in hot tropical climates was challenging. We were directed to sell the mix in one-pound cardboard boxes, overwrapped with Bencoseal, an expensive, imported laminate of paper, aluminum, and polyethylene.

Test-market results in the city of Armenia were disastrous. A pound of Quaker's mix was four times the price of the degerminated white corn from which the homemade version was made.

Product quality was also a disaster. The traditional version was slow-cooked overnight. In the early morning, the soft, cooked corn was run through a meat-grinder-type device to create a soft, smooth, moist masa formed into a patty to put on the grill. It's delicious. The inside of an arepa is still somewhat wet and flavorful. Outside it has a firm but not crispy, cohesive crust. The outer skin of the Quaker product would crack, and the inside would dry out and crumble. It was terrible.

Time to Get Creative. Resourcefulness was called for. The city of Medellín is reputed to have the best arepas in Colombia. Solution? Hop on an Avianca DC-3 and go up into poor barrios on the city's hills to interview housewives, asking, "How do you make your arepas?" Maybe we could pick up a clue for a solution.

Eureka Moment

Those homemakers in the barrios showed me how they made masa from the corn they'd cooked overnight. They used a meat-grinder device with a pair of counter-rotating, serrated metal plates that sheared the soft, cooked corn kernels into mush to be formed into patties. That's it!

It was a eureka moment! I had a flashback to studying the cell structure of plants in eighth-grade biology class. The corn was not cut up or blasted apart by hammers; it was sheared without rupturing cell walls. The Quaker process destroyed the cell structure of the corn with the knives of a 3,600 RPM hammer mill. Ruptured cells don't retain moisture to form either a cohesive crust or a moist masa interior.

Back at the pilot plant in Cali, we installed some industrial-sized versions of what the housewives were using. The dried instant arepa we produced made a product that tasted as good as homemade. *Voila!* It had worked…almost. We had the product, but what about distribution?

How do we get it into consumers' hands at a reasonable price? We had to somehow eliminate that costly, triple-film-laminated box.

Time to Get Creative again. The answer was right in our plant. One of our products was Ful-O-Pep animal feed, which used 70-lb., multiwalled paper sacks. We also imported oat groats from Argentina, Australia, Canada, and the US—the oat "berry," without the husk—which we steamed and rolled into Quaker oats. These groats came in 70-lb. polyethylene-lined jute sacks.

Grains were traditionally sold in a galleria's many small market stalls from one of these large sacks. The stall proprietor would fill 10 to 20 one-pound bags of beans, rice, etc., to put on the shelf—the number being what he could sell during the day. Meanwhile, the bulk of the product would stay protected from infestation and moisture contamination in the large, sealed sack.

So how do you project any brand identity in those small, brown paper bags? OK, "So, what if we supplied branded, bright white paper bags for the seller to package what was needed for the day? Then we could sell ArepArina in 70 lb. polyethylene-lined Kraft paper bags. Before sewing the top of the Kraft bag shut, we insert 72 (let them cheat a little) crisp white paper bags branded with 'ArepArina by Quaker.'"

The net result was: we got arepa quality to equal homemade and got the price down to a level close to the cost of the basic corn in a white bag that stood out from the other plain paper bags on the shelf. The sales in the test market took off like gangbusters. Quaker built a nice new plant in Cali, its largest investment in a manufacturing facility in Latin America.

Alianza Para el Progreso

Flashback! Here was this gringo in a khaki suit going up into the barrios, allegedly trying to figure out how to make arepas. Well, it wasn't long before a curious crowd gathered and started asking questions about what was happening. Learning that I was an American, they started bombarding me with questions about President Kennedy's recently announced Alianza Para el Progreso in Latin America and how they might benefit.

I expounded on how US foreign policy was trying to help improve their standard of living, schools, and employment opportunities. Upon returning home to Cali, I shared with Mary the thought, "It's too bad young Americans"—me being 27—"are so coddled that some enterprising college grads couldn't be persuaded to come down to just live, interact, and talk with these people for short periods. Wouldn't that be so much more effective than Foreign Service people sitting in consular offices?" Maybe it was *Time for the US government to Get Creative.*

Imagine how thrilling it was for me about a month later (September 22, 1961) to learn that Congress had passed the Peace Corps Act, naming Colombia as one of the first two countries to receive volunteers.

US State Department

Some of our best friends in Cali were State Department employees at the US Consulate in Cali. I and general managers from other American subsidiaries, like Container Corporation, Corn Products Refining Company, Colgate-Palmolive, Home Products, and Goodyear, formed an advisory board for the consulate. A primary US Foreign Service mission was to foster American business abroad. We'd kept in touch with Marian and the late George Tolles since our particularly memorable trip hiking to the top of the Andes, 14,000 feet up, between Valle del Cauca (elevation 3,200 feet) and the port of Buenaventura, on the Pacific.

I was packing a pistol, as there was a smattering of the "violencia" in the area. These were violent gangs extracting protection money from local *campesinos*. We were lucky that our friend Paco Rojas, Quaker sales manager, knew of a young, local Indio guide with a packhorse that could lug our tents, some water, food, and cooking utensils, as this would be a three-day trip: the first day climbing up an old trail to the campsite on top, the next day exploring the area and an abandoned gold mine, then back down on the third day.

Ever try that? When nearing the top of the trail, I'd struggle to go 30 steps and then have to rest for 30 seconds.

Once on top, the body becomes acclimated to functioning with less oxygen. On the way back down, being able to process oxygen more efficiently, I was so energized I felt could almost fly. The photo shows us at the peak, celebrating, drinks in hand. This was taken above the clouds during sunset on the second day. It wasn't Mount Everest, but for us, it was seven better.

Peace Corps

Columbia One was the first Peace Corps group to be assigned any-where in the world. They came to Cali in September 1961. Mary and I were invited to the welcoming reception. Our friend John Burdick, the local CARE administrator, was the host of this highly competent group.

Chris Sheldon became director for Colombia after a horrendous personal tragedy. He had been the owner-captain of the brigantine school ship, *Albatross*, which capsized in a "white squall" and sank in seconds, with the loss of his wife, Alice, and five others. My first cousin, Tod Johnstone, was at the wheel and miraculously survived because he was on deck. The book *White Squall* details the tragedy and was made into a movie starring Jeff Bridges.

The Sheldons had met on Irving* and Electa Johnson's* *Yankee* on its last cruise in 1956. Had it not been for attending Fort Sill, Mary and I might have been on that same cruise of the *Yankee*. Before kids came along, one of our ideas for an adventurous early married life was to ship off with the Johnsons on *Yankee* as seamen and teachers. Was that another *almost entering the marine industry* moment?"

Incaparina

Another way to make the world a better place was by improving Colombia's eating habits. A unique cereal mix called Incaparina provided such an opportunity. Kwashiorkor, a protein deficiency, was killing 40,000 preschool children per year in Colombia. Milk would have provided the protein but was too expensive and not readily available.

Incaparina had been developed by the Institute of Central America and Panama (INCAP) to be a whole-food cereal, similar to diet foods like Metrecal but made primarily of corn, soybeans, cottonseed oil meal, and Torula yeast. A bowl full of that and a banana were all an infant needed for sustenance.

The challenges to overcome were to make this mix with all-local ingredients and also make it tasty. The latter proved a challenge.

Time to Get Creative. Incaparina was launched and promoted with the help of Catholic priests from their pulpits and the Ministry of Health; it was cited by the World Health Organization primarily for the cost-effective, unique, 70-lb. bulk sack and individual branded paper bag distribution, similar to ArepArina.

The project was written up in a 1964 Harvard Business School publication, *The Protein Paradox: Malnutrition, Protein-Rich Foods and the Role of Business*, by Gail Chester Belden.

Unfortunately, after mild success and much hoopla, the product didn't taste good enough to succeed in replacing the local cereal-based *coladas*. Quaker Oats were often prepared as one of the *coladas* that were preferred.

Profitability

In 1964, after six years, I left Productos Quaker SA profitable. This was my first business venture as a CEO. Revenue, in Colombian pesos, was

Ps30.6 million, with a profit of Ps2.3 million. Coincidentally, those peso amounts were the same as the US dollar amounts of MJM Yachts' revenue and profit 57 years later, in 2019, as my last business venture. Even more coincidental is that, after adjusting for inflation, the companies were the same size.

To explain: The 1963 peso-to-dollar exchange rate was 9:1. A 1963 dollar is worth nine times more in 2022. So Ps30 million Colombian pesos in 1963 was equivalent to about US$30 million in 2019. If the Company I was running at age twenty-eight was about the same size and as profitable as MJM Yachts was 55 years later in 2019, when I was 85, it doesn't say much about my life's progress as a business manager. But there was a difference. I didn't have to relinquish earnings to Quaker stockholders. They could stay home in the family.

Venezuela

My next assignment from Quaker was an awkward one. I had to fly to Venezuela, walk into the offices of Productos Quaker CA—the manufacturing subsidiary in Valencia, two hours west of Caracas—and tell the general manager, whom I'd worked with earlier in Colombia, "Really sorry to inform you, Quaker has terminated your employment. Here's the confirming letter from the boss. I've been given the unwanted task of saying you must gather your personal items, hand me the keys, and not return to the premises."

I escorted him out of the gate and told security not to let him back in.

Two weeks later, I picked up Mary and the kids in our Ford Falcon and drove up the mountain from Maiquetia Airport into the city of Caracas to the entrance of the Hotel Tamanaco. It was the inauguration week of the democratically elected President Raul Leon. Security was tight. Delegates were arriving from all over the world. Four soldiers armed with automatic weapons stopped us as we headed up the drive to the hotel.

This had to be a very elaborate ruse if we were terrorists. Mary, me in a poplin suit, and our three small, towheaded kids: Stu (6), Drake (5), and Helen (3).

They shouted, "Everybody out! Open up the trunk! What are you doing here?"

Quite shaken after about five minutes of grilling and having the car thoroughly searched, we climbed back in to drive up into the porte cochere to unload. There was a lot of kid stuff, as you can imagine.

Going up in the elevator, the door opened on every floor. We could see what were a pair of security guards wearing dark, ill-fitting suits, white socks, and scowls sitting scrunched into the small, decorator love seats opposite the elevator door on each floor. Our suite was on the same top floor as the Presidential Suite.

Then I remembered, "Oh my God, the car!" So I hustled back down the elevator and out the entrance door. Facing away from me was the head doorman. I knew he was the doorman because he wore a typical doorman's uniform, trimmed with a gold braid. So I tapped him on the shoulder and asked, "*Perdone, senor. Puede decirme, donde se puedo estacionar un carro?*" (Excuse me, sir. Can you tell me where one can park a car?) As he turned toward me to respond with a frown, I saw the ribbons and stars. Horrors! It was a Venezuelan army general! I mumbled and stammered apologies and drifted off, acting like the dumb gringo I was.

Once the car was parked and I was back up in the room, after a bourbon to settle nerves and restore ego, the kids' dinner was delivered in a stainless warming cart. My Ian Fleming thriller education chimed in. Oh my goodness, the perfect place for a bomb!

Time to Get Creative. Has Venezuelan security anticipated a terrorist ploy of coming up the service elevator pushing one of these dinner carts rather than up the main guest elevator?

Maybe I could restore my stature with the Venezuelan military by assisting with their security arrangements.

So I went out the door in my khaki suit to share this concern with the security guards seated next to the elevator. "If there's a plan to put a bomb in an ambassador's room, it's not likely to be coming up the main elevator you are watching. Have you considered it would be smarter for a bomber to use the service elevator, with the bomb inside one of those metal dinner carts, disguised as a hotel waiter?" Startled, they thanked me profusely with rapid head nods, instantly grabbing their phones to talk with supervisors.

Un Americano in a khaki suit? Must be US Secret Service sent down to check on security preparations. It would be a creative first for the Secret Service to include the wife and kids on such a mission.

The story gets better. Mary and I were scheduled to meet friends for dinner at the city's premier French restaurant, Hector's—made famous by his haughty response to a woman's question in his cooking class, who had asked exactly how many teaspoons of a certain spice should be added to the pot. Hector's prideful answer was, "Madam, please, we are chefs, not chemists!"

A call to the front desk to arrange a babysitter got a "*Lo siento mucho, senora. Pero es imposible.* They've all been spoken for. We are very busy, as you can appreciate."

Time to Get Creative again. What are we going to do? We can't take the kids with us. Wait a minute! What about those two goons sitting outside our door by the elevator? Making this probable US Secret Service agent happy would surely be rewarded by their boss. So with a positive, "*Sí, senor. Con gusto. No es un problema,*" they readily agreed to be babysitters for the evening.

We had a wonderful dinner, then got back and asked how things went. Our two government babysitters pulled out a notepad with about six entries describing sounds they'd heard, questions from the kids they answered, etc.

Best and lowest-cost babysitters we'd ever had *to date*! They'd soon be upstaged.

Sunfish Fleet-Building

Once settled in Valencia and having become members of nearby Club Lago de Guataparo, we purchased a Sunfish to sail there at the club and on weekend family trips over the mountains and down to the beautiful Venezuelan coast, with its horseshoe-shaped coves with beaches and overhanging shade palms.

It wasn't long before Mary and I were invited to beach resorts like Puerto Azul and Camuri Grande, where guest apartments were provided. We'd depart after work on Friday, one Sunfish on top and a borrowed one for Mary to sail on a trailer. It was about two hours east on the *autopista* through Caracas down to the coast. We'd stop at a shoreside kiosk for grilled, fresh fish and Club 60 beer (made by Heineken), get a good night's sleep, wake up, put on our bathing suits, and race Sunfish for two days. Paradise. But what could we do for babysitters?

Time to Get Creative. Peace Corps to the rescue. This was in 1964, three years after the first tough bunch arrived in Cali. Peace Corps volunteers sent to Venezuela were placed at the Universidad de Carabobo to teach English as a second language. They had no responsibilities on weekends and a very little spending allowance. So they were delighted to hang out in an American home with a pool and take care of the kids while Mary and I took off sailing.

My life of creating new one-design fleets and regattas for more people to have fun sailing—while not getting far with model Stars in Cali—finally got traction at Club Lago de Guataparo. This was mostly a swimming club, and a few of us got a tennis court built. I had been the Club Campestre Tennis Champ in Cali. But sailing was my game.

Time to Get Creative. So we lobbied for and built an enclosed concrete boat shed with a launching ramp for a dozen Sunfish on dollies. This was a fantastic lake to sail on during the winter trade-winds season of November to April.

You could see the clouds coming from the Caribbean, creeping over the mountain range to the north. They'd start making their way down the slope toward the lake.

Soon it would blow 25 knots with smooth water, and you'd be off on a screaming plane in your Sunfish.

The New Year's Regatta (Copa Ano Nuevo) in 1965 attracted about 30 Sunfish from all over Venezuela. We'd constructed a new set of floating docks for the event.

A British submarine commander from WWII was recruited to be the race committee chairman. On one day, it was blowing those 25 knots.

Two things happened. First, a Sunfish ran into the side of the committee boat, putting a hole in the 18-foot outboard launch.

While those aboard were frantically bailing, Mary capsized about 50 feet away. She was wearing a heavy sweatshirt that had become waterlogged, so movement was restricted even with a life jacket. In response to her request for assistance, the proper British naval officer turned, stood up in the launch, and, with a stiff upper lip, shouted, "Good lord, woman, can't you see we're sinking!"

Mary finished fifth in the Venezuelan Nationals, while yours truly won them twice and wrote the first of the "Tuning to Win" series of articles for the magazine *One-Design & Offshore Yachtsman*.

Bruce Kirby* was the editor and the eventual designer of the Laser; his admitted motivation was to one-up the Sunfish with a better-performing race boat.

Little did I know then that in nine years, I would become VP of marketing for AMF Alcort, hired to revive Sunfish sales after AMF's inept response to the introduction of the Laser.

Schooner *White Wing*

During the summer of '65, we decided that a family cruise from Stonington, Connecticut, to Maine on a larger vessel would be fun.

Brother Rodney was a yacht broker at the time and had lined up a 1920s Alden (Design #219B) classic for us: the 43-foot schooner *White Wing.* It had solid spruce masts with checks you could sink a knife into, hoops around the masts to attach the mainsail, a gaff-rigged foresail, and belaying pins instead of cleats.

With Mary at the spoked wheel, it would take me about half an hour before entering port to start reducing sail. I remember going for our indoctrination sail in Stonington, taking along Mom and Dad. They were visibly intimidated and petrified we'd be taking a cruise on such a labor-intensive ship with their young grandchildren, ages 6 to 9.

Maybe the good Lord was also concerned with our lack of crew because, unbeknownst to us then, he'd added a fourth to the crew, Peter LeGrand Johnstone, on the eve of our *White Wing* voyage.

And if we give credence to studies of women who are active during pregnancy, reported in the National Institute of Health by Professor May, mentioned later as an explanation for daughter Helen's agility, then it's not surprising where this modern-day Pierre LeGrand acquired his swashbuckling nature. He was born nine months later, on April 5, 1966, just before our leaving Venezuela for Chicago.

The most dramatic event of the *White Wing* voyage occurred on Buzzards Bay. We had sailed from Stonington to Newport, where we witnessed 12-meter America's Cup trials, which were won by *Constellation,* helmed by Bob Bavier*. Our paths would cross eight years later on the US Olympic Yachting Committee and then again with J/Boats. Bob went on to successfully defend America's Cup.

I've always felt some kinship with another America's Cup skipper, Sir Thomas J. Lipton. The letter "J" in his middle name is for "Johnstone." He was also in the grocery business and the founder of Lipton Tea. Sir Thomas also had a habit of finishing as a runner-up, having lost five times in his efforts to win the cup.

We anchored in Newport Harbor's Brenton Cove and walked around the Swiss Village Farm, foreshadowing our lives there, at Beechbound, thirteen years later. The next day seemed ideal for our sail to Marion to visit Mary's cousins Per and Bunny Henrikssen.

Under full sail, we thundered along the Rhode Island coastline, rail down on a beam reach. I was at the wheel, marveling at what a wonderful old craft this was. As we cleared Sakonnet Point and entered Buzzards Bay, visibility had dropped to less than a quarter mile. But no worries, we'd mapped out the course. It was a glorious sail, and our next mark was Can #1 to clear the shoals. I was feeling in such good spirits I declared to Mary, "I'll have a shot of that rum with lunch. Yo-ho-ho and a bottle of rum!"

Perfect! "Down to the sea in ships!" *White Wing* was thundering along at about nine and a half knots. We'd just passed Can #1 to port. My navigation was spot on...although that mark did seem to appear a bit sooner than expected.

This is what sailing is all about! I was steering from leeward, right hand on the wheel, marveling at the proximity of the wake streaming past. But no sooner had this euphoric moment occurred than did I seem to be hallucinating. "That couldn't possibly be an old man standing up to his knees in the water, appearing out of the fog about 100 yards ahead, could it?" Reality hit like a sledgehammer. The yellow crescent of a beach started to materialize out of the gray mist behind him.

"Holy mackerel! We're about to drive up on a beach!"

As I threw the ship into an all-standing, 180-degree crash tack to reverse course, I yelled to Mary below, "*Dear*, come up and grab the wheel, *quick*, to hold the boat on this reverse course while I try to figure out what's happened."

First, I saw from the chart that we were about to go up onto Horseneck Beach. Then I noticed another Can #1 closer to shore than our intended Can #1. How could the US Coast Guard do such a thing: two Can #1s in such proximity?

The next question was, how could the compass be about 25 degrees off?

But then I remembered being told at Dodson's that the Seagull outboard engine, normally clamped to a board between the shrouds, was placed in the deck hatch right in front of the binnacle.

Oh, boy! That big chunk of iron was probably the culprit. I pulled the Seagull out of the hatch and secured it on the board in the rigging. The compass swung back 25 degrees in the correct direction! Whew!

The rest of the cruise that summer of 1965 was a piece of cake! But it was the last time we went family cruising on a boat that large until introducing the J/42 thirty years later, in 1995.

S&S Rainbow in Venezuela

Off a beautiful crescent beach in Venezuela, we pushed the family capacity of a Sunfish to its limits. We got all five of us aboard at one time for a short voyage of exploration to an uninhabited island with a shipwreck near Puerto Cabello. When shortly thereafter, a friend offered us use of his 24-foot Sparkman & Stephens-designed Rainbow sloop in Puerto Cabello, we accepted. That made much more sense for a family daysailer than a Sunfish.

It's a small world when you consider that our first boat upon returning to Lake Michigan would also be a Rainbow, sailing out of Wilmette Harbor, the Chicago suburb that would be our next home.

CHAPTER 6

Quaker Oats Chicago

B ack in Venezuela, with child number four, Peter, on the way, the frequency of family off-the-beach Caribbean Sunfish racing was not significantly reduced and may have further contributed to the development of Peter's sailing skills. But managing this growing family's logistics, schedules, and responsibilities got me thinking more about our future. Where do we go from down here in the tropics?

The resourcefulness required to be on the firing line, profitably managing Quaker subsidiaries in Colombia and Venezuela for eight years, surely compared favorably with the benefits of two years of paper case studies at Harvard Business School. But it had become clear that one skill set that could be improved upon was marketing. How does one minimize the risk of placing bets on a promising new product or business strategy? I struggled with this and wasn't getting much help from otherwise-creative ex-pats at the local branches of J. Walter Thompson, McCann-Erickson, and Grey Advertising. Help with business disciplines and skills for selling, accounting, engineering, and production can readily be found, but when it came to creative marketing—coming up with new products and product strategies—I felt like a babe in the woods or, in this case, the jungle. My conclusion was, "You can't live long enough to become good at marketing if you have to learn by making your own mistakes."

Also, I was beginning to have doubts about Quaker's long-term business strategies. Management sent a policy initiative asking subsidiary CEOs to recommend interesting acquisitions. My recommendation for acquiring PAN, the instant arepa brand in Venezuela, and combining it with our ArepArina brand in Colombia to monopolize the product seemed to fall on deaf ears.

Time to Get Creative. How smart were they up there in Chicago? If I'm going to make Quaker Oats my career, wouldn't it be a good idea to get transferred up there to find out? Besides, Quaker had about 20 different product areas and must be making all sorts of mistakes I could learn from. So I requested to be transferred back to Chicago in domestic marketing.

Thrown to the Dogs

Upon arriving at Chicago headquarters, I was somewhat put off by Quaker assigning me as brand manager of Ken-L Ration canned dog food. Shortly thereafter, I was almost put out on the street. My office was a glassed-in cubicle in the Merchandise Mart, reputed to be the largest office building in the world when built.

My ex-boss from Cedar Rapids, Arch McClure, lent us his house in Kenilworth until we were able to purchase and move into our new home at 1306 Greenwood Avenue in Wilmette, a beautiful town on the shore of Lake Michigan. It was an easy 25-minute train ride to Chicago with a healthy half-mile walk on both ends.

It wasn't long after getting settled into this new routine that President Bob Stuart wanted to increase Quaker's earnings forecast in hopes of improved stock-analyst ratings. One move was to raise the case price of canned Ken-L Ration. KLR canned was enjoying good sales increases due to supermarket discounting six-packs to under $1.

The president reluctantly accepted my logic that a price increase would rapidly kill supermarket discounting and sales. But he was not pleased. Seems I hadn't subscribed to big-company politics. "To get ahead, do what the boss wants, even if wrong. Then, if it goes sour, you are not to blame; it is shared, and you get promoted for always agreeing with the boss."

180-Day MBA Wonder

President Stuart had a scheme to shape up his rebellious brand managers. He contracted Walter Salmon, a professor of marketing at Harvard Business School, to show us how to profitably manage our brands. And a brand was needed to try out the latest strategies. Perfect!

Time to Get Creative. I was the first to volunteer as the guinea pig. Here was my chance to get a Harvard professor on my side with pricing strategies and fast-track an HBS education. Imagine going one-on-one with Professor Salmon for six months. It was great fun. Super guy. We improved profitability and product image by eliminating horsemeat in the formula. Then we came up with a Ken-L brand umbrella advertising strategy: just advertise the newest exciting product, which will carry the line more profitably than running ad campaigns on each product within the brand. This umbrella advertising strategy was successfully applied to both J/Boats and MJM Yachts. And having gotten back into the boss's good graces, I was promoted to brand group supervisor of all dog food, including semi-moist Ken-L Burgers and dry Ken-L Biskit, sponsor of the Westminster Dog Show.

Ken-L Cheeseburgers

Gaines-Burgers looked like hamburger patties and were killing us with a 35 percent market share of the semimoist dog food category. Quaker's Ken-L Burger had only a 15 percent share.

Time to Get Creative. To me, the solution was a no-brainer: Ken-L Cheeseburgers. What could be more logical? Everyone knows dogs love cheese, and cheeseburgers taste better and demand a higher price than hamburgers.

Upper management pooh-poohed the idea. "That's silly, Johnstone; get serious, forget it!"

I couldn't believe what I was hearing. "Silly? You guys have already anthropomorphized dog food by introducing Ken-L Burgers, and if you ever owned a dog and served cheese hors d'oeuvres on a coffee table, you'd know it's a constant battle to keep them away."

To convince them, we invested in national consumer research among 200 dog owners to prove the point: over 55 percent knew dogs loved cheese.

The biggest concern was the likely General Foods' response to Gaines-Burgers: putting a yellow piece of cheese on their patty to make it look like a real cheeseburger. Quaker's product was extruded strands of red, meat-like material in a plastic bag. So what were we to do? Throw in some square, yellow cheese hunks, or maybe some yellow strands among the red? Let's find out.

So we made up some Gaines-Burgers with a slab of cheese on top and sent samples to a test panel of dog owners. We needn't have worried. The dog owners were horrified. The dogs would bite into the patty, and the cheese slab would stick to their upper fangs. The dogs would then try to slap it away with their paws onto the floor, away from the bowl, or run around the house with it flapping there. We decided to go with the yellow strands among the red, secretly hoping Gaines-Burgers would try the slab version.

Quaker management dragged their feet before investing in extruder capacity to meet the high demand after launching the product. Ken-L Ration Cheese Flavored Burgers for dogs were a huge success, cited as one of the top five grocery products of the year, hitting $30 million in sales—that's $247 million in 2022 dollars— and overtaking Gaines-Burgers in share of market.

That success earned yours truly the coveted "Donold B. Lourie Quaker Oats 1968 Marketing Man of the Year" trophy. This was another keeper!

I implemented pet-food marketing strategies over four years to triple operating income on a sales gain of 67 percent to $170 million. What was my reward? I was to become the "Willy Wonka Candy Man."

Willy Wonka Candy Man

After receiving the "Marketing Man of the Year" trophy and a handshake, I was assigned to a rescue mission to save the Willy Wonka candy division managed by the president's son, Jim Stuart, a strapping, 6-foot-3-inch-tall, 240-pound Princeton '63 rugby player. His dad must have figured I was the only one in the company who could manage him since Jim had followed this captain's orders for two years as the middle man for our 1972 Soling Olympic Trials crew.

But like Snapple and Marx Toys later, Quaker had the misguided notion that their relationship with supermarket-chain buyers would more than makeup for lack of distribution through the jobbers that serviced all those convenience stores, gas stations, theaters, vending machines, and other small mom-and-pop outlets. And because of Cap'n Crunch cereal's success, corporate hubris existed: "We know how to talk to kids."

To top that, they bet that media advertising wasn't necessary. A movie could do the job. *Charlie and the Chocolate Factory* would replace the need for a conventional TV advertising campaign for the initial two products, Willy Wonka *Super Scrunch* and *Oompa Loompas* (M&M-type) candies. They'd gotten it wrong, and I was to fix it.

After I'd accepted the challenge, they confessed, "Oh, by the way, Bob, there's $2 million worth of aging candy bars that have a six-month shelf life in warehouses. And right now, most of it has reached month five."

I can see why the president was concerned about the impending doom of his son's reputation in the company. But I wasn't about to become the "fall guy" and figured I had lots of leverage at the time.

Time to Get Creative. I was miffed. "Thanks a lot, guys! But to make up for that curveball you threw me, I want the entire Quaker sales force assigned to Willy Wonka for a week. They're going to stand in the aisles of supermarkets all across the country and hand out all that candy as a massive free-sampling program. Better to hand it out for people to eat than have Quaker eat it."

Luck doesn't hurt. The stars were aligning. Amazingly, that same month of June, Sammy Davis Jr. singing "The Candy Man" was number one on the Hit Parade. Willy Wonka's sales doubled for the June–July Nielsen report. But as I feared, success was to be short-lived. The August–September Nielson report came in with sales dropping back to prepromo April–May levels.

The night before getting that raw data by phone from my Nielsen contact, our president, Bob Stuart, got headlines in the *Chicago Tribune* following a stock analyst conference. He couldn't resist.

Despite being cautioned not to say anything about Quaker's candy business until we had the Nielsen data, he announced, "Quaker is about to launch a fantastic new Willy Wonka candy bar called *Scrumdiddlyumptious.*"

Time to Get Creative. With that morning's *Chicago Tribune* in hand, I went to my boss, Ken Mason, and asked, "Are you going to tell the president, or am I?

We needed to get out of this business ASAP, and I recommend we sell or "give" the brand to Quaker's contract manufacturer before the situation even worsened.

This was one benefit of not owning the factory. The risk could be minimized if the product did not succeed in the marketplace. As you will read later, this experience influenced my later business strategies.

The late Ken Mason and his author wife, Cherie (*Wild Fox*), were friends Mary and I visited at their waterfront cottage on Deer Isle, Maine. He had retired as president of Quaker Oats and owned one of our J/32 cruising boats. Ken gave me one of the most important pieces of advice in the business world. A Yale grad and former advertising executive, he counseled me, "Bob, if you have an idea or product to sell and can't get the message across in a one-page advertisement or proposal, forget it. Because it means you've yet to figure it out yourself."

Quaker's Futurist

What's next? President Stuart asked, "How did we screw up with Willy Wonka? How about you doing a white paper outlining where Quaker went wrong?"

The result was not flattering to top management and didn't win me many friends. Upon returning from a Caribbean cruise where he'd finally read the white paper, the president was sufficiently impressed to say, "Bob, brilliant job! Very helpful. What job would you like in the company?"

Needless to say, I was flattered and relieved. My answer was, "The fun part of your job…coming up with strategies for existing products and identifying promising new product areas."

President Stuart then created a dream job: Director of Market Strategy and Analysis, reporting to the president and his long-range planning committee to recommend investment priorities and marketing-divestiture plans for thirty business areas worldwide. I was given an office and a secretary.

Earlier, I'd been offered and declined the job as president of Quaker Oats Canada, based in Peterborough, Ontario. This might have been fun for the family, as both boys were all-star hockey players, and our daughter, Helen, was a figure skater. But it would have taken me away from my beloved sailing activity on Lake Michigan. And the job was mostly administrative, more like a glorified Quaker Colombia assignment, with little opportunity for developing innovative products or marketing strategies. The goal would be to implement products already developed by Quaker for the US market.

I recommended they pick Frank Morgan instead, which they did. After Canada, Frank became president and CEO of Quaker Corporate. While the sales of Quaker Canada were about $100 million, less than the pet-food division I had been running, it was being looked at as a way to evaluate a manager's capability for the number-one job in the company.

Time to Get Creative. I started by publishing a comprehensive analysis of major consumer and product trends in the US market

Best-Performing Brand Strategy

That assignment had a profound impact on my business future. I developed a "Business Quality Rating Chart" that paralleled Harvard Business School's "Profit Impact of Market Strategies" (PIMS) program. This helped identify businesses impacted by changing demographic trends.

Quaker was considering an investment in recreational sports. A strategy had to be decided upon in that field. A review by product category indicated three ways to go: low-priced, midpriced, or best-performing brand. Low-priced brands sold well through mass merchandisers when the economy was strong, and people had time and dollars to take up a new sport. Midpriced brands try to stay "fresh" with styling changes year after year but with no remarkable innovations.

Best-performing brands are generally higher-priced, incorporate the latest technology, and are owned by aficionados of the sport—a category most participants gravitate toward as they become more proficient. Jean-Claude Killy holding up his Rossignol skis after a win is a perfect example. Even beginners would buy Rossi's, thinking they'd ski better. Another benefit of a best-performing brand strategy is that sports devotees are the least likely to cut back on their sporting activity in hard times. The category is thus more recession-proof.

This work and the earlier project with Professor Walter Salmon formed my J/Boats and MJM Yachts marketing strategies.

Goodbye, Quaker

I presented a five-year plan (F74–F79) for Quaker to improve return on investment from 20 to 25 percent with $196 million less capital than the $608 million initially planned. I had ranked 30 Quaker brands and potential acquisitions on a "Business Quality Rating Scale." The acquisitions listed were Crate & Barrel, L.L. Bean, Coast Catamaran (Hobie), Coleman Co., and Schwinn Bicycles.

I used Boston Consulting Group's (BCG) matrix to categorize Quaker product categories as either a *Dog* (to get rid of), a *Problem Child* (needing work), a *Star* (to invest behind), or a *Cash Cow* (to milk).

The ranking used a five-point rating scale for Brand Strength, Industry Growth, Demographic Trends, Societal Image, and Investment Risk (e.g., exposure to the fuel crisis, urban unrest, or a "down" economy).

The 1973 oil crisis did not bode well for my new job as director of market strategy and analysis.

Top management went into a state of paralysis, verging on panic. Investment plans were put on hold.

When Quaker decided to circle the wagons and delay all plans, I was put in limbo. What was I to do? Dust off what I'd just recommended to resubmit the following year?

Time to Get Creative. The handwriting was on the wall. It was time to go. Quaker was a great family company chaired by Donold Lourie (Princeton '22), an All-American and College Football Hall of Famer. Business-wise, it was like a caring family. Each of the 20+ business divisions got equal and fair treatment as offspring.

The divisions weren't callously treated like BCG *Dogs, Problem Children, Stars,* or *Cash Cows.* Few loving parents would demand better results from the brightest kid while kicking a problem child out the door.

The Stuarts had been like family to me. John Stuart was a big supporter of my father at Princeton. He was a 1900 graduate of Princeton and CEO of Quaker from 1922 to 1953. He was keenly interested in the trees on the Princeton campus. As the university's business manager, Dad oversaw a project to protect and expand upon this arboretum-like setting.

I was very much encouraged by John Stuart, who periodically sent me letters of support saying how happy he was with my job.

I felt I'd done well by Quaker in hiring several recent MBAs for the pet-food product-management group. Pete Rhodes became executive VP and managed Quaker's successful Gatorade acquisition, a reason for PepsiCo's eventual acquisition of Quaker Oats.

Doug Mills, a scow sailor, also became an executive VP of Quaker's $2.5 billion US and Canada Foods Division until 1998.

David Chamberlain became president of Quaker's frozen-foods division and later the chairman of Eddie Bauer. I recall him sailing Hobie Cats. He was a member of St. Francis and Larchmont Yacht Clubs.

My philosophy was that racing sailors made better businessmen and decision-makers. One of my proudest moments at Quaker was when the Kepner-Tregoe "IN Basket Test" rated all product-management groups for critical decision-making skills.

In this test, you are told the manager of your company has suddenly died. You are now in charge at his desk and have been given 10 minutes to go through the "IN basket" and decide how to deal with the deceased's family and 20 other items.

My pet-foods group of four brand managers scored in the 98th percentile of the entire country, while other Quaker groups were about 10 points lower.

That result reflected my training technique: load up my brand managers with twice the work they could reasonably finish in the time allotted. Assigning priorities became an essential part of their job.

It was critical decision-making, like in a sailboat race. Making decisions without knowing all the facts and not wasting time on the unimportant or irrelevant. It was what Kepner-Trego's test measured.

It didn't hurt group profitability either. Fewer high-priced brand managers were needed to do the job.

My overall concerns about Quaker Oats when leaving Venezuela had come to pass. Having given them another seven years, the infamous "itch" had set in.

I wasn't ready to change my ways, to become a "corporate man." Nor did I see a path to gaining enough influence in the company over the next ten years to change its culture.

Time to Get Creative...to seek new horizons. So, regretfully, I resigned.

Thanks to a previous Quaker director of personnel, I was offered an attractive "heir apparent" job by a large company in San Francisco. But even that hotbed of sailing couldn't offset my age-40 time in life, a need to sink or swim on my own. Quaker generously granted me a year's severance pay and the use of an office.

They'd provided me with the ultimate business education: the combination of (1) an eight-year MBA graduate course in entrepreneurship as CEO of remote manufacturing subsidiaries in Latin America and (2) a seven-year deep immersion in US corporate product management... the top of the marketing world.

Maybe I was a bit impetuous. Only eight years later, Bill Smithburg became the president and CEO; in 1983, he became chairman.

He joined Quaker as a brand manager in cereal when I returned from South America to be a brand manager in pet foods. We'd both risen to be product-group managers. Pet foods had grown and contributed considerably higher earnings than cereals. So accepting the Canadian job could have been my fast track to the top.

Old-Fashioned Quaker Oats

I may have abandoned the company, but not the product, of which I've remained a dedicated daily user and advocate ever since.

It's hard to imagine a healthier or tastier breakfast, particularly when topped by Wyman's frozen, wild Maine blueberries and a ring of pure New Hampshire maple syrup with a dollop of milk or cream. Other, larger, sour blueberries don't work. Quaker needn't have bothered introducing the less flavorful "Quick" or "Instant" versions. The best way to cook "Old-Fashioned" oats takes less time (three to five minutes on "high," depending on the lidded saucepan) than it takes to boil the water you'd have to use for the instant variety. Let it sit covered for a minute to absorb excess water. Then put it into a bowl.

Top it with three to four table-spoons of frozen blueberries right out of the bag. There's no need to thaw them ahead of time. Watch the steam rise as the oatmeal does the job. Add a tablespoon of milk or half-and-half, then pour a ring of maple syrup.

The initial portions are easy for two people: one cup of oats and two cups of water.

CHAPTER 7

Sailing on Lake Michigan

Needless to say, since we had moved back to the US, to the shores of Lake Michigan, the chance to get back into sailing was not to be missed. But some obstacles had to be overcome. There was a long wait time for moorings in Wilmette Harbor, which was so crowded that boats were moored by the bow and stern with padded canvas bumpers on either end.

Time to Get Creative. The only apparent option for a "family size" sailboat in the harbor was to partner with a recent widow who was reluctant to give up ownership of her Rainbow #180 *C-Bird*. She was happy for us to cover maintenance and mooring costs. As we learned on our initial Rainbow sail in Venezuela, its long cockpit and cuddy with two berths were perfect for a family crew of five. It would be several years before our youngest, 1-year-old Peter, would be hauling lines.

Rainbow Nationals

The Rainbow had more than its share of shortcomings, mainly having to do with the rig. Olin* and Rod* Stephens designed it, and Jerry Wood^ and his Annapolis Sailing School had them built. Several had lost their masts in Northeast blows with big waves on Lake Michigan. Class rules or not, my family would not be at risk. *Time to Get Creative.*

Problem #1: The boat had in-line upper and lower shrouds connected to a single chainplate abeam the mast and no offset lower shroud to keep the mast from pumping out of line, buckling, and going over the side. Solution: install a set of forward lower shrouds so that, with backstay pressure, the mast would not pump.

Problem #2: The mast was deck-stepped, and the mast step was sinking down into the deck because the underdeck aluminum support tube was mounted on top of an athwartships wood frame in the bilge with an eight-inch-wide limber cutout instead of limber holes under it. This allowed the frame to deflect downward with pressure. OK, we put an oak block in the gap underneath to support the frame.

Problem #3: The mast was still pushing the deck down. Now what? Turns out the underdeck aluminum support tube was bending out of column. Horrors! I hammered an oak dowel down inside the tube to stiffen it. Now we had a rig we could tune with headstay tension and even some mast bend for heavy air.

Problem #4: That wasn't the end of it. We won the Chicago to Waukegan Race. The mast was no longer sinking into the deck or going out of column. But the transom was being pulled inside out by pressure on the backstay. Strange design! The backstay, instead of being attached to a tang supported by going over the arc of the transom and bolted to its aft face, went through the deck and was attached to an internal tang, fastened to a knee glassed onto the inside-forward face of the transom. Amazingly, the knee didn't simply rip away instead of inverting the transom! But it might have been just about to happen! The solution was obvious. Bolt a stainless chainplate strap to the outside of the transom and then bend it over the arc of the transom's upper edge.

We finally had a boat that *safely* won the 1967 and 1968 National Championships.

"Pass the Crackers"

My favorite Rainbow story happened at the 1967 Championship in Annapolis. Legendary Chesapeake Bay sailor Arnie Gay had future J/24 North American and J/41 SORC Champ, young Charlie Scott, as crew. They were the hometown ringers and the boat to beat.

On one downwind leg, Arnie was ahead, and we were slowly overtaking him under spinnaker in light air.

Our family crew of Mary, Stu (9), Drake (8), and Helen (6) was hardly of the professional caliber of Arnie's.

As we came abeam, slowly passing them, the tension was palpable on both boats.

Helen picked this moment for a classic icebreaker comment, saying in a voice everyone could hear, "Daddy, can we have some crackers?"

I replied, "Sure, please pass them around." We went on to win the race and regatta.

Arnie—who became a friend, later helped create the J/22 Feet at the Annapolis Yacht Club, and campaigned a J/33,—never failed to remind me of that incident.

World Champ #8700 *Rabbit*

Our other Chicago-area sailing action was on Skokie Lagoons in a Penguin fleet of about 30 boats.

This was a "frostbite" sailing opportunity in spring and fall featuring great competition with Star silver medalist Dick Stearns^ and Lightning World Champ Bruce Goldsmith. Salentine Boat Works in Wisconsin built me a beautiful, wooden, minimum-weight, sky-blue Penguin with a white bottom, *Rabbit* #8700. It was parked in our garage on its trailer during the week. I eventually became fleet captain.

As with the Rainbow, family safety again became a concern, particularly in near-freezing waters.

The Philip Rhodes-designed Penguin didn't have any side decks, so it could not self-rescue. You didn't have to heel over very far for the water to instantly pour over the leeward gunwale, start filling up the boat, and surge to the bow. Crew weight on the weather rail, instead of helping the boat recover upright, would drive it down deeper until it sunk.

The crew would have to hang on until they were rescued, with the boat being towed ashore and emptied.

Needless to say, it was not a safe boat for family sailing.

Time to Get Creative. The challenge was to make it self-rescuing within the rules of the class, with light enough materials that performance wouldn't be hindered.

My solution was to put two-inch sheets of Styrofoam under the floorboards and fit Styrofoam blocks under the thwart seat. Then I fit Dacron over the foam blocks filling up the bow section to deal with waves on Lake Michigan.

It worked and was submitted to the Penguin Class! You can see the foredeck created in the photo of #8700 (courtesy of Murphy & Nye and IPCDA).

The foam delayed the "quick sink" nature of the boat sufficiently for the crew to recover from a knockdown with only a partially flooded boat or, worst case, a boat that was floated high enough by the positive flotation so that when it flooded, the Elvstrom bailers were able to help drain the boat.

The Skokie Lagoons had a unique method of splitting their fleet for a manageable starting line. The top 10 boats were the "Black Watch," and the rest were the "Main Fleet." The winner of the Main Fleet could challenge anyone in the Black Watch the following week to move up, with the loser relegated to the Main Fleet.

The Skokie Lagoons Fleet hosted the 1969 Penguin Internationals (Worlds) at the Sheridan Shore Yacht Club on Lake Michigan. Consistent sailing, with a 5th place average finish in the 47-boat fleet, was enough for *Rabbit* to win with Stuart as crew.

Soling Olympic Campaign

After winning the 1968 Rainbow Nationals in Wilmette, we set our sights pretty high by getting excited about campaigning an Olympic Soling for 1969. The Soling was selected as the three-man keelboat for the 1972 Olympics in Kiel, Germany. Wilmette harbormaster Bill Wente devised a unique mooring system to circumvent the crowded harbor scene: mooring eight Solings bow-in, toward the outer breakwater, with the stern held out and tied to mooring balls. Dick Stearns flew Stu and me up to Milwaukee in his private plane to meet with Jack Van Dyke.

The plan was to purchase fleets for Wilmette and Milwaukee from Bill Abbott in Sarnia, Ontario, as the first step of a regional Olympic effort.

Jack Van Dyke, a 1932 classmate of Dad's at Princeton, hosted Mary and me at his house in Milwaukee as my surrogate father for weekend regattas.

He was later instrumental in recruiting Buddy Melges* as our area J/Boats dealer and eventually purchased a "J" himself.

Family Crews

US-180 *Gull* became our first Soling, but it wasn't much of a family boat. The International Soling Class Rules and competitors didn't want to see more than three crew members on the boat, no matter their weight, gender, or age. So two of our young, flyweight Rainbow crew had to be left behind.

This noninclusive, antifamily experience weighed heavily nine years later when we drafted the International J/24 Rules. We implemented a weight limit rather than a crew-number limit.

Nevertheless, we finished a respectable 9th in the 1969 North Americans at the Milwaukee Yacht Club, with Mary at 130 pounds and Stu (11) at 110 pounds. Some competitors threatened to protest us because Mary would take the helm downwind so I could do foredeck with the spinnaker, with Stu in the cockpit tailing. The interpretation of Soling rules was that the registered skipper had to be at the helm all the time. Imagine. Hard to believe we were considered that much of a threat.

Buddy Melges* then became involved. He had imported and commissioned three boats from Dufour in France, touted as much lighter than the Abbotts. They needed 60 pounds of corrector weights. We purchased US-430 *Houqua* and sold US-180 to Dick Dobroth, whose son Brendan became a successful IOR yacht designer.

Soling North Americans

At the 1970 North Americans at Texas Corinthian Yacht Club in Kemah, Texas, our lightly crewed Soling was fast in light air. When leading one race. going around the first weather mark, 12-year-old Stuart turned to me and said, "OK, Dad, don't blow it!" You can imagine my shock. *Time to Get Creative.* "Well, son, if that's how you feel, maybe it's time you and your brother, Drake, sailed your boats just to see how good you are. Maybe a couple of Sunfish?"

We got each their Sunfish to sail from Gillson Beach in Wilmette. They were that good and started winning everything. That incident was the first step in how the United States Youth Sailing Championship came about in 1973.

Soling Worlds 1971

Sticking with a family program, my brother Rod was recruited from Stonington to join Mary and me for the 1971 Soling World Championship on US-430 *Houqua* at Seawanhaka Corinthian Yacht Club on Oyster Bay, Long Island.

Bob Mosbacher won. Fellow Wilmette Fleet member Bruce Goldsmith was 2nd in an Elvstrom-built boat. The Great Dane himself, Paul Elvstrom, was 3rd in *Bes* (which became our next boat). We were 7th in US-430, fast in the first three light-air races, and 2nd just behind Mosbacher after four races. But we were slow in waves.

We are pictured (courtesy of ISCA) with a good leeward start in the windy last race. *Boom! Boom!* The hull "oil-canned" loudly over each of those waves.

I suspected that Dufour saved weight by lightening up the hull laminate and structure over the keel. As the hull twisted and deformed, the keel had to be wobbling.

Time to Get Creative. Do we repair #430 or buy another one for the '72 Trials? Fortunately, we had the answer in about 60 days. Elvstrom sold his Soling *Bes* to Gordon Lindemann after the Worlds. Gordon had a tough time making it go in Milwaukee's light airs and sold it to me.

Elvstrom hadn't done well in earlier light-air races, either. But *Bes* had won the Europeans, had the quasilegal, glassed-in double bottom, and was fast, with finishes of 1st and 2nd on the breezy last day of the World Championship.

1971 SOLING WORLDS							TOTAL
US 504	Bob Mosbacher	5	4	2	(10)	7	34
US 501	Bruce Goldsmith	3	8	(35)	9	1	35
D 42	Paul Elvstrom	16	13	(29)	1	2	44
US 95	John Dane	(dnf)	2	13	8	9	51
KC 97	David Miller	1	17	17	(dnf)	3	52
N 53	Eivid Koefoed	6	15	5	(21)	10	59
US 430	Bob Johnstone	8	11	3	20	(31)	63
K 85	Robin Judah	9	3	11	22	(22)	66
KC 84	Sidney Dakin	2	5	(dnf)	3	42	67
S 65	Stig Wennerstrom	22	1	(24)	17	11	68

Bruce Goldsmith, in his Elvstrom, was fast in a breeze too. With the Olympic trials taking place on San Francisco Bay's windy Berkeley Circle the following June, this seemed to be the way to go.

1972 Soling Olympic Trials

Diane Beeston Photo

108

Our Elvstrom Soling didn't make a sound going through waves in heavy air. Getting serious about the Olympic trials, I recruited 220-lb. Scott Stokes and 240-lb. Jim Stuart as crew. Elvstrom had done the boat in gold gelcoat. We got number US-549 for "49ers" and were going for Olympic gold, so *Gold Rush* replaced *Bes* as the name.

We qualified from the Midwest District along with sailing luminaries Melges*, Goldsmith, and Dick Stearns^.

The highlight of the week and probably my best race ever was winning the heavy-air second race on the Berkeley Circle by over two minutes. It was gusting 30+ knots. Buddy Melges*, Stuart Walker*, Jim Coggan, and Ti Hack had all lost their masts. Maury Rattray sank.

Lowell North* planed through our lee on the second reaching leg and rounded the bottom mark ahead of us and just behind Bruce Goldsmith, who was leading. The three of us were in front of the 35-boat fleet, starting the second weather leg.

Goldsmith, in the lead, continued out on port tack toward the favored starboard layline. North, in 2nd, tacked onto starboard to clear his air. We rounded behind North, hesitated a bit, then also tacked onto starboard so as not to be directly behind Goldsmith or North.

When North came back onto port, we did also, at the same time, below him. So the three lead boats were now all on port tack: Goldsmith to the right and out ahead, us in the middle, and North out to windward abeam of us. Then the magic happened.

We sailed out from under North with his 260-lb Los Angeles Rams tackle crew and over Goldsmith with friends Bob Barton and Robbie Lansing aboard. *Gold Rush* was motoring. Goldsmith tacked onto the starboard layline. We tacked ahead and in front of him, crossing North to round the second weather mark in the lead. We held our position on the wild, surfing spinnaker run to the leeward mark. Then, as we rounded the mark, the wind seemed to increase. I could barely see.

A stinging slipstream of water was coming over the droop-hiked bodies of my two crew and spraying right into my eyes. Squinting, I was sailing by feel. Because I was blinded, it was strictly heel angle that guided me, threading us through the waves.

Total 35	1972 SOLING OLYMPIC TRIALS								PTS
1	Buddy Melges	5	(dnf)	2	1	1	1	2	16.0
2	Lowell Noth	2	2	(8)	2	2	3	5	27.7
3	Bruce Goldsmith	1	3	5	5	3	2	(9)	34.4
4	John Dane	6	4	3	3	(dnf)	5	1	41.1
5	Earl Elms	3	6	1	10	4	(dnf)	4	49.4
6	Bob Johnstone	11	1	7	9	(dsq)	6	3	62.4
7	Warwick Tompkins	4	5	4	(19)	7	4	14	67.0
8	Sam Merrick	8	8	9	(13)	5	10	8	83.0
9	John Kolius	(dnf)	3	12	8	13	8	7	102.0
10	Dave Curtis	13	(dnf)	10	11	9	11	13	103.0
11	Dick Stearns	(dnf)	9	6	4	8	7	dnf	104.7

Gold Rush was smoothly cutting through them. We pulled farther away, upwind, stretching the lead to two minutes to get the gun at the finish. We couldn't even read the sail numbers on the two boats behind. The rest of the fleet was way back.

It was not surprising that others were amazed, curious, and probably a bit suspicious. At the San Francisco Yacht Club docks after the race, Lowell came over to inspect *Gold Rush* with his builder, Carl Eichenlaub*. You can just guess what they were thinking. "Johnstone couldn't be that good a sailor. That ratty-looking Murphy & Nye mainsail couldn't be a match for the latest North sails…ergo, *Gold Rush* had to be an extra-fast, illegal Soling!" This was both ironic and amusing. Rumors were circulating that Eichenlaub* had built Lowell a "special" Soling.

Lowell said, "Bob, nice sailing. You sure had this boat moving. Mind if we check it out?"

"No problem, Lowell, come aboard."

Lowell stepped onto the foredeck. It bounced up and down under his feet. You know he was checking out how lightly built it might be. Sure enough.

"Wow, Bob, this deck is really light!" I'm thinking, *Elvstrom, you sly fox. You really built this boat right.* Lighten up the deck and put the extra glass and resin in the bottom and keel structure, one-upping whatever Eichenlaub might have done. It was the boat Elvstrom built for himself, the legality of which was challenged by the Europeans and later approved as the first Soling with a glassed-in double-floor structure over the keel.

Not sharing my theory, I shrugged my shoulders, saying, "Golly, Lowell, couldn't be much more legal. The boat on the scales was 60-lbs. overweight. It passed measurement inspection here and also at last year's European and World Championships."

That was the end of it. Lowell's boat was going fast enough. He probably abided by the adage, *People who live in glass houses shouldn't throw stones.*

This was not the end of top sailors wanting a piece of what made *Gold Rush* fast in heavy air. Buddy Melges replaced his mast and handily won the Trials with Bill Bentsen* and Bill Allen^ as crew.

Buddy had also replaced his lightly built Dufour with a new Abbott-built boat. Being a builder himself, Buddy probably suggested a few "improvements." Lowell was 2nd but declined to go to the Olympics as the alternate and as Buddy's trial horse. So the 3rd place finisher, Bruce Goldsmith, agreed to go in Lowell's place. Therein lies a story. Bruce hadn't forgotten the upwind speed of *Gold Rush* in that rough second race. Bruce was a friend and our sailmaker at Murphy & Nye in Chicago. Before the trials, he'd convinced me to order a new mainsail made out of a miracle fiber called Aquino cloth. It was miraculous all right… in how slow it was. In heavy-air, side-by-side brushes against other boats before the trials, the mainsail stretched and wrinkled in weird shapes. We were the slowest boat on the water.

In desperation, before the official sail-measurement deadline, I tracked down Bruce in the yacht club parking lot. "Bruin, help! There's no way I can race with this Aquino cloth mainsail. It's terrible! We're now the slowest boat out there. We might as well pack up and go home. What can you do?"

"Bob, sorry, I didn't bring another new mainsail. The only way I can help is to give you the first mainsail I ever made for a Soling, which is somewhere in the back of my station wagon. It's yours if you want it."

Disappointed and resigned to our fate, knowing anything would be better, I accepted.

He opened the back of the wagon, dug under a bunch of junk, dragged the sail out, swept off the dust, and said, "OK, well…here it is. Good luck."

Our local Midwest region did well, with half of the top six finishers: Buddy, Bruce, and me.

After the awards ceremony, Bruce said, "Bob, about that mainsail I lent you. We need to get Buddy up to speed in heavy air at Kiel. Can you give me back the mainsail now?"

"Bruce, you're kidding. Lent? You gave it to me like I was doing you a favor to clean the junk out of your car. It was to replace that Aquino cloth disaster you made me for the Trials."

"Bob, please! I feel bad about that Aquino sail and apologize. But we need to do everything we can to ensure Buddy wins, and nobody was faster than you in the heavy air forecast for Kiel. Tell you what, I'll build you a new suit of sails of the good stuff if you let Buddy and me take that race-winning mainsail with us to Kiel."

"Well, OK," I agreed.

Buddy won the Olympic gold medal at Kiel convincingly, by 23 points, with finishes of 1-2-3-(4)-1-1. Stig Wennerstrom of Sweden won silver. Stig had finished behind us in the Worlds and wasn't particularly fast in heavy air.

It was fun to think we might have had a chance for Olympic glory. I was gratified to know *Gold Rush* played a part in bringing home the gold medal, albeit in a more indirect fashion than I'd dreamed.

470 Midwest Championship

Déjà vu all over again. When selection of the 470 was announced for the 1976 Olympics, many of America's best sailors jumped into the boat.

We'd taken the first step by getting sons Stu and Drake a new, Harken-built 470 US-301 just before the Soling Trials. The idea was to challenge the boys, who'd been winning all the local Sunfish regattas.

When we returned to Wilmette after the Trials, the boys dared to ask, "Dad, can we go sail in the Great Lakes Championship next week?"

"What? Give me a break! You've had your 470 *Flying Cloud* for three weeks, and you think you're good enough to compete in a major championship against forty other world-class Flying Dutchmen, 505, and Fireball champs...all those hot shots from dinghy classes jumping into this new Olympic class? You're going to get killed! Plus, I need a break from all this Olympic-class racing pressure."

They kept pleading. Eventually, I relented. "OK, I'll go help Art Mitchell of Harken run the races on the Committee Boat, and we'll drag you up there."

We trailed *Flying Cloud* up to Milwaukee. It was a light-air series. They had a set of baggy Murphy & Nye sails. In those conditions, it was a happy M & N error.

The wind never got over eight knots. The two boys together weighed about 215 lbs. Nobody in the fleet was trapezing, except Drake, flat out on the wire. Boats have a way of living up to their name. *Flying Cloud* it was, and they were!

The boys did a horizon job on the forty-boat fleet. It wasn't close. As 470 Midwest Champions, they qualified for the region's single entry to the 1972 World Championship in Montreal.

470 Worlds 1972

"Daddy, can we go to the Worlds?"

It was pretty hard to deny them the chance after winning the Midwests. Mary drove them to the Nationals in Hingham, then up to Lac de Deux Montagne, south of Montreal, for the Worlds.

What a turnaround! At least some family members would reach the pinnacle of their class that year.

The organizing committee enlisted me as an international judge for the event. To fulfill my duties and for us to spectate from, we purchased a Zodiac inflatable with a 9-HP Mercury outboard.

Friend Ding Schoonmaker* was also a judge. Among our duties was the daily inspection of the top three finishers to ensure they were legal.

One day, Ding was to inspect the winning French boat crewed by a well-endowed woman. Ding approached them and asked, "Were you wearing any extra ballast?"

Grinning, the female crew pulled open her wet suit to reveal her ample breasts. "You mean these?"

You can imagine Ding's red-faced reaction!

The boys finished an impressive 2nd and 3rd in two light-air races, but it was a windy regatta. So they ended up 32nd with a prize for being the top junior crew in the event.

Family Olympic Syndicate

Now what? Should we keep the Soling and accompany the boys on the 470 circuit? Or do we sell the Soling and get another 470 so Mary and I could race together and do the regatta circuit as a family?

Time to Get Creative. One doesn't usually equate an Olympic campaign syndicate with a husband, wife, and four kids under age 15. But we weren't normal.

We sold the Soling and ordered two new 470s. The 470s went deck-to-deck on a trailer, with the Zodiac on our wagon's roof.

Helen (age 12) and Peter (age 7) would drive the Zodiac team support boat, towing the two boats to and from the race course. There were no coach boats in those days.

In the interim, while we waited for our new boats, Peter Harken* generously lent us his 470.

We found room for ten 470s on dollies in a little-used corner of the Star boat in the dry-sail lot across from the Sheridan Shore Yacht Club.

Gerard Pender Photo

115

Our two-boat family syndicate participated in many regional and national 470 events: SPORT, CORK, the North Americans, Nationals, and regional regattas.

The most memorable race was on Carlyle Lake, a large body of water east of St. Louis. We were up against some good competition, including a young University of Michigan student and future yacht designer, Bruce Nelson^.

In one race, the wind gusted to 50 knots. I can still see Mary flat-out on the trapeze. To keep from capsizing, I was feathering the fully trimmed sails, almost into the wind, with both jib and main whipped into a constant, high-speed flutter.

The boat stayed in limbo, not going forward but drifting sideways. Luckily, we stayed upright until the gust passed, survived, and won the race and the regatta.

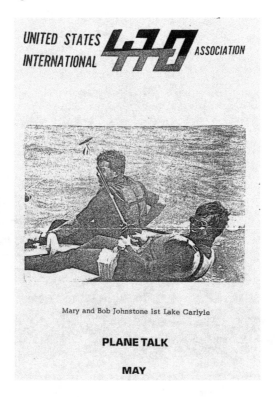

Mary and Bob Johnstone 1st Lake Carlyle

PLANE TALK

MAY

The win was impressive enough for us to make the front cover of *Plain Talk*, the 470 Class newsletter.

Before one race at SPORT on Apollo Beach, 7-year-old Peter decided to tease Augie Diaz* by tossing a ring-ding into the cockpit of Augie's boat on the beach, so he might think a clevis pin from his rigging would come undone during the race.

It was blowing 15–20 knots that day. Sometimes it's not *Time to Get Creative.*

Mary and I reckoned we'd be much faster if we switched roles: I'd put my 175 lbs. on the trapeze wire while Mary's 128 lbs. steered.

We were fast for about two minutes, motoring right out from under Dave Ullman* and so far in front of other starboard tackers we could tack to cross the entire fleet in 1st place.

The trouble was, we hadn't practiced this new program. In her new role as the driver, Mary got the hiking stick tangled up in the mainsheet in the middle of the tack, and over we went, capsized and swimming. Skip Whyte crossed behind us, convulsed with laughter.

In a race on Lake Michigan, a strong westerly squall hit us. It was fun for a while! Mary and I were close to flying on a beam reach without a spinnaker. Then we were overpowered and flipped. Fortunately, our standard garb for this 60-degree water was lightweight "surfer" wetsuits.

The challenge then became how to right the boat. It was impossible to pull it up into the wind by standing on the centerboard, as there was too much wind pressure on the hull and rig.

Time to Get Creative. So why not try in the other direction? Get the wind to help by blowing the boat upright. The trick was to dive under the boat and grab the leeward rail so when the wind caught the sail to push it upright, and the windward rail came out of the water, I'd be lying on the deck of the boat and rolled into it. That became standard operating procedure. Both boats qualified to be members of the United States 470 team at world championships in 1973 and 1974, which we did not attend.

Besides Ullman*, Diaz*, Whyte, Proctor*, and ourselves, shown in the CORK results, the others in December 1973 were Pete Commette^ and Rick Grajirena.

Shown are results from the 65-boat 470 fleet in the 1973 CORK, a year into our program. You can see that Mary and I weren't doing badly. After four races, we were right in there with Augie and Skip behind Dave Ullman. The boys sailed a great regatta.

PLACE of 65	1973 470 CORK OLYMPIC TRAINING REGATTA							PTS
1	Dave Ullman	1	3	2	1	(3)	1	9
2	Stu & Drake Johnstone	2	4	(DNF)	2	4	2	25
3	Augie Diaz	5	2	1	(19)	1	12	31
4	Skip Whyte	(17)	1	6	5	11	4	47
5	Mauricio Bolens (Ita)	(28)	12	3	3	2	17	55
6	Bob & Mary Johnstone	9	8	4	4	(17)	6	57
7	Colin Park	6	6	(33)	10	12	5	67
8	Ched Proctor	10	9	(34)	7	10	9	75
9	Jerry Roufs (Can)	30	10	20	(31)	5	3	94
10	Gilles Casaubon (Can)	(35)	33	9	9	6	10	95
19*	Rod & Lucia Johnstne	(41)	20	22	8	21	20	121

By that time my brother, Rod, had also gotten a 470 to sail with his wife, Lucia. That 4th race was a family affair with finishes of 2-4-8.

CHAPTER 8

US Youth Champs

Witnessing the performance of our kids at ages 13 and 14 in an Olympic class at the Worlds, I thought, "It's too bad more youth in America don't have this same opportunity."

Team USA would do much better at World Youth Championships and the Olympics by fast-tracking youth in Olympic boats. Another example of America's youth talent was John Dane, Marc LeBlanc, and crew from the Southern Yacht Club in New Orleans. They won the Sears Cup in 1967, the Soling North Americans in 1969 at age 19, and a silver medal in the Soling Worlds in 1970, and they finished 4th at the 1973 Soling Olympic Trials.

Time to Get Creative. The concept of a US Youth Sailing Championship was taking root. In my youth, nobody encouraged me to sail in the Lightning North Americans, even though I was winning many events locally. It was unheard of for 15–17-year-olds to compete in Olympic classes at the national level.

I hadn't forgotten, 20 years later. Why couldn't an event be created for young sailors to discover how good they were or what they had to learn? The founding concept of the 1973 US Youths was to scour the country to identify 150 youth, as I'd once been, and invite them for a chance to compete against each other at the highest level.

They'd learn quickly by sailing against the best. Let's not let them get bored and drift away from sailboat racing.

OK, how did we pull it off?

In 1972, the previous year, NAYRU (now US Sailing) had sent the top Florida Optimist sailor, who was about 14 years old, to compete in the single-handed class, and sent 17-year-olds from the Sears Cup—winning crew from a small rotate-boats series to compete in the IYRU Youth Worlds. They were up against 19-year-old winners of big fleet events.

We needed a qualifying event for America's best youth aged 19 and under—not just from Florida and the East Coast but from all over the US, no matter what class of boat they'd been sailing.

Like sons Stu and Drake, they needed to be motivated to compete in exciting new 470s and Lasers. We'd bring them all to a central Midwest location like our Sheridan Shore Yacht Club in Wilmette and conduct the event in June 1973, between the end of the school year and when they'd start summer jobs as sailing instructors.

I called my fellow 470 Worlds judge and friend, Ding Schoonmaker*, to get the ball rolling. He was then chairman of NAYRU's Junior Sailing Committee. It helped that Ding had witnessed the boy's performance in a 470 at the 1971 Worlds.

After describing the event concept and proposing it become the official NAYRU qualifier for the US Youth Team for the 1973 World Youth Championships, Ding agreed to take it up with the board of directors.

He replied two weeks later. "Bob, NAYRU doesn't have the personnel or capability to organize an event of this scale on such short notice. But the board agreed that if you organize and run it at Sheridan Shore Yacht Club, we'll put the USYRU name on it. You can call it the United States Youth Sailing Championship."

I accepted, and I am forever indebted to Ding for that administrative coup. He had a deal!

We were off. I ordered eight new 470s from Harken to charter and make available for post-regatta sale, saying, "Get ready. You will probably be getting even more orders."

I did the same with Ian Bruce of Performance Sailcraft for Lasers. The Bruce Kirby-designed Laser wasn't introduced until 1971, so fewer than 5,000 boats existed. Youth all over the country who didn't own a Laser now wanted to sail one. The US Youth Champs put the Laser on the map.

Sheridan Shore Yacht Club was psyched. The next challenge was getting the word out so no deserving youth would be missed.

US Olympic Yachting Committee

Time to Get Creative. As I had been appointed by Class President Larry Lewis as the 470 Class Representative to the United States Olympic Yachting Committee (USOYC), the answer was close at hand.

I just had to get my hands on some USOYC letterhead.

The first meeting of the USOYC for the 1976 Olympiad was in March 1973 at the New York Yacht Club on 44th Street.

Flying with my friend Dick Stearns^, an Olympic silver medalist and the Star Class representative, I asked him, "Out of curiosity, do you have any aspirations for a role on the Olympic Committee...like maybe being the next chairman?

Dick thought for a moment, brightened, and said, "Well, yeah, that would be great!" I said, "OK, let's see how things develop. As a first-time rookie, I can ask some first-timer questions to steer the committee in that direction."

The meeting was conducted by Star legend Paul Smart, age 80, who'd been chairman since 1964.

I wanted to understand what the USOYC did, thinking how important it was to have the USOYC behind the launch of a US Youth Championship.

My newbie questions started with, "What is the role of the US Olympic Yachting Committee? What are their plans to develop talent?"

Chairman Smart's answer, echoed by other old-guard committee members, was, "We have a lot of outstanding sailors in the US. They are so talented we have little we can teach them. Our role is to provide them with financial support for international competition and a good venue for the trials."

I asked, "Has the USOYC considered being proactive in offering programs to bring up, develop, and improve on the talent pool?"

Again, they said, "No, no, we're not into that. We're hands-off. We're not into any programs except to administer the trials."

So I was rolling my eyes along with other new committee members. A silent consensus was building: USOYC was missing the boat here. They were essentially doing nothing to develop talent or increase the chances of the US winning more Olympic medals...an "it is what it is" laissez-faire posture.

When it was time to elect officers for the 1976 Olympiad, the expectation was that the old guard would again rubber-stamp themselves back into control.

I was thinking, *No way!* To rattle the cage, I nominated Dick Stearns^ as chairman to lead a "new, proactive" USOYC. It was seconded and followed by some shocked, back-and-forth emotional responses.

But the tide had turned, with building support for the more proactive stance. Stearns^ was voted in as chairman. He then nominated me for secretary-treasurer, figuring, "OK, Johnstone*, you got me into this job. Now you're going to have to help me do it." Seconded and passed.

Another Midwesterner and friend, Bill Bentsen*, who had crewed for Buddy Melges in the Soling, was appointed special advisor. The Olympic power center shifted to Middle America to begin a new era.

I had my stack of USOYC letterhead and the contact info for all the top sailors in America.

Before that meeting adjourned, Bob Bavier*, editor, and publisher of *Yachting*, said, "Sorry, gentlemen, I've got to go; we're closing the magazine. I have to make sure everything is OK."

I raised my hand to plead, "Bob. Please. This new US Youth Championship is coming up in June. It's key for developing Olympic talent. Can you run an announcement in this issue? The event is just 90 days away. Every second counts to get the word out."

He turned to me halfway to the door, saying, "No! Sorry. It's too late. The book's done. Just closing up."

I was crestfallen. But before Bavier* left the room, Dick Stearns^ said in a stage voice, "Bob, don't worry about it. *Yachting* is just for old farts anyway."

With that, Bavier* mumbled a weak denial and bolted from the room. So much for *Yachting*'s help. We'd find some other way to get the word out.

The rest of us adjourned for lunch downstairs at the club. I was seated with Stearns.

About halfway through lunch, Bavier* showed up and hustled over to our table with a notebook and a pencil in hand, clearly flustered by the "old farts" jab. He declared, "OK, *Yachting* will do it. What should we say about this Youth Championship?"

That's how word first got out in the national press. Interested youth were asked to apply to the Youth Championship Committee with their resume.

Uncle Sam Wants You

Time to Get Creative. As secretary-treasurer of the US Olympic Yachting Committee, I had a couple of potent weapons: USOYC stationery and contact addresses for all prior and aspiring Olympians.

Along with sailmakers across the country, they got a letter requesting help identifying the top two or three young sailors in their area, age 19 or under.

We ended up with a couple of hundred names and addresses for Bill Bentsen and me to sort through and decide whom to invite.

Once we'd selected those to invite, we sent them the following "Uncle Sam Wants You"–style letter of invitation on US Olympic Yachting Committee stationery:

You have been identified as one of the top youth sailors in the country who represent the future of the United States success in the World Youth Championships, as well as Olympic and International classes.

We are therefore pleased to invite you to compete in either Lasers or 470s in the inaugural NAYRU US Youth Sailing Championship at the Sheridan Shore YC in Wilmette, IL. See the attached Notice of Race.

You may use this letter with your yacht club or YRA to help secure sponsorship and travel funding. The top 3 finishers in each division shall receive USYOC funding to the Youth Worlds or for World and National Class Champs.

Be assured that everyone will return home as a winner. Buddy Melges, Dave Ullman*, Bruce Goldsmith, Bruce Kirby, and Manton Scott are some world-class sailors who will be there to observe, video, critique, and discuss your performance and convey their racing experience every evening after racing.

Housing and food is arranged at no charge for all contestants. 8 new 470s are available for purchase. Other 470s, as well as Lasers, are available for charter.

We had 100 percent acceptance. Two of the 117 wanted to attend but were denied the chance. A doctor told a New Jersey Laser sailor who had broken his leg that he couldn't sail with a cast. The other was the top single-handed sailor in New England, a cadet at the Coast Guard Academy in New London.

On a phone call with the academy's commandant, I couldn't convince him the event would be better for the cadet and the academy than a week on the *Eagle*. That's how it all came about. The Sheridan Shore YC membership pitched in.

Tragically, Manton Scott, who was going to be a seminar leader, was electrocuted while putting up his 470 mast a month beforehand.

The 115 youth in that 79-boat fleet (36-470s and 43-Lasers) are credited with unifying the sport under the US Sailing banner, putting America's best young sailors together for the first time. Previously, NAYRU had an East Coast bias. Sailors from this first 1973 event, like Dave

Perry*, Mark Reynolds*, Peter Commette^, Augie Diaz*, Greg Fisher^, Alison Jolly*, Carl Buchan*, and the rest, became leaders in the sport.

See the Appendix for the complete Laser and 470 results from the 1973 Youth Championship, courtesy of Pete Commette, who saved them. Note that 21 of the 43 Laser sailors and 25 of the 36 470 sailors finished in the top 10 in at least one race. There was lots of future talent in those fleets.

US Sailing named the single-handed US Youth Championship trophy the Robert L. Johnstone III Trophy in honor of my founding of the event and my contribution to one-design sailing.

Top of the Youth World!

The US Youth Champs dramatically raised America's level of success on the world stage. The USOC funded the top finishers in each fleet to the World Youths and 470, 420, or Laser Worlds.

Augie Diaz* won the 1973 World Youth Championship in Lasers. Terry Neff and Kevin Lofstedt finished a close fourth in the double-handed World Youths in 470s.

Peter Commette^ wanted to sail the Laser Worlds, but the first Worlds weren't until 1974, which he attended and won. In 1973, he went to the 470 Worlds and took silver with Mike Loeb.

Here's a sampling of how that first 1973 US Youth Championship event has impacted US sailing.

➤ 4 Olympic Gold Medals (Allison Jolly, Mark Reynolds, Carl Buchan)
➤ 5 National Sailing Hall of Fame Inductees (Diaz, Buchan, Reynolds, Perry, Jolly)
➤ 2 National Sailing Hall of Fame Nominees (Commette, Fisher)
➤ 4 Rolex Sailors of the Year (Diaz, Reynolds, Jolly, Jud Smith)
➤ 14 ICSA All-Americans
➤ 3 ICSA Sailors of the Year (Diaz, Stu Johnstone, Buchan)

➤ 1 inductee in the ICSA Hall of Fame (Nina Nielsen—Princeton)
➤ 13 World Championships in Laser (Commette), 420 (White-hurst), Snipe (Diaz), Star (Reynolds, Buchan, Diaz), J/24 (Charlie Scott, Johnstone), J/70 (Smith), J/22 (Fisher), FD (Buchan), Etchells 22 (Smith), International OD (Smith)

Within two years, the US swept the 1975 World Youth Championship. Bob and Tom Whitehurst won the double-handed, and Carl Buchan* won the single-handed.

Nathaniel Philbrick

One of my favorite stories from the first Youths, which vindicated the concept, is about National Book Award–winning author Nathaniel Philbrick.

The "selection committee" of Bentsen and I had been turning down several applicants to keep fleet sizes manageable.

There was this kid from an inland lake near Erie, Pennsylvania, who'd won some local Sunfish regattas.

We went back and forth on whether to accept him, finally reminding ourselves, here's a classic case: giving a youth who's dominated the local scene a chance to go up against the best in the nation.

Nat had to charter a Laser, a boat he'd never sailed before. He finished last. But by 1978, he'd won the Sunfish North Americans and become Brown University's first Intercollegiate All-American.

We connected many years later at a Boston book signing for his award-winning *Mayflower*.

When asked if he'd be willing to write a short commentary for the participants about his time in the Youths, he did so, confessing, "You know, it was actually a good thing I came in last. All that time in the back of the fleet gave me the chance to study all those great sailors ahead of me. I learned a lot."

He also provided a signed copy of *Mayflower* to be presented to the last-place finisher in the Laser Class at the 2007 Youth Championship on Lake Pontchartrain.

In 1976, as VP of Marketing at Alcort, I'd commissioned Eric Schweikardt to get a shot in Bermuda, when the tall ships were there, of a Sunfish in front of a tall ship. That photo became a large AMF Alcort promotional poster.

Nat later confessed, "That poster on my wall was what convinced me to become a writer of history." He received Mystic Seaport Museum's America and the Sea Award in 2015, the year before Rod and I did for J/Boats.

CATCH THE SPIRIT

CHAPTER 9

Sail 73 Wilmette

H aving reached out to identify and motivate the best young sailors in harbors and lakes across America via the network feeding talent into the US Youth Championship, how do we increase the talent pool of youth at the local level?

Time to Get Creative! The most obvious answer was, "By growing the sport of sailing." We didn't have to wait long to see how that might happen at home in Wilmette.

Even before the kids become less of a full-time job, the biggest challenge for a married couple is ensuring both partners *get a life.*

Mary's studies at Smith College were interrupted by our marriage after her junior year. She promised her mother that she'd complete her college education.

Ultimately, to do so, she had to take two years at Northwestern instead of the final year she'd missed at Smith. Because? The provost considered Smith to be a "finishing school" rather than a proper university.

She graduated with a degree in music education and initially pursued a career in music by teaching "required" junior high school music for a semester. After running afoul of some parents for including the Beatles' "Maxwell's Silver Hammer" in the curriculum, she decided that teaching obligatory junior high music was not her thing. She mentioned the possibility of becoming an entertainer, playing evenings at a piano bar or working as a waitress at a diner on Skokie Boulevard. I was horrified.

Time to Get Creative at home, too. This hubby went into overdrive as a career counselor.

I contacted my friend Burt Manning, Quaker's pet-food account supervisor (later chairman and CEO) at J. Walter Thompson, to set up an interview for her with Dick Marx, a jazz pianist, composer, and arranger who produced some famous radio and TV jingles and film music, including "My dog's bigger than your dog" (Ken-L Ration), "Double your pleasure, double your fun" (Wrigley's Doublemint Gum), and the soundtrack for the movie *A League of Their Own*.

That job appealed to Mary's creative side, but the hours were a turn-off. Dick warned, "You might have to burn the midnight oil frequently to meet the demands of clients, who always want their jingles yesterday."

So I started scanning classified want ads in the *Chicago Tribune* and *Wilmette Life* for jobs that might be fun.

She perked up at the possibility of being a sales clerk in one of our favorite stores, a nearby Crate & Barrel in Plaza del Lago.

In addition to being accepted as one of two among fifty applicants, she was promoted to buyer's assistant at headquarters and then assistant store manager.

Since I'd also heard some beefs from Mary about city management, open space, freezing to death at the outdoor ice rink, etc., I hinted that if she had some spare time, maybe it would be worthwhile to do something about it.

Mary got involved politically, taking a leadership role in two private-citizen initiatives: Save Open Space (SOS), acquiring the Northwestern University golf course to preclude real estate development, and building an indoor ice rink.

You can't imagine how welcome the rink was after having had to suffer through nearly zero-degree temperatures at the town's outdoor ice rink for seven winters, with two sons on all-star hockey teams and a daughter figure skating.

Mary became forever famous, with her name etched in granite on the cornerstone of the rink building.

Those accomplishments led to Mary being elected as a Wilmette Park Commissioner with support from both political parties, garnering a larger popular vote than the mayor.

Community Sailing Program

This was fun, being the spouse of a rising political star. While Mary had to put up with the cigar smoke in the Wilmette Park District conference room, I was not beyond applying undue leverage to the commissioners to support a community sailing program.

We labeled it SAIL 73 Wilmette. This could be a model program for not only Chicago's North Shore but the entire country. Turns out it did more than that. It became a turning point in our lives.

Wilmette owned about half a mile of the Lake Michigan waterfront. The rumor before we arrived in 1966 was, "Normal, law-abiding citizens are arrested for sneaking onto that beach with small boats."

When we got there, a rack was available for storing private Sunfish and Hobie 16s. Formal sailing instruction was only available at two private clubs: the Sunfish Club on the north end of the beach, where members would drop off their kids age 8 and up for morning lessons, and the Sheridan Shore Yacht Club. They ran a junior sailing program. In total, maybe 100 people were learning how to sail each year.

Time to Get Creative. If the town was going to get more people out sailing, the populace had to become aware that sailing and sailing lessons were available to everyone.

The solution seemed logical enough: treat sailing like tennis, golf, bowling, swimming, nature hikes, or other community recreation. List the schedule, rates, qualifications, etc., in the Parks & Recreation summer program booklet.

Since Wilmette had the best beach on the North Shore of Chicago, and there was no residency requirement, that booklet could be distributed to towns 10–20 miles inland. The word got out. It had never happened in sailing before that you could sign up yourself and your kids in advance for a season's participation.

We'd gotten the park commission's attention with Mary on the board. SAIL 73 offered a three-part program. The Sunfish Club offered beginner instruction and capsize drills for children starting at age eight. The park district on Gilson Beach offered instruction and rentals of Sunfish, Hobies, and Windsurfers to anyone who could swim, no matter their age, at any time of the day.

Sons Stu and Drake, with friends, were instructors. The Sheridan Shore Yacht Club offered a learn-to-race program in the 470s.

When developing a pricing strategy, it became clear that a one-to-one instructor-to-student ratio on a 470 dinghy or a Hobie would not be as profitable as a one-to-four ratio on a 24-foot sloop.

We didn't have keelboats to pull it off in 1973. But that was the founding premise later for J/World Sailing School using J/24s.

The second key was providing an incentive to the local boat dealer, Hedlund Marine, to sell the park district boats for $1 each to cover liability. In return, the city promoted Hedlund as the place to buy a boat after learning to sail. Hedlund Marine became one of the country's largest dealers. The park district had a resource to maintain and periodically renew its rental fleet.

A third key was showing the park district how sailing could be a moneymaker. After all, the water and beach were free. Private-boat storage fees on the beach and small boat rentals would be gravy. It worked. Here are the reported numbers from June 15 to Labor Day, 1985:

- 17 instructors operated seven days and three nights per week.
- No residency requirement. Parking for 385 cars.
- Racks for 455 privately owned Hobies, Lasers, and Sunfish.
- 1,600 students.
- 27 Hobies, Sunfish, and Windsurfers in rental fleet booked.
- 10,000 rentals, earning the city more than $250,000.

CHAPTER 10

Naturescapes Inc.

T ed Turner* is reported to have commented about his son, Teddy, "He's become an entrepreneur, which means he doesn't have a job."

"Photo Wall Murals of Nature" was at the top of my list of high-potential business areas before departing Quaker Oats. That probably said more about my state of mind than my financial acumen. Nevertheless, I decided to put my money where my ranking (a.k.a. ego) was and go with one of the top products on the list.

The inspiration was a black-and-white photography exhibit of nature scenes in Quaker's cafeteria in the Merchandise Mart.

The Quaker offices, occupying the entire third floor, had been "modernized" by Skidmore, Owings & Merrill. Initially, there were wide-open spaces, with many small offices having glass partitions. Everyone could see what the weather was doing outdoors.

The latest architectural theory, however, was that windowless private offices, beige rugs, and modern art hanging on white walls would impress visitors and motivate management.

It sure didn't work for this occupant. Days went by in winter when I never saw daylight. I'd get to work at sunrise and leave after dark for the 30-minute train ride on the Chicago Northwestern to Wilmette. I was living the life of Alvin Toffler's book *Future Shock*, with an emotional need to relate to the natural world.

The potential cure was revealed during a coffee break in Quaker's cafeteria. An exhibit of large, four-by-six-foot, black-and-white photographs of nature was on display. Sitting there looking at those images, I felt a sense of peace and relaxation. Priorities started to fall into place, putting me in a positive mood to tackle the afternoon's work.

Time to Get Creative. A business concept began to form. In this brick-and-mortar urban environment, wouldn't natural images like these contribute to an improved state of mind and increased productivity?

An article by a Yale psychology professor reinforced the concept. Naturescapes was born, a collection of photographic murals by America's leading environmental photographers.

OK, what were the images going to be? My first thought was, "If I weren't in this office, where would I most want to be? And wouldn't it be nice if a wall were like a huge window looking out into that place?"

Indeed, everyone must carry in their mind a vision of a favorite place: a beach, forest, lake, or trout stream.

Gerald French Photo

My consumer research wasn't very sophisticated. I started asking friends and others, "If you had a choice right now, where would you most like to be?" And "Can you describe some of the details of the scene?" The feedback consistently described one of about twenty different natural scenes.

Ecopsychology

I learned later there was a name for what I was becoming involved with: "Ecopsychology"—how immersion in nature benefits one's health.

Research by Rachel and Stephen Kaplan at Michigan's School of Natural Resources and Environment concluded, "Those with a view of nature felt less frustrated and more patient, found their job more challenging, expressed greater enthusiasm for it, and reported higher life satisfaction as well as overall health."

Lack of windows was a major complaint, as windows are a source of light, sunshine, or information about weather and happenings in the world outside.

Contract Manufacturing

Who could produce photo murals as large as 9x14 feet? The printer of outdoor billboards had to be the answer. The largest in America was the Gugler Lithographic Company in nearby Milwaukee.

Gugler could print and perfectly color-match the eight panels that made up the full-size mural. Could they print at a resolution of 60 dots per inch (DPI) instead of the 20 DPI used for billboards?

Environmentalists depressed outdoor billboard sales. So Gugler was motivated to print and then inventory finished murals until drop-shipped upon receipt of orders.

It's an axiom of business that specifications for one's initial product are rarely those of the product that ultimately succeeds. Naturescapes was no exception.

I was so convinced of our black-and-white (B&W) product's appeal and the execution of the concept that a direct-marketing approach was deemed viable.

The first ad was a double-page B&W spread in *Chicago Magazine* for an incredible 8x12 foot forest image priced at $75. The first mail-in order didn't arrive for two weeks! The initial product line of five B&W photo murals was short-lived. At the Chicago Home Show, people would look at a stunning B&W Redwood Forest image by Philip Hyde—the sun filtering in onto ferns and a fallen log—and say, "Oooh, too bad it's not in color!" We ended up dumping 75 percent of them.

People wanted nature scenes in natural colors to consult with interior designers and reinforce their ideas. Bypassing traditional interior decorator outlets didn't work. *Time to Get Creative.* We doubled the price to distribute sample books through interior decorators and wallpaper outlets, giving them a 50 percent margin. Involving the entire family once again in the decision, we started all over again in four-color, taking out a second mortgage on our home to finance $10,000 for a single run of a four-color image of Walden Pond.

The business started to grow as proceeds from that one image were reinvested in runs of additional color images.

Naturescapes was still a home business on a shoestring. Our garage became the distribution center. Pages for our sample books were collated, punched, put in loose-leaf binders, then packed 25 into a box for delivery to distributors.

The workforce consisted of Peter's 7-year-old friends after school and our three older kids working for maybe $2 per hour when they had time. When interior decorators called to complain of a missing page, I had to confess, "It's tough finding skilled workers these days."

CHAPTER 11

AMF Alcort

I received a call from an executive-recruiting firm in the spring of 1975. It was a game-changer.

Fellow Soling sailor and then Barton & Cormier sailmaker Bob Barton was the one who put the headhunter on to me. I was asked, "Would you be interested in accepting a job as VP of marketing for AMF Alcort, maker of the Sunfish?"

"Would I? Sounds very interesting. Please tell me more."

I was leaning toward carving out a career in the marine industry. Plus, I was a strong advocate of the Sunfish as the best boat to learn how to sail on, as evidenced by SAIL 73. I was ready to accept the offer and move the family east to Connecticut. Even the prospect of working for another Fortune 500 company didn't raise any red flags, as it probably should have.

An AMF Alcort job selling Sunfish could be great fun.

Sailing was exploding in the early 1970s. Sailing was what I did in my spare time. I'd started a Sunfish fleet in Venezuela and was twice their national champ.

I'd started up 20-plus-boat Soling and 470 fleets under nearly impossible circumstances. So it seemed I had a knack for selling boats.

Why not align my hobby with a vocation? Maybe it was time to act out my ministry full time. David Brooks would describe it as "The beginning of one's ascent up life's second mountain, after scaling the first and being disillusioned with the view."

Windsurfer Dealer

My first step into the marine business was to become Lake Michigan's earliest Windsurfer dealer. I had a lot to learn.

We'd been to Association Island, where I'd officiated at the US Youth Championship and pre-Olympic regatta. Hoyle and Diane Schweitzer* of Windsurfing Inc. had sent out a half dozen Windsurfers for us all to flop around on.

This new form of sailing was both challenging and great fun, so much so that I tried to contact a local dealer upon returning to Wilmette. But there weren't any in the Chicago area, let alone Lake Michigan.

So I called Hoyle Schweitzer. He answered, saying, "There isn't a dealer in your area. Would you like to be it?"

Hesitantly, I asked what was involved. Hoyle said, "It's easy. Order six boards, which I can airfreight to you tomorrow."

I accepted and drove my Penguin trailer to O'Hare the next day to lash all six boxes on top. That marked my entry into the marine industry as a "dealer."

I didn't waste any time trying to promote the product. That same weekend, Dick Tillman^, Mary, and I entertained the fleet of Laser sailors by trying to remain standing on those tricky boards during the Great Lakes Laser Championship off Winnetka.

My first ads were under "Boats" in the *Chicago Tribune*'s classifieds. I advertised that Windsurfer sailboards were available by calling my number.

Many enthusiastic calls came in until I mentioned a price of over $400. The all-too-quick response was, "That's ridiculous. I can get a surfboard for $100."

To not waste my time, the next classified ad included the price. The result: no calls.

Like Naturescapes, direct marketing wasn't going to work. Friends had to recommend them, and they had to be seen on the water. I'd be far more successful marketing the iconic Sunfish.

Naturescapes' New CEO

Mary agreed to run Naturescapes if I accepted the AMF Alcort job in Waterbury. She'd worked her way up at Crate & Barrel from store clerk to buyer at headquarters and to assistant store manager.

Her retail-business experience and personal skills proved ideal for growing Naturescapes' dealer-designer network and sales. Receiving the magazine *Progressive Architecture*'s "Top Inquiry Award" was proof of the concept and market interest.

Naturescapes profits paid for our kids' college education and bankrolled the first-year startup of J/Boats Inc.

AMF Alcort Troubles

The Sunfish had been very profitable for Alcort founders Alexander Bryan* and Cortlandt Heyniger* when selling 15,000 per year. But after buying Alcort, AMF was at a loss on how to respond to emerging competition.

You hear stories of profitable small companies being taken over by big corporations like AMF. The founder goes happily off into the sunset with his cash. The Fortune 500 is stuck with a business they know little about, neither the consumer dynamics nor what made it successful in the first place. The first time something goes wrong, the company goes into a nosedive. Next thing you know, it's gone. That was happening to AMF Alcort.

Laser Intro

Hobie Cat and Laser made huge inroads. Take the Laser, for example. Alcort management, rather than creatively coming up with winning product strategies, had given traction to one of their future primary competitors, the Bruce Kirby–designed Laser.

It happened at the 1970 America's Tea Cup Regatta at the Playboy Club on Lake Geneva, Wisconsin. This event was a comparative "test" for small sailboats selling for less than $1,000.

It was a brilliant move by Kirby, editor of the magazine *One-design & Offshore Yachtsman,* which sponsored the event.

He entered his prototype Laser, the "Weekender," built as a "one-off" by Ian Bruce of Performance Sailcraft in Canada and sailed to a decisive win by Canadian Olympian Hans Fogh. The prototype was 25 pounds lighter, at 109 pounds, than a production Laser.

AMF Alcort, with its Sunfish, was snookered, even more so by a light-air series on Lake Geneva and the failure to have lightweight, 120-pound son Stu sail the boat. Stu had been winning just about every Sunfish race on Lake Michigan. Had Alcort put him on the Sunfish rather than doubling him up with his brother Drake on the smaller Mini-Fish, there's no telling how history may have changed.

Most likely, AMF wouldn't have needed to hire me as their marketing VP to solve their problems.

AMF was looking for a top sailor with Fortune 500 product-management experience to revive Sunfish sales and profits, which had plummeted from an output of 15,000 per year to less than half that.

AMF didn't understand that Sunfish's success mainly involved beginners and recreational fun. The Laser was introduced, as admitted by Kirby, as a "one-up" of Sunfish performance for racing. AMF management fell into the trap of ineffectually playing the Laser "racing" game rather than building on the larger, recreational, "fun" franchise they owned.

They introduced the Force 5 and Super Sunfish, which had Laser-type rigs. These offshoots never had the national-class support of the Laser and were only a distraction from Sunfish promotional efforts.

Meanwhile, Hobie was gobbling up the "fun" market. AMF Alcort was losing on two counts.

In addition to the Alcort Sunfish, AMF corporate had acquired a couple of small cruising boats from Nova Scotia, the Paceship 23 and 26, which were typical of the sluggish, small, overly equipped cruisers then populating the mid-20-foot market.

With a dozen or more similar brands like Ericsson, Columbia, O'Day, and Catalina dominating, AMF's share potential in the small-cruiser category was no more than 8 percent.

We'd soon learn it was half of that. AMF's marine group office in Stamford was in charge of Alcort, Slickcraft, Crestliner, and Hatteras. The group VP wasn't an entrepreneur or marketer. He was an administrator trying to please AMF's board by milking the businesses for short-term profits instead of investing in new product concepts for the perpetuity of the brands.

You can't replace passion with spreadsheets. It happened with Harley-Davidson and Hatteras as well.

In 1975, the Baby Boomer generation was getting married, having kids, buying camping gear, etc. Nearly 100,000 small sailboats were being sold each year: Hobie Cats, Sunfish, Lasers, and Styrofoam Snarks, the latter for $100 and the label from a carton of Kool cigarettes.

Once people learned the thrill of sailing fast on those off-the-beach boats, they wanted to share their fun with girlfriends, wives, or kids and spend more time on the water. But all these go-fast sailors had no larger boats to transition to if they wanted the excitement of sailing in street clothes rather than freezing in a bathing suit.

Alcort 3-Year Plan

Time to Get Creative. Comprehensive long-range planning was rare in the corporate world at the time. I walked into my job at AMF in July 1975 with a plan for Alcort to more than double their business by reviving Sunfish sales and leveraging that franchise to introduce an easy-to-sail, high-performance keelboat of 23–25 feet with overnight accommodations.

The added $10 million in revenue would take Alcort from a loss to an annual $1.6 million profit.

About 80 percent of America's population lived near cold water. Even on Long Island Sound in the middle of summer, one could suffer hypothermia after sailing a Sunfish for an hour or so in a bathing suit.

You had to get to Florida or the islands in winter or to an inland lake in summer to find warm water to sail in a bathing suit.

The next step for all these new sailors had to be a larger family boat that was stable as well as fast.

I recalled our family day-sailing experiences. When owning a pair of 470s, thoughts of going out on Lake Michigan for a family picnic sail were out of the question.

The boat wasn't large enough to fit the entire family. It was inconvenient to launch from its dry-sail storage trailer with a crane, park the trailer, then rig the sails.

Then there was the safety concern of being in a small boat that could capsize if a big wind came up. So you couldn't be very adventurous, sailing far from your home port.

The solution was a boat larger than twenty feet with the stability of a keel to minimize the chance of capsizing. Before owning 470s, we allowed Stu and Drake, ages 14 and 13, to take our 27-foot Soling *Gold Rush* out into Lake Michigan. If heavy winds came up, they could always aim the boat at the harbor and get back.

If you wanted to sail safely with the family, a seaworthy boat similar in size to our former 24-foot Rainbow was the answer.

Time to Get Creative. My first step to gain management support was to revive the base business of Sunfish sales by going national with the SAIL 73 Wilmette community boating program.

A unique opportunity existed to introduce, for the first time, a display of sailboats and sailing as a sport at the National Recreation and Park Association (NRPA) annual conference at the Dallas Convention Center.

I got my friends to join me on a sizeable four-boat display that featured all SAIL 73 program craft: Olaf and Peter Harken came with their Olympic 470, Bob Brown of Coast Catamaran with a Hobie 16, and Hoyle and Diane Schweitzer with their Windsurfer. Of course, I was there with a Sunfish.

We passed out hundreds of pamphlets with "proven" program details, an organizational guide, financial projections, sample advertising, and scheduling forms.

The tally, after the week, was about 50 park districts expressing interest.

I then redirected Sunfish promotion away from racing, toward the beginning sailor, with 20,000 copies of the *Fun of Sailing* going out to Alcort's 150 dealers nationwide.

Included were more colorful sails. That was 7-year-old Peter's initial contribution to the sport. Mary was featured sailing the Sunfish in "Learn to Sail in 3 Days," a step-by-step illustrated self-teaching instructional guide.

Another aggressive step to reposition the Sunfish as the ideal "first" sailboat was cooked up with sailing friends Tim Dolman and Bill Sandberg of Benton & Bowles. Two full-page ads were run in *Sports Illustrated* in 1976.

AMF 7.3 Meter

With Sunfish marketing revamped, the next step was to convince management to approve a move forward with the key feature of the three-year plan: a performance keelboat.

I'd described it to my brother Rod and others as an "all-out fun," high-performance recreational boat under 25' overall, having an 8' trailerable beam, 7/8's rig, lift keel or keel/centerboard, and an adjustable backstay.

I was looking for a speed advantage over a Poitin, Soling, or Hobie 16. Sitting headroom belowdecks was acceptable, similar to many of Europe's small ¼- and ½-ton IOR boats.

Rod had been working on his 24-footer since 1974, periodically updating me on progress. His design had a fixed keel and 9' beam, which exceeded the 8' trailering and required a "wide load" sign. Neither feature was convenient for easy launching or trailering.

Wanting to be sure Rod remained a candidate to be the designer of an AMF 7.3 and assuming I could convince management of a sail-off among several leading designers, I'd encouraged him to start designing a prototype. He did and later built it, calling it the J/23.

I'd also talked with Scott Kaufman, Bruce Kirby*, and Gary Mull^ for the sail-off. I still have Gary Mull's design, dated March 1976. It was similar to Rod's but had an 8' beam, a 1.5' longer waterline, a heavier 1,200 lb. keel, and a 2.5' higher foretriangle, and it was lighter at 2,250 pounds. It would have been quick, but also had the fixed keel.

Market dynamics and imagination were beyond the grasp of AMF's number-crunching management. They rejected the project, saying, "No, the AMF Alcort sailboat division had to first improve sales of the AMF Paceship 23 and 26 designs by doing a better job with dealers, improving the interior, etc., before considering any new boat project."

I argued, "Look, the AMF Paceship 23 and 26 are like every other small cruiser on the market, and there's minimal potential upside no matter what we do. We need a boat to excite all the Sunfish, Hobie, and Laser sailors wanting to share their newly found sailing passion with their families."

"How about this? Let's give $20,000 each to Gary Mull, Scott Kaufman, Bruce Kirby, and Rod to build their 24-foot design. Give them a date and place for a sail-off. AMF can go with the winner, just like the IYRU does with new Olympic classes."

That plan got shot down. "Sorry, Bob, we're not going to approve the $80,000 for a sail-off. Even if we did, your brother's design would be out of the running as a conflict of interest. Furthermore, if we did anything, we'd want a design from a famous name like Ted Hood*."

My response was, "Fine, include Ted Hood as well. But he designs heavy boats, nothing like the fast, planing boat needed."

"No, Bob, you must realize that the Alcort division has had a poor new product success rate. Why should we expect it will improve?"

"Well, guys, thanks a lot. That's why you hired me, remember?"

Consumer Research

We're now getting into July 1976. Rod, in the meantime, built his 24'
Ragtime and was starting to win races.

Time to Get Creative. Remembering my "dogs love cheese" con-
sumer-research program to convince Quaker management of Ken-L
Cheeseburgers for dogs, I recommended that an independent research
firm verify interest in a 23-to-25-foot performance sailboat. They
agreed, most likely to appease me.

The research went out to ten cities, asking people at marinas, boat
shows, yacht clubs, and dealerships whether they planned to buy a boat
between 20 and 30 feet in the next few years.

If "yes," they were shown four storyboards with a photo, specifications, and bullet points listing features and price for each of four boats: a
Catalina 22, an AMF Paceship 23, a Farr ¼ Ton World Champion, and
an AMF 7.3. The latter had a photo of Rod's *Ragtime*.

To anyone with an ounce of marketing sense, the results were as-
tounding! Fifty percent of respondents split their choice evenly between
the two performance boats that weren't on the market: the Farr ¼ ton-
ner and the AMF 7.3.

The other 50 percent of the market consisted of similar small cruisers like the AMF Paceship 23 or Catalina 22. Fifty percent divided by 12
results in a rather unattractive 4 percent share opportunity.

Compare that to taking over 50 percent of the market with a new
performance boat. Still looking for a reason to scrub the project, AMF
management asked, "What's so special about the Farr and AMF 7.3?"

I said, "They sail about a knot faster to windward."

"What's a knot?" they asked.

I replied, "1.15 miles per hour."

Having had their Harley-Davidson brand dusted off by Kawasakis
and Hondas that were 10+ MPH faster, they weren't impressed and
directed me to kill the project.

In desperation, I pleaded, "Look, 20 percent faster on the water to windward is more impressive than 10 percent faster over the road. And what about that 50 percent market share opportunity versus maybe a 4 percent share, which is the most we can expect even if we do great with AMF Paceship models?"

"Sorry, the answer is *no*. Maybe in several years after you've revived the Paceship brand."

I should have known. Just another Fortune 500 company run by bean-counting custodians, not customer-oriented entrepreneurs!

Island Time

I wasn't happy about having the AMF 7.3 put on ice and having to plod on as a caretaker for Alcort small boats.

So there was nothing like a week in tropical Nassau during a cold Connecticut January to escape winter, get out of the office, clear the mind, and let priorities all fall into place. My role was to be a judge at the 1977 Sunfish World Championship along with the colorful Nassau Mercedes dealer and Olympian Bobby Symonette.

To mark what would become a life-changing occasion, I purchased a Tag Heuer Skipper Automatic Chronograph watch for $175. It's still on my wrist, 46 years later, having timed countless races. A duplicate on eBay goes for $9,500.

CHAPTER 12

J/Boats Inc.

R eturning home from Nassau, I called Rod to confess, "I've had it
with AMF. Let's create a new company—J/Boats Inc. I'm willing
to resign from AMF Alcort now and can afford to work full time at J/
Boats as president, running the business until we have enough revenue
to pay us a salary."

He agreed, and we were off. Research revealed the J/24 design to be
a winner, even with a fixed keel and a 9-foot beam. Olin Stephens* and
I were blessed with a younger brother and business partner named Rod,
creating many great sailboats. While Roderick Stephens* was a Cornell
graduate, my brother Rodney was Princeton '58, a Fort Sill Artillery
School grad, and a history teacher at the Millbrook School.

Rod ultimately returned to Stonington, Connecticut, where he's
lived ever since. He was passionate about yacht design and took the
Westlawn Institute of Marine Technology of Yacht Design correspondence course. He didn't qualify for a naval architecture degree since he
dropped out after completing the curriculum dedicated to hull design.

Later, Westlawn wanted to attract new students with a magazine ad
claiming some credit for Rod's design achievements. Rod agreed on the
condition that they grant him an honorary degree in naval architecture,
which they did.

In Stonington, Rod had a brief stint as a yacht broker and as a supervisor at Electric Boat Company. He ran a sailing school in Essex and
was an ad rep and design editor for *Soundings* magazine.

Rod is a world-class sailor. In 1954, he followed Dad and me to
compete in the Sears Cup National Junior Championship. He crewed

with Mary and me in the 1971 Soling World Championship and competed on the 470 regatta circuit with his wife, Lucia.

Richard Frank Photo—Continental Airways

When Lucia rebelled at being in a wet suit all day on a 470, and Rod became reluctant to leave the rest of his family at home on regatta weekends, he was inspired to design a performance 24-footer with bunks he could sail with the family.

Rod's design project was started in 1974, put on hold for summer sailing in 1975, and then restarted in March 1976.

Planing reaches on Thistles, 505s, and 470s influenced the hull shape of Rod's design. The Soling's adjustable fractional rig at the '73 Worlds and my less-than-happy experience with the Rainbow's masthead rig probably factored into Rod's decision to go with a shorter version of the

Etchells 22 fractional-rigged mast, built by Kenyon. The 24' length and 8'11" beam were mandated by the depth and door width of his Stonington home's garage, where the boat was to be built.

Friends labeled it the "Garage 24." I shipped him a box of excess deck hardware and stripped off my Elvstrom Soling, *Gold Rush*. With the contribution of materials from various other sources, his 24-footer, called *Ragtime*, was completed in time for the 1976 summer sailing season.

He won the ECYRA Offshore Season's Championship, finishing first in 15 of 17 races.

Rod persuaded me to race *Ragtime* a couple of times. The first time wasn't too impressive. We won the second time in late August 1976.

Time to Get Creative. With AMF dragging its heels on the AMF 7.3 project and with us having been asked by a sailor at the postrace party if he could get a boat like Rod's, it made sense for Rod to go forward with making copies.

Everett Pearson of Tillotson-Pearson was the consensus best choice. At Brown University, he was captain of the 1955 football team. After graduation and the Navy, he started Pearson Yachts to become the *grandfather* of fiberglass sailboats.

Everett introduced the 28-foot Triton in 1959 at the New York Boat Show and sold 30 of them. Later, he introduced the popular Ensign and numerous other designs under Alberg and Pearson brand names.

He was building the Etchells 22 and tried, unsuccessfully, to persuade Skip Etchells to introduce a family weekend cruiser version with a cabin and bunks.

Aware of *Ragtime's* winning record, Everett agreed in October 1976 to accept Rod's invitation to visit Stonington and check out *Ragtime.* He'd been concerned that Rod's boat might be too similar in size and thus create a conflict of interest with the Etchells. However, the 22-foot waterline length of the Etchells translated to 32 feet overall, so it was considerably longer than *Ragtime's* overall length of 24 feet and had a mast that was 4 feet taller.

Everett, sitting on *Ragtime*'s deck at its mooring and then having his wife, Ginny, approve the looks, concluded there was no conflict. He told Rod, "Let's do it."

Shortly after that, Ragtime washed up on shore in a storm and was lifted by crane onto a trailer for delivery to Warren, Rhode Island. The hull became the plug to make the production tooling. That was the end of the "Garage 24."

After a modest marketing campaign of three ¼-page ads in *Soundings,* courtesy of his supportive publisher, the almost-complete first J/24 made it to the Hartford and Boston Boat Shows in February 1977.

J/24 Start-up

Starting a boat company is tough. Warranty card analysis shows that whether it's a Sunfish or an MJM Yacht, 80 percent of people get interested in a boat because "a friend recommended it" or "I saw it on the water or at a boat show."

Trouble is: if there's only one boat on the water anywhere, only a handful of friends would see it, and any boat-show presence would be small. It's a wonder a boat company can ever get off the ground.

Time to Get Creative. You have to start somewhere. Our start was a bit shaky. My first encounter with a J/24 was hull #1 at the February 1977 Boston Boat Show. Tillotson-Pearson was in a rush to complete the boat. The "hit list" included:

- Glass bulkheads to hull and deck.
- Lower rudder gudgeons.
- Reposition lifeline stanchions.
- Move the galley locker to widen the main bulkhead opening.
- Put limber holes in the bilge.
- Make the rudder the same color as the hull, so the boat looks "less toylike."

Everett's team made all those corrections in two weeks. We commissioned the first production boat, Dennis Murphy's *Red Pepper,* in New London on a beautiful 70-degree, early-March day.

Before the racing season got underway on Memorial Day weekend, the only major glitch was the rudder design. In an early Off-Soundings regatta, the first time any J/24 had raced in strong winds, four had rudders snap off at the lower pintle. Horrors! About the worst thing that could have happened. The competition and press had a field day.

The rudder laminate was beefed up to withstand a test of placing a 900 lb. lead keel on the lower blade, with the rudder clamped sideways on a bench at pintle locations.

Time to Get Creative. I panicked and created a 1,672-word, triple-page, foldout ad, "What's Different about the J/24?" which was run in May 1977 boating publications, trying to convince everyone to own a J/24.

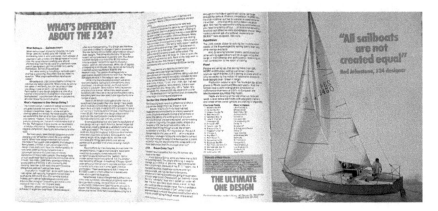

We repeated the ad 11 months later with a picture of Larry Leonard's *LL Express* in *Yacht Racing & Cruising* magazine.

There was a lot to talk about after that first year. We'd already chartered or were forming the 40 fleets listed in that 1978 repeat of the ad.

It's interesting to look back on that broad-gauged rationale. I've often been accused of putting too much copy in ads. Guilty as charged! This ad took the cake. Here's the copy boiled down to 337 words:

WHAT'S DIFFERENT ABOUT THE J/24?

What Sailing Is...Sailboats Aren't

We believe J/24, by solving family needs, becomes an ideal one-design class for yacht-club sponsorship. Open cockpit designs under 20 feet dominate the local sailing scene, but *a high percentage don't have inherent stability for safe open water sailing by inexperienced or lightweight sailors and usually require outside assistance for rescue after capsize.*

Some yacht clubs tried lighter, self-rescuing boats such as the 420 or 470. But, *owners soon discover racing isn't everything, and there's little chance to relax in "hot" trapeze boats.* Greater participation may occur with keelboat fleets, but they cost over *$5,000 ($22,500 in 2021) while still not offering broader recreational opportunities than smaller daysailers* and can't be classified as having offshore stability and seaworthiness. Sailing activity is restricted to the harbor.

Sailing is evolving from a male-dominated, one-design racing, yacht club base activity to a broader, more diverse, family recreation. Sales of 20-30 foot cruising boats are now three times greater than one-design class boats. People seem more willing to invest $10,000 [$45,000 in 2021] in a boat the family can sail six or more months of the year. The problem is: *The majority of small cruising boats are designed to appeal to first-time boat owners rather than experienced sailors.*

Dream come true? J/24 comes very close to the ideal: Fast as a Soling with a 5/6ths rig, less complicated than a Lightning. With 8'11" beam, 4-foot draft flared bow, and light displacement, it has the reserve buoyancy, resistance to heeling and dryness going through seas of much larger boats. One ecstatic gal claimed it to be the only "non-barfy" boat she'd sailed on under 40 feet. Hull pounders could break a wrist. The hull is quiet and stiff going through waves. She's small enough for the kids or gals to sail alone, yet large enough for serious offshore competition. At 2600 lbs., the club hoist can put her on a trailer to take home or trail off to some vacation spot. She has weekend cruising accommodations for a family of four. What more could one ask, especially for $9,850* race-equipped less sails.

Faulkner Island Race

J/24 #1 doesn't exist. As the designer, Rod uses USA-1 on all his J/24s, naming them *Ragtime*. USA-1 is also on the sail of the dramatic, full-size J/24 display in Newport's new Sailing Museum.

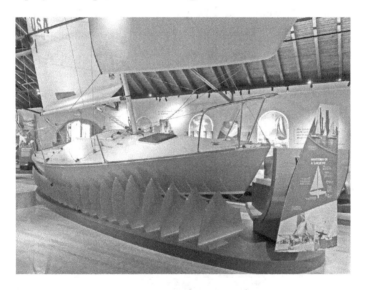

My first J/24 was #21 *Top of the World*, delivered just in time for the Storm Trysail Club's 100-mile overnight Faulkner Island Race out of Larchmont Yacht Club.

The race was for Midget Ocean Racing Class (MORC) boats 30 feet and under. I was sailing with an all-family crew of Stu, Drake, and Helen.

Rod won, sailing with friend and sailmaker Sandy Van Zandt. We were 2nd. That started the buzz.

Block Island Race Week

To get the word out in Marblehead, I invited Dave Curtis* from that town to helm *Top of the World*. I crewed with my son Stu and Major Hall. We slept on the boat the entire week.

The main competition for J/24s in the MORC Division was Bill Soverel and his son Mark in a Soverel 30, a family boat enterprise from Florida.

In the end, J/24 *Top of the World* won. At the time, we'd sold approximately 60 boats and were trying to motivate owners to enter the MORC Nationals in Annapolis. After Block Island and September's MORC results got out, J/24 went viral. Many factors fueled J/Boats' growth.

After this regatta, Marine photographer Fred Nakajima instigated negotiations with Nissan for a licensee to build J/24s in Japan. His photo below is of my J/24 #21 *Top of the World*.

CHAPTER 13

Formula for Success

A race-winning boat design was an important starting point but wasn't enough to build a global business alone. What set J/Boats apart from other brands with fast designs were 24 other factors described below in this chapter.

The results are unprecedented in the sport: 20+ Boat of the Year Awards among 52 models launched, five World Sailing International Classes in 30+ countries, more than 35 percent of entries in US Race Weeks, and most recently, 25 percent of entries in the 2022 Newport to Bermuda Race...four times that of the previous dominant offshore brand, Nautor Swan.

A copy of the Harvard Business School case study *J/Boats, Inc.* is available on the Harvard Business School website: *hbs.edu/faculty/Pages/item.aspx?num=5050*.

(1) A Passion for Sailboat Racing

A love of sailboat racing is in the family's DNA. We always dream about how to make boats go faster or how a new boat can be even better.

Being immersed in the culture makes one more sensitive to both shortcomings to correct and possibilities for innovation.

Sailboat design is fertile ground for innovation. Arguably, it's more art than science. Researchers acknowledge there's much to be learned about surface-vessel hydrodynamics.

Add air as a second medium with the flow of wind along a sail's surface: the scale of the problem and computational power to effectively model the shapes is beyond the capabilities of today's most powerful machines.

(2) Timing

Being in synch with demographics was a big help. Our parents brought us into the world at the perfect time…10 years ahead of the Baby Boomer generation. By the time we figured out what we'd like for our next boat, designed, and launched it, the market of like-minded sailors was right there, ready to join us.

As we grew older and wanted larger boats, so did the sailors among all those Boomers. Among 70 million of them in the 1970s, there were 100,000 new sailors per year buying Sunfish, Hobies, Lasers, and Snarks to sail off the beach.

The off-the-beach sailing phenomenon started in 1949 with *Life*'s August 15 feature "World's Wettest, Sportiest Boat." The subtitle was, "Crew of the new Sailfish are in the water as much as out."

Life Magazine Centerfold
8/15/1949

Life Magazine Centerfold 8/15/1949

A 35,000-household panel of the National Sporting Goods Association in the mid-1980s revealed that the number of sailors in upscale households earning more than $50,000 ($130,000 in 2022) had nearly tripled, with 609,000 new participants. Sailing fulfilled the needs of Boomers entering their 40s with teenage kids. Leaving them behind to pursue "couple" sports, like tennis or golf, was out of the question. New sailors wanted to share their fun, new sport with their families.

(3) Best Performing Brand Strategy

The recreational product strategy developed while at Quaker Oats was followed. The J/Boats design mandate can be described as, "Create the fastest family-friendly boats for their length and use because speed, responsiveness, and ease of handling are qualities sought by all sailors, whether beginner or expert."

Even cruising sailors enjoy displaying their superior sailing skills when next to another boat. Nobody wants to hear that status-threatening question, "Daddy, why is that boat going faster than ours?"

J/Boats' dominant race-week and offshore regatta participation as well as the brand's numerous local one-design fleets worldwide underline the validity of the "Best-Performing Brand" strategy.

(4) Umbrella Brand

Instead of a name like Comet or Sonar as the trademark and sail insignia, we used an underlined "J/" over the model length, as in "J/24" or "J/105." Advertising efficiency and better owner-resale value resulted.

In this way, the excitement created by ads for the latest new design adds luster to all prior J/Boats.

The letter "J" for "Johnstone" had a positive connotation in sailing, reminiscent of past America's Cup "J Class Yachts" of the 1930s.

The US Patent Office registration of the J/24 trademark graphic, combining the letter "J" with a bar underline and boat length, predated Elizabeth Meyer's^ restoration of the "J Class Yacht" *Endeavor* by seven years.

(5) Market Research

AMF Alcort's consumer research, previously described, gave us the confidence to move forward in a new life, successfully invest our few dollars with minimal risk, and motivate a building partner.

(6) In-House Venture Capitalist

Money is critical to the start-up and survival of any venture. We founded J/Boats Inc. on a shoestring. My $10,000 and an assigned value of $10,000 for Rod's design capitalized the 50/50 partnership.

The business needed more than that $10,000 in cash to get rolling. Fortunately, we had an "in-house" venture capitalist, Mary. She was earning $140,000 per year ($630,000 in 2022) running Naturescapes.

Mary's income allowed me to work full time without salary, building the business and covering initial J/Boats advertising, a demo J/24, boat shows, and administrative expenses. J/Boats didn't have a positive cash flow to pay ourselves a salary for nine months.

After delivering 254 boats in the first fiscal year of 1977, the company lost $14,000. Since we had paid ourselves $25,000 in salary, the net for the year was $18,000 each.

Mary was generous enough not to insist on a venture vulture's 50 percent stake.

(7) Talented Start-up Team

Is there another boat company fortunate to have had all three critical disciplines at start-up? There was a Westlawn-educated designer, the country's most efficient production boatbuilder, and a Fortune 500 Marketing Man of the Year.

In addition, all three were and continued to be champion sailors as role models for their J/Boats customers.

(8) Supportive Builder

Everett was excited to be involved in the project. Our consumer research vindicated his concept of modifying an Etchells 22 to be a performance-oriented family cruiser. His financial partner in Tillotson-Pearson Industries (TPI) was Neil Tillotson, inventor of latex products. TPI covered the cost of J/24 tooling and plant start-up expenses.

Rod originally contracted for a $200 royalty per boat for however many he could sell. That 2 percent wasn't enough to gear up a sales office, a national dealer network, advertising, and additional designs. Even 6 percent barely covered design and marketing. Later, when J/Boats paid for the tooling of new models, 12 percent became the number.

Everett expressed anxiety at our initial meeting, saying, "Bob, to come up with a retail selling price under $10,000, including a 20 percent dealer margin and bigger slice for J/Boats, TPI has to produce lots of boats. How many do you figure on selling the first year?"

Time to Get Creative. "Well, Everett, you know Rod designed a fast boat. We have research indicating a 50 percent share potential. The most successful boat to date, retailing for less than $10,000, is Bangor Punta's O'Day 25. They sold 250 boats in the first year.

"PHRF rates that O'Day 25 at 230 seconds per mile. That's 60 seconds per mile slower than the J/24's projected 170 seconds per mile. Think about it in football terms. Six knots is 8.8 feet per second. After sailing a mile, 8.8 seconds times 60 seconds is 528 feet or 176 yards. So in just one mile, the J/24 would leave the O'Day behind by more yardage than you ever ran as a fullback in a game. No contest!

"Call it $9,850 at retail with your selling price to the dealer of $7,880 and $500 to J/Boats. So net of $7,380 for TPI."

Everett said TPI could do it. As sales mounted, he dialed up operations in two plants, Fall River and Warren. We took orders for over 750 J/24s in the first 14 months. That spring of 1978, to catch up with orders, TPI was producing six J/24s per day, six days per week…36 boats per week total.

To Everett's credit, and thanks to nearly tripling the initial sales estimate, TPI held the price of the J/24s for two years. On January 1, 1979, it was raised by only 8.6 percent to $10,700.

I ran the business and took all sales orders from our Beechbound harborside condo in Newport. I sent the order specifications to TPI before getting payment. It was frantic: sales orders were coming in at an average of two per day.

I remember one call from our Flathead Lake, Montana, dealer. After assigning him the next available hull number, I asked for color selection. He said, "Red hull with a yellow boot stripe." Not bad.

"OK, what about the deck?

When he said, "Red deck with yellow nonskid," I lost it!

"Wait a minute! What?" He repeated the combination.

I reacted, "No way! Not unless you send full payment for that boat ahead of time."

"But Bob, you don't understand. It will be OK. You don't have to worry about it."

"Look, what I do understand is the risk. If you can't come up with the money after the boat is built, there's no way I can ever resell it with that color combo! So I'll worry plenty about it if you don't send me cash up front."

"OK, Bob. Look, apologies for not letting you know something at the outset. Maybe it will explain the situation, so you understand there's not much risk here. The buyer's name is Ronald McDonald!"

Well, McDonald's colors! That was good for a laugh and reason enough to put the order in line with the rest, risking a truckload of Big Macs if I was wrong.

(9) Professional Dealer Network

"Nothing happens until somebody sells something." The importance of dealers was made clear after the Naturescapes direct-sale fiasco and by what I learned managing one of the largest marine dealer networks for AMF Alcort. Dealers were vital to building a profitable boat business.

First, enough sales volume must be generated to achieve efficient production rates for a competitive price. While J/Boats didn't need 150 dealers like Sunfish, Hobie Cat, or Laser, we certainly had to match the 80–100 dealers of our performance-oriented brand competitors: C&C and the Kirby-designed San Juan 24.

We had to break out of the "cottage industry" of race boat designs like the Poitin 29, Santa Cruz 27, Olson 30, and Moore 24. The designer-builder sold those boats from their shops to several dozen friends in the local region.

Launching the first design of a new brand is challenging. You don't know where the business will take hold. Dealers are good if you can sign them up. But it's like pulling teeth with a new design from a company that doesn't have a sales track record. I knew of most good dealers that weren't handling AMF (to avoid conflict of interest). When contacting them, a typical response was, "Bob, it looks like a fun, exciting boat to sail. It's a boat I'd love to own. But I'm afraid it won't sell in this market."

Interpretation: "Nobody had ever sold one around here, and I'm not going to be the first."

Time to Get Creative. "Wait a minute! Are you saying that your appreciation of what makes a good sailboat differs from that of your customers? That doesn't make sense. Why wouldn't they get excited the way you do? Why not get a J/24 for yourself, race it, and see what happens?"

Before Block Island Race Week, we'd sold one boat in Narragansett Bay, six boats on Lake Minnetonka (thanks to Dad's Princeton '32 classmate, John Savage), four boats in Eastern Connecticut, and a few others around the country.

We hadn't sold any of the hotbeds of sailing like Marblehead, Larchmont, or Annapolis.

It wasn't until Rod and I went planing past Peterson 34s (the hottest IOR boat at the time) at Block Island Race Week that J/24 went viral.

McMichaels Yacht Brokers (McM), a major dealer in Mamaroneck, New York, still wasn't convinced. Eventually, I cornered Bill Kelly, Howie McMichael's brother-in-law, and Rob Ball, C&C's marketing man (McM was a C&C dealer), belowdecks on a J/24 for a beer. We were scrunched together on the berths, knees touching. The pitch that broke the ice was, "See, you can even go cruising on it."

Rob Ball probably figured this was no competition to C&C and might feed more customers into his brand's successful offerings of larger racer-cruisers.

McMichael, from that moment, started on the path to becoming one of J/Boats' largest dealers.

The phenomenon was repeated on the Chesapeake after half a dozen J/24s dominated the September 1977 MORC Nationals in Annapolis.

The local Annapolis dealer commented, "It's like selling shoes. People come in and say they want a J/24. We ask, what color? They tell us. We say OK. They sign the check."

Texas wins the prize. A crazy bunch of sailors had formed a "Texas Racing Circuit," trailering custom IOR ¼ tonners to a different lake each weekend for a chili cook-off, sleeping off their hangovers on the boats to race again the next day.

J/24s enabled them to level the playing field with a single-boat design. The four bunks were there. It had a faster IOR ½ ton speed, and they didn't have to deal with the measurement issues of an IOR handicap rule or get a new boat every other year to stay competitive. That first year we sold 150 boats in Texas thanks to the enthusiastic J/Boats dealer in Dallas.

Periodically, owners looking for a deal complain about paying dealers a margin. Even 30 years later, MJM Yachts builder Boston Boat-Works (BBW), previously a custom boatbuilding shop, challenged the wisdom of granting a 20 percent margin to dealers, saying, "It could be better used to improve our BBW builder margin." Or, a customer would argue, "Lower the retail price."

How does one persuade potential buyers or business partners that dealers are essential for creating value?

Time to Get Creative. Do the math. Of 195 boats sold by MJM by 2012, BBW was involved in selling 58, or an average of five boats per year. That sales rate is on a par with The Anchorage building Dyer 29s or Coecles Harbor building four Shelter Island 38s per year. On such a low volume, management salaries and overhead expenses alone would drive each boat's price up by more than $100,000.

And somebody still has to sell the boats. A sales agent, as used by Hunt or Grand Banks, would still demand 5 percent or more.

Then, "Who will accept, maintain, and market a trade-in? There's a trade-in with 90 percent of MJMs sold."

"Who takes the place of dealers to advertise, display, stock boats, and conduct sea trials?"

"Where will the working capital come from to build the boats?"

"How many buyers are willing to advance cash to a small-volume builder?"

"Dealers don't net 20 percent. It's more like 10 percent after paying for boat shows, brokerage commissions, trade advertising, and office expenses."

"If sales drop, where's the capital coming from to invest in tooling for new designs to reinvigorate the brand and sustain owner-resale value?"

J Boats' aggressive dealer strategy paid off. Eight years after introducing the J/24, Performance Handicap Racing Fleet (PHRF) database showed there were 631 brands of sailboats. Not boat models but brands!

The top 15 brands accounted for 85 percent of all boats. The top three brands accounted for 35 percent: J/Boats, low-cost Catalinas, and the competing performance brand, C&C.

(10) Network of Sailing Friends

From my Olympic Soling and 470 campaigns, my duties as secretary-treasurer of the US Olympic Yachting Committee, and my role as founding chairman of the US Youth Sailing Championship, I was already in contact with or knew most of the country's top sailors and sailmakers.

Sailmakers were a key building block of our strategy to grow the J/24 class. I'd sent a letter to every major sailmaker in the country before the August 1977 MORC International Championship in Annapolis, stating,

If you aren't already building a sail development program for the J/24, look out! Twelve others are. 40 boats have been sold in the past 60 days. What better way is there to make a name for yourself than to design better J/24 sails than anyone else? There must be a dozen people you know who are struggling to win, blaming on your sails because they don't...Why not do them and yourself a favor? They can probably sell that old crate, buy a whole new inventory of sails, win all the time, buy you drinks for being so smart, and come out ahead financially.

Sailmakers responded with a great turnout and dominant performance in J/24s. I had 470 World Champion Dave Ullman* helm my boat as a way to get the word out in Southern California.

The stage was set for the first J/24 one-design regatta, the Key West Midwinters, in January 1978.

Eighty-one sailmakers, friends, and customers arrived in Key West. Among the skippers, in order of finish, were: Mark Ploch, John Kolius^, Vince Brun*, Gary Weisman, Larry Leonard, Scott Allen^, Dave Ullman*, Bob Barton, Charlie Scott, Charlie Fowler, Bill Allen^, Gordy Bowers^, Jim Scott, Rick Grajerina, Neal Fowler, Jon Wright^, Tom Whidden*, and Carter Gowrie.

My son Stu was sailing with the winner, Mark Ploch. Rod* was racing as well.

Mary and I operated the photo boat for Eric Schweikardt.

At a meeting under the Storm Trysail tent, we debated and then hammered out the initial J/24 one-design class rules. Then everyone departed for home and spread the word: "J/24 was *the* boat!"

(11) Pros Welcomed

We didn't forget who put J/Boats on the map. Sailmakers had families, too, and loved sailing the boat.

Selling sails for all those J/24s was big business. A friend commented, "Bob, you may have created a popular racing boat, but the people who will be making money over the years are sailmakers." That figures. J/Boats sells 5,500 boats once. Sailmakers sell a new suit of sails every 2–3 years. Do the math. After 44 years, they make three times what J Boats had.

But we had to set limits to avoid having pros who weren't owners and dues-paying class members jumping into boats for major championships,

taking the helm from owners. At the same time, there were boat owners who were just as talented as racing skippers as sailmakers and could
spend just as much time or more sailing.

Time to Get Creative. The solution was: it's OK for sailmakers to drive,
provided they become bona fide owners and class members.

We got pushback. Some amateur ("Corinthian") sailors claimed it
wasn't fair, as they couldn't possibly win sailing against the pros.

The challenge was to convince them otherwise, so they'd retain their
enthusiasm for being members of the class and having fun.

Having been there and done that—experiencing the thrill of crossing tacks with my legendary idol, Paul Elvstrom, and finishing ahead of
Lowell North* in the Soling Worlds and heavy-air race at the '72 Olympic trials—I found it difficult to sympathize with those who wanted to
make winning easier. Nothing could be more satisfying. Because?

Winning isn't everything. Time with friends and learning something
new every day when racing is hard to beat. Could we be persuasive with
this philosophy?

Maybe by eating a little crow, we'd grab their attention. This two-page
ad shows Greg Fisher^ and my son Drake "shrimping" *Top of the World*'s
chute with Mary and me in the cockpit during the 1979 North Americans.

The 598 words of the ad are reduced below to 268:

165

Sailors come to realize that to become really fast, you've got to have more than boat speed. You've got to have smarts.

For this, you need to spend time in a boat where your ability to sail intelligently is as important as your boat's ability to sail fast. And few boats have proven themselves better suited to impart both kinds of knowledge than the J/24.

Sheer boat speed might let you get away with making errors in some kinds of racing. Make mistakes in a fleet of J/24's and it's tubesville.

There will always be faster boats. With money, you can buy into all the custom boat speed you want. But what makes faster sailors isn't fast boats. It's learning from other fast, smart sailors. J/24 attracts the most intelligent racing talent in the world. If you're serious about reaching your highest level of competence, you've got to get in there and mix it up with the best.

The 1984 Midwinters probably had more National, North American, World and Intercollegiate Champions together than any other one-design regatta in history. There's a reason. Even the best in the world can still learn something. There aren't many classes competitive enough for them to do that.

The J/24 is one fun boat to sail. It's time in the boat that shapes your ability to read wind patterns and tidal flows, to play the waves and sails. The average J/24 sailor spends 54 days a year on the water. The J/24 concept of racing is not just for the best, but for anyone who wants to improve by sailing against the best.

Twenty-two years later, Geoff Moore was quoted in *Sailing Scuttlebutt* #305 (4/7/99) as saying, "So, it should come as no surprise that the greatest sailors on earth have learned their craft from the people who sail J/24s."

(12) Long-term One-Design Value

A key to sustaining a J/24's competitive life is the rigid Baltek-cored hull that doesn't distort with frequent trailering, age, or "oil can" going through waves.

Each "J" is rigged as though for a world championship, using the best hardware available.

The J/24, as the first offshore one-design to use its ball-bearing dinghy hardware, put the Harken brothers on the big-boat map. The gear had to hold up under years of hard racing and still function smoothly. High-quality hardware made it easier to insist no changes be made from one boat to the next, the true essence of one design.

So older boats could compete with newer boats, and strict one-design rules stated, "Any modification from standard, not specifically allowed, is illegal." The self-defeating C&C "quick money" design strategy of making this year's model a bit faster than last year's was avoided. Such a practice pulls the rug from under an aspiring class association, owner-resale value, and one-design competition.

Dave Curtis* trailered his three-year-old J/24, *H.J.*, over 36,000 miles. He raced his J/24 as hard as any boat could be raced, winning the 1984 J/24 Midwinter Championship, two North American Championships, and the Pan American Games with six bullets.

Ed Baird*, with a 5-year-old chartered boat built by Westerly in the United Kingdom (UK), won the 1983 World Championship in Malmo, Sweden. I was runner-up with the other Laser guru, Dick Tillman^, in my crew sailing a brand-new, TPI-built US-3700 *Rabbit*. That fantastic crew also included Matt Ciesicki and my son Stu.

(13) Popularizing Offshore One-Designs

Before J/24s, one-design racing boats were "harbor" or yacht club boats with open cockpits unsuited for "offshore" sailing.

Some larger boats had been promoted as one-designs but were not easily trailered to regattas to build a national class. Nor were they affordable enough to become popular family boats locally.

The North American 40, Tartan 10, and Peter Barrett's* North Sails Omega 30 project fit that category.

J/Boats bridged that divide by introducing "offshore one-designs" that gave owner families the chance to engage with and make friends beyond local yacht-club circles…like attending Block Island Race Week, trailering their boat to Key West Race Week, or rafting up with another boat during a weekend cruise.

In *SAIL Magazine's* tenth-anniversary issue (January 1980), "The Breakthrough Boats" recognized the dual-purpose concept. The J/24 was runner-up to the Cal 40 among cruiser-racers as an offshore design. Then, as a one-design keelboat, the J/24 topped the runner-up Star.

(14) Family "Performance"

Sailing is a family-lifestyle recreation. The President's Commission on Americans Outdoors conducted a survey in 1986 to identify the primary motivation for participation in various sports.

The psychographic profile of frequent sailors shows them to be 2–3 times more active than the US population. Sailors were primarily categorized as either "Excitement-Seeking Competitives" (26 percent) or "Get-Away Actives" (36 percent).

Half the former group belonged to a sports club or team. The latter group, 41 percent of whom were Baby Boomers, rated "social activities with family" and "experiencing nature" more highly than "competition" or "risk-taking," as in racing.

Our personal experience fit the crossover demands of both profiles. The implication is that a sailboat design that addresses both profiles could be a big winner.

PL	1979 J/24 WORLD CHAMPIONSHIP							TOTAL
1	Charlie Scott	Smiles	2	2	6	2	10	22
2	Ed Adams	Trio	13	1	4	6	7	31
3	Will Whitmore	Popeye	5	12	9	4	5	35
4	Scott Allan	Razzle Dazzle	1	6	19	1	13	40
5	Larry Leonard	L. L. Express	12	7	24	5	4	52
6	Bill Jorch & Bill Shore	Stark Terror	17	8	20	14	1	60
7	Bill Menninger	Expoobident	3	14	3	11	44	75
8	Bob & Stu Johnstone	Top of the World	41	10	1	21	8	81
9	John Kolius	Honky Tonk	77	3	18	8	2	108
10	Dave Hirsch	Ukelela Lady	21	30	38	16	15	120
11	Rod & Jeff Johnstone	Ragtime	20	38	2	12	49	121

The boat had to be nonintimidating and manageable by anyone in the family: suitable for diverse family adventures like day sailing, racing, and weekend or extended cruising beyond the local harbor.

It also had to be fun and exciting, with good response at the helm and a sense of acceleration…e.g., not a slug.

It had to be predictable. A navy jet pilot described the perfect airplane as a "two-finger plane," easily going wherever you directed it. In other words, the boat had to be forgiving, with a wide groove to sustain speed in varied sea and wind conditions.

This Karin Olson photo shows Charlie Scott planing in #407 *Smiles* during the 1979 World Championship in Newport.

Winds were gusting over 40 knots in the low-pressure system, which became the Fastnet Storm on the other side of the Atlantic.

The results of the third race in the Worlds were particularly sweet. Our two family crews finished 1-2 in the boat we'd created. My sons Stu and Drake were sailing with me for the win. Rod was 2nd with his boys aboard.

And lastly, comfort is a factor. That's more than just physical comfort. Comfort aboard a boat is just as much a state of mind as it is physical.

Not being panicked by a boat's potential bad behavior is essential. Light ends avoid the hobby-horsing that contributes to sea sickness. Full "U" sections prevent the bow from burying and wipeouts when diving down a steep wave.

Easily adjustable rigs minimize the need to change sail shape or put people on the foredeck to change sails over a range of conditions.

Since there are situations where boats are sailed by one person (crew asleep off watch), single-handed ease of operation from the cockpit is a crucial design element. That calls for exceptional helm control and visibility to minimize fatigue and handy rig-sail control systems.

The goal was to design "nonintimidating" manageable boats that sailed fast upwind with a low center of gravity for offshore stability.

An early family example of our confidence in offshore safety and manageability? We let our 15-year-old son Peter and two friends sail our J/24 #2424 *JJ* on a 30-mile overnight from Newport to Buzzards Bay.

Or take the case of a 52-year-old mother, Heather Gregg Earl. She won the J/70 North American Championship and placed 5th in the inaugural J/70 World Championship. As the top-finishing female skipper, she won the Helen C. Johnstone Memorial Trophy that honored her dear friend.

For success on the local level, all members of the family must be capable of sailing the boat. If designs are too extreme, requiring greater athleticism, only regional or national events attract enough participants for a decent regatta.

Fellow Princetonian Dick Rose* ('60) described how the Seattle International 14 Fleet had enjoyed one-design class popularity with about 30 boats. The fleet later dissipated completely when the I-14 class went to the double trapeze. Its remaining adherents had to travel long distances for good racing.

(15) Institutional Fleets

Encouraging the development of J/24 sailing programs is a highly efficient way to expose many people to the joys of sailing the boat. I remembered all the Sunfish, Hobie Cat, and Windsurfer sales that resulted from the SAIL 73 Wilmette program.

The most challenging problem institutions have with creating fleets is financing the boats. Here are some of the fleets we helped start:

J/World Sailing School After we'd moved east for my AMF Alcort job and were living in Woodbridge, Connecticut, Drake started SAIL 76 New Haven, modeled after the SAIL 73 Wilmette program. Then later, after graduating from Yale, he was ready to start a dual-season sailing school business with his brother Stuart and cousin Jeff, Rod's son.

I encouraged the use of J/24s to not only supplement our marketing efforts, but to be more profitable for J/World, teaching in boats with a 4:1 students-to-instructor ratio rather than a 1:1 or 1:2 ratio.

J/World was founded as a family affair in 1980. Rod and I, as J/Boats, signed a note for bank financing of the boats. The program spent summers in Newport and winters in Key West. Later, San Francisco, San Diego, and Annapolis programs were added.

In 1998, *Practical Sailor* published their readers' "overall satisfaction rankings" of sailing schools. J/World was ranked #1. The Olympic Circle Sailing Club on San Francisco Bay, which used J/24s, was #2. And Colgate's Offshore Sailing School, using Solings, was #3.

More recently, the boat of choice for J/World has been the J/80, which is more modern and has more comfortable seating for an instructor and students.

Sail Newport was founded in 1983 to fill the void of sailing excitement after losing America's Cup. Sail Newport's mission was to promote and operate affordable public sailing instruction and sailboat-rental programs.

With J/Boats in the same town, we offered to help establish a fleet of J/22s for the 1987 season. Sail Newport couldn't afford to buy them outright.

Time to Get Creative. The only way Sail Newport could acquire boats was to finance them with a bank loan, secured by Rod's and my personal guarantees.

Sail Newport became a major success as a sailing center and host to countless major regattas.

College of Charleston also acquired a fleet of 10 J/22s for intercollegiate events and a community sailing program similar to Sail Newport. Their board was able to raise funds for the purchase.

The US Naval Academy acquired a fleet of 12 J/24s in time to sponsor the USYRU Sears Cup Championship in 1985 and to allow midshipmen to compete in the large Annapolis J/24 fleet. By replacing an older Shields fleet, the academy was able to attract potential All-American sailors. J/24s gave more cadets a chance to hone their helming skills instead of being assigned to grind winches on the larger yawls.

The US Coast Guard Academy created a J/22 fleet when J/Boats offered them a 100 percent financing arrangement using the Sail Newport model. The academy could then host the Intercollegiate Yacht Racing Association Keelboat Championship.

They have now acquired a fleet of J/70s. It didn't hurt that my son Stuart had earlier served as the sailing coach for the Coast Guard Academy team.

(16) Yacht Club Fleets

The broad appeal of a versatile, family one-design racer made it possible to establish large yacht club fleets overnight. How did we manage to pull that off?

Time to Get Creative. Would you believe "easy money" and "J/24 neckties"?

Noroton Yacht Club J/24 sailor Jack Couch saw an opportunity to have more J/24s to sail against in his club. They needed 10 new boats to host the Sears Cup.

My sales pitch had to be in a building other than the main clubhouse, where commercial activity was taboo. I gladly accepted the challenge, knowing that Noroton was the home club of Bruce Kirby, designer of the competing 23' Sonar.

I arranged with a local bank to offer 20-year boat loans with no down payment for about $250 per month upon approval of creditworthiness.

On stage, I'd erected a large display board with graphics of 40 hulls with different color combinations. After a slideshow, I outlined the deal. "The first person to come forward, agreeing to sign up at the bank next week, gets first pick of colors. By taking one of these J/24 neckties, it's your solemn pledge, witnessed by all present, that you'll go through with the deal."

About 20 people came forward, picked a color, and took a tie. I was elated.

But the next morning, I got a call from the club commodore, who gravely informed me, "Bob, we have a big problem with your presentation last night."

I was thinking, *Oh no! Here comes the violation of the club's commercial code. Kirby has gotten to him, and I'll have to cancel all those orders.*

He said, "I've had numerous calls from upset members."

It was getting worse. It's not good to get a commodore in trouble!

But then the situation vaulted in a positive direction when the commodore said, "It's the members who didn't know about your meeting who are upset about missing out on the deal."

"Whew!"

He then asked, "To cover all the bases, I like to send a letter to the entire yacht club membership giving them the chance to buy a J/24 on the same terms. Would that be possible? Would you agree to do that?"

Breathing a sigh of relief and trying not to sound too pleased, I said, "Yes, certainly, commodore, I think we can arrange that."

We sold another half dozen boats.

I made a similar pitch to St. Petersburg Yacht Club and Sheridan Shore Yacht Club to enable those clubs to host US Sailing Championships in perfectly matched J/24s.

Manhattan Yacht Club (MYC) In the spring of 1987, Michael Fortenbaugh founded this unique sailing club at the South Street Seaport, figuring that young investment bankers had few attractive recreational opportunities in New York City. After all, the city is surrounded by water.

His board of directors supported a plan to acquire a dozen J/24s, but they weren't willing to sign a note to finance them.

Unbelievable! Here were these titans of Wall Street leaning on a small boat company in Rhode Island to come up with $150,000 worth of boats for them to sail.

Time to Get Creative. Just another challenge! I arranged a loan with Key Bank for the value of the entire fleet, signing a buyback agreement on behalf of J/Boats.

If Manhattan Yacht Club defaulted by not paying off the note by August, our bailout position was that MYC would sail all the J/24s to the Stamford Boat Show, where we'd blow them out the door as "Boat Show Specials."

Fortunately, we didn't have to do it.

Boothbay Harbor Yacht Club (BHYC) We moved from Newport to Boothbay Harbor, Maine, in 1994 when the bishop of the Episcopal Church in Maine called Mary to be the vicar of Boothbay.

We purchased, then remodeled, an old Maine farmhouse overlooking the BHYC anchorage.

There was talk of starting a club fleet of Kirby-designed Ideal 18s. There's no way I could be happy looking out from my front porch at a fleet of those boats.

Time to Get Creative. The solution became a model for community and yacht club fleet programs across the country.

Wealthy, semiretired club members could buy a J/22 on its trailer at an attractive "fleet special" price and would be able to name the boat and skipper it in Wednesday evening races, Saturday race days, and any day it wasn't being used by the club. The owner would have a crew pool of club juniors and members available.

BHYC would use the boats for its youth, ladies, and weekly teaching programs. In return, the club provided a "free" mooring, launch service, insurance, maintenance, and winter storage.

Older members of the Club could take visiting grandkids for a sail on "my boat"...yet have none of the hassles of ownership.

Moscow's Spartak Yacht Club (SYC) A German lawyer, the first foreign lawyer to be accredited in Moscow, was a sailor. He wrote asking for my help in starting a fleet at SYC on Lake Wodnik, north of Moscow.

The hope was that sailing would somehow be accessible for sailors among the 48,000 or so foreigners living there. This was in 1995. Foreigners were not allowed to travel outside of the highway that circled Moscow.

Time to Get Creative. After agreeing to help, I flew to Moscow with the BHYC J/22 program in mind.

Keen sailors among the expatriates would buy 10 J/22s and 10 One Design 14s, making them available to Soviet members of the SYC for their various instructional and recreational programs.

In return, SYC would allow these foreigners to race the boats at the club on weekends.

 I visited the club in the middle of winter and hoisted our red J/Boats show banner up their flagpole in place of the hammer and sickle. Hey, it was a "red" flag. Maybe it would sway their decision.

While there, I was shown a storage building with some interesting boats. One was the sailboat owned by World War I's Kaiser of Germany. The Russians made off with more than valuable paintings as a spoil of WWII.

We prepared all the formal contracts to put the deal together and presented them to the Moscow Trade Union of Sports commissar, the same group that controls one of Russia's hockey teams.

The program offered was a win-win proposition. In effect, foreigners would provide the boats "free" to SYC members for its activities.

This commissar, a tall, fit-looking gent who spoke fluent English and was pleasant enough, firmly replied, "We're not going to do it, even though it's a good program. So do you want to know why?"

Crushed, I replied, "Well, we certainly do."

He said, "I'll tell you a story. I'm a professional squash player. A major event on the tour was to be held in the United States. I was denied a visa to compete. So why should Spartak get involved with buying American boats or treating foreigners like guests at our yacht clubs?"

Eventually, the sailors prevailed. Before the invasion of Ukraine, the scene had improved considerably. Forty-eight J/70s sail in Moscow, Saint Petersburg, Sochi, Tuapse, and Sevastopol. Russian crews have excelled in various J/70 European League events.

(17) Forming Local Fleets

It's easier to get people excited about buying a fleet of boats than to sustain their interest and enthusiasm for fleets to thrive and grow.

Good fleet administration, programming, and communications are critical. Fleet success is less about running good races than making sailboat racing secondary to fleet-related social activities and networking.

The initial advertising campaign of our Japanese licensee used the phrase "Sailing Is Friends."

Sailboat racing should be the game sailors play at the party amid camaraderie and fun, like "musical chairs." Being serious about playing musical chairs in a parking lot on a cloudy day without dancing, candles, and cake is not much fun.

Too often, a new fleet becomes another gun on the starting line during Saturday races, with the fleet captain's function being nothing more than to buy trophies and assess dues.

It takes more work than that. The formula for fleet growth starts with preseason organization. For instance: Schedule a summer weekday evening series of nine Thursday-night postrace potluck dinners at different houses or the club. Have a pair of short, 3-to-4-mile races starting at 6:30 p.m. Leave weekends free for major regional regattas or family activities.

If there's a social obligation to show up after racing, people are likely to respond, "We may as well race! "

The fleet captain or secretary should email everyone after racing with the results plus amusing anecdotes.

(18) Class Administration

Once dealers are in place, a few hundred boats have been sold, and local fleets have formed, the next step is regional, national, and world championships. What's needed is an effective one-design class office.

The class office is like an additional marketing and customer service department in support of the class, brand, and sales efforts of local dealers.

Having served as fleet secretary of the Skokie Lagoons Penguin Fleet, secretary-treasurer of the US Olympic Yachting Committee, and J/24 class executive director at the outset before hiring Dick Tillman for the job, I can say that the value of organization, communications, funding, and networking among members to build an effective governing body had become apparent.

Being the founding chairman of the J/24 class during its first six years and guiding it through the approval process to become an International class was a time-consuming challenge. Approval depended on having National J/24 Class Associations (NJCAs), and official class measurers set up in at least six other countries.

One-design classes cannot officially conduct hemisphere or world championships without the blessing of the IYRU (now the World Sailing Association). Many builders don't seek international status for their designs because they don't have national class organizations in place or are reluctant to pay the royalty to the WSA for such recognition, builder control, and class-rules oversight.

Having navigated the process, J/Boats had the advantage of being able to expedite approval for another four international classes.

One of the great benefits of international status is lower import duties in countries without builders.

This process requires a set of class rules, a constitution, and bylaws approved by the WSA Keel Boat Technical Committee and then the WSA Board of Directors. Good class organization and communications precede that step.

The services provided by the National (NJCA) and International (IJCA) Class Association offices are a reason for a design's enduring popularity. They include keeping a record of all members, collecting dues and sail royalties, setting the regatta schedule, issuing notices of race, and overseeing class rules.

For the past 10 years, Chris Howell and his One Design Association Management firm in Tampa, Florida, have done a great job with six J/Boats classes: J/24, J/22, J/105, J/70, J/111, and J/88.

(19) Networking

Communications are essential to encourage networking, provide recognition, and keep owners updated on the latest happenings, regatta results, etc.

With only the J/24 to talk about at the outset, Mary and I published a slick, biannual *J/24 Magazine.*

As new designs were introduced, biannual class newsletters were published by J/Boats and then by class offices.

One-design class communications are essential to conducting class business.

In 1997, son Stuart used his internet skills to help Tom and Craig Leweck set up *Sailing Scuttlebutt*, the sailing world's most popular daily email newsletter

Soon after that, he launched *J/News*. For a brand umbrella publication, there's nothing like *J/News* in the sailing world. This weekly 15-to-30-page newsletter is emailed to 15,000 subscribers and J/Boats dealerships worldwide every Friday with an estimated readership of one million, considering the dealer customer base and social media multipliers.

Half a dozen major J/Boats events are featured weekly from around the world. Racing victories, photos of winners, cruising stories, and people's profiles are all covered.

"The sun never sets on J/Boats" is the caption on the opening photo.

This newsletter rallies owners behind the brand, builds participation in regattas, and generates excitement about meeting new friends at harbors worldwide. Stuart's time-consuming labor of love has kept the J/Boats brand dominant in the sport. To receive a copy of *J/News* weekly, email editor@jboats.com.

News of all the models keeps them fresh. When boats don't seem to age, demand for preowned boats is sustained, resale value is improved, and trade-ins on newer models are facilitated.

(20) Licensed Builders

Fleets and owners worldwide must be supplied with boats in a timely fashion and at competitive prices.

Having managed Quaker subsidiaries in Colombia and Venezuela, licensing builders overseas was a logical and not unfamiliar step in creating an "international" class.

Seeing one's creations appreciated in distant ports is a thrill. I remember how emotional it was to see two of the first J/24s at the San Diego Yacht Club, 3,000 miles away.

Imagine my emotion the morning of my first visit to Italy for the Italian J/24 Spring Championship. Looking out a window of the Hotel Nazionale Portofino at the small, ancient horseshoe-shaped harbor, there were J/24s all over the place. They were rafted alongside or parked on the quay, interspersed with colorful old fishing boats. I'm thinking, *Christopher Columbus was born in nearby Genoa; Italians, regarded as master artisans, picked the J/24 to be their one-design race boat?* Heady stuff!

It was right up there with Buckminster Fuller mooring his J/24 in front of his cottage on Bear Island in Penobscot Bay, Maine. A J/24's humped deck without a cabin trunk was perhaps the closest thing "Bucky" could find to a boat resembling one of his geodesic domes.

To build boats elsewhere, Everett agreed to provide facilities or sell us master plugs, tooling, and jigs for cost plus 20 percent, not exceeding the retail selling price of one standard boat less sails.

Westerly Marine—Europe The international push began as early as May 1977 in discussions with Westerly Marine in the UK.

By November 1978, they had sold 124 boats and delivered 72. While 30 boats had been sold to Sweden, it could have been more if I hadn't granted the license for all of Europe to Westerly.

At the first London Boat Show at Earl's Court, 30 J/24s were sold. Impressed, Albin Yachts approached me at the show and asked if they could have the J/24 building license for Scandinavia.

I had to say, "Sorry...I've committed that territory to Westerly from the UK." Undeterred but liking the concept, they returned to Sweden and got Peter Norlin to knock off the J/24 as the Albin Express. To launch the Express, Albin Marin AB took just about any used sailboat that floated in trade on the new boat.

Two years later, after selling 700 Expresses (which could have been J/24s), Albin Marin AB went bankrupt, drowned in their unsold trade-in inventory.

One of the highlights of that first Lon-don show was the visit of Kingman Brewster Jr., past president of Yale University and the recently appointed ambassador to the Court of St. James. Son Drake had called the US Embassy to extend the invitation. Drake accompanied us to the show and at the time, was a student at Yale. Ambassador Brewster was certainly doing his job promoting the US industry with the press coverage of him sitting on a J/24.

Performance Sailcraft—West Coast I had known Don Trask^ since 1973. He was the Laser builder on the West Coast and was consulted when trying to identify the best young sailors in his area to invite to the US Youth Championship.

Don built 11,000 Lasers, 300 J/24s, and 30 Star boats. The expense of shipping J/24s cross-country put a damper on sales, so it made sense to find a willing builder for the class. A J/24 was the logical next step up for a young Laser sailor. Don did a great job functioning as the builder and regional West Coast distributor, setting up a good dealer network, and representing J/Boats as we expanded the line.

He also founded and then ran the International Masters Regatta for many years, first in J/24s, then in J/105s.

I remember winning in 1986, crewing for Charlie Dole^ of the Waikiki Yacht Club. Then I drove a J/105 to 3rd place in 2000, with a dream crew of Dave Perry*, Bill Martin*, Dave Irish, and Mason Chrisman, taking on the other 18 skippers pictured. Malin Burnham* won, with Bruce Munro as runner-up.

FRONT ROW: Johnstone, Leweck, Harvey, Trubovich, McDell, Bouzaid, Dickson, Dever. BACK: North, Petterson, Trask, Elvstrom, Kirby, Easom, Jennings, Burnham, Isdale, Munro, Buchan. (Courtesy of St. Francis Yacht Club).

During dinner at the event, Paul Elvstrom confessed this would be his last regatta. An incredible career!

Recently, the event has been hosted by the San Diego Yacht Club in J/105s. To illustrate how time flies: the winners in 2021 and 2022 were Carl Buchan and Augie Diaz, graduates of the inaugural 1973 US Youth Championship, both winners of the World Youth Championship. They are both inductees in the National Sailing Hall of Fame.

Nissan Marine—Japan It was June 1977 at Block Island Race Week when marine photographer Fred Nakajima looked at the J/24 and said, "Perfect for the Japanese market. Headroom, no problem."

Fred trained as a kamikaze pilot, but the war ended before his mission was called. He dispelled my long-held impression. "Bob, don't believe all those stories about heroic Japanese kamikaze pilots wanting to die for the Emperor. We didn't want to die any more than anyone else. They didn't give us parachutes, so we'd try to figure out how we could crash-land on the beach or along the shore of some small island without blowing ourselves up."

Fred's best friend, Shuji Watanabe, was Japan's WWII submarine designer and Nissan Motors' marine consultant. Shuji was our contact in negotiating a builder licensing agreement with Nissan to build and sell J/24s through Nissan car dealers in Japan.

They were tough negotiators, with much haggling back and forth. It got down to Nissan not wanting to pay the 10 percent royalty. Finally, they relented when I threatened to walk out on the deal, pointing out, "That means you're not going to be able to sell this boat with a "J" on the sail…a "J" that can stand for *Japan*."

I can understand why the Japanese have done so well in international trade. Once they've agreed to terms, they stick to them. Every three months, we got a check, on time, with a full accounting of the hulls sold by whom, with their addresses for class records. We never had to hound them about paying on time. That wasn't our experience in the US or the rest of the world.

The one glitch in the relationship came at the outset—a case of technological one-upmanship gone bad, with the potential loss of face.

The Japanese have great pride in their technical ability. Nissan sent four technicians armed with SLR cameras to Tillotson-Pearson in Rhode Island. They spent two weeks photographing and taking notes on every detail and phase of building a J/24.

The last step was loading six new J/24s plus a set of tooling on a large Nissan car carrier in the Port of Providence. My initiation to Japan was sharing their native menu for lunch with the ship's captain in his wardroom.

Two months later, we got an urgent fax saying, "The tooling is unacceptable for molding a J/24. It cracked. You must provide us with a new set of tools at your cost."

How was that possible? We flew TPI's molding foreman, Duarte DaSilva, to Japan to solve the problem.

He reported his findings. "In the building where J/24s are molded is a huge oven compartment, big enough to roll in a J/24 hull or deck mold."

The Japanese refused to admit they'd attempted to "one-up" TPI by accelerating cure time. The trouble was that the resin to make the mold was not designed to survive oven temperatures and cracked.

Time to Get Creative. I can't remember the financial solution to replace the tooling so nobody lost face in Japan. We probably gave up something, like splitting the cost. But it was worth it, and we more than got our money back.

Nissan Marine went on to build over 100 boats, hosting three World Championships: Atsumi Bay 1985, Osaka 2001, and Wakayama 2016.

J Composites—France It wasn't until 1989 and the introduction of the J/44 that my son Stuart had the foresight and initiative to set up J/Boats Europe. With financial backing from his then-father-in-law, Kent Johnson, Stu and his wife, Shelley, moved to England in July 1990, intending to win a series of major regattas starting with Cowes Week.

When their J/44 *J-Hawk* won Class A, the British tabloid press ballyhooed their victory as the "second coming" of the yacht *America*. Emblazoned across the front page of *The Sunday Times* and other independent newspapers was a spectacular photo of *J-Hawk* finishing under a spinnaker in front of the Royal Yacht Squadron.

Because these races were witnessed by Europe's top sailors from France, the Netherlands, Belgium, Spain, and Germany, it wasn't long before Stuart got the word out about J/Boats, and sales started to come in. The timing was fortunate. Sales in the US had plummeted with the luxury tax.

Stu's major regatta campaign strategy in England, Scotland, France, and the Netherlands paid off. Forty-five J/Boats were sold in the first five years, from J/92s to J/44s. Many of the strong dealers established then still handle J/Boats today.

A championship-winning couple, the late Paul Heyes and his wife, Marie Claude, ultimately became J/Boats Europe's biggest dealer, having done an exemplary job organizing J/Boat fleets and regattas.

Fortuitously, at the 1994 IYRU World Keelboat Championship in La Rochelle, France, where Stuart had organized 12-boat fleets of both J/24s and J/22s, he met the outstanding French sailor and boat builder Didier le Moal.

Together, they would establish J Composites as a J/Boats licensed builder. That partnership had a major impact on brand success in the European market. Furthermore, J Composites contributed greatly to J/Boats' product-development and production capabilities to deal with US currency fluctuations and market cycles.

The results of this two-year effort are seen in the dramatic number of J/Boats racing at major events such as Spi Ouest, with nearly 100 J/80s or large local fleets, like 30 J/80s, in such prestigious locations as the Club de Yates in Barcelona, site of the 2023 America's Cup.

The recent phenomenon of sailing leagues, which started in Germany with fleets of 6 to 12 J/70s, has exploded to hundreds of sailing clubs and thousands of sailors. They participate in four to six events per summer, all exclusively racing J/70s in the United Kingdom, Ireland, Spain, France, the Netherlands, Germany, Denmark, Switzerland, Italy, Sweden, Norway, Finland, and even Russia.

The latter has nearly 80-J/70s between fleets in St. Petersburg, Moscow, Sochi, and Konakovo. Today, thanks mainly to Stuart's prospecting, J/Boats is the dominant one-design brand across Europe, with fleets of J/22s, J/24s, J/70s, J/80s, J/109s, and J/111s in over 20 countries.

Other Licensees Ultimately, J/Boats added licensed builders in Brazil, Argentina, Australia, Italy, South Africa, France, and China.

To discuss setting up the original Australian licensee, Mary and I were visited by builder Kanga Birtles and journalist Rob Mundle. They test-sailed our J/24 in Newport. It was blowing a good 25 knots out of the northwest. They planed at high speed down the bay under spinnaker to cinch the deal.

The Aussies have a great knack for naming boats. The first was *What a Difference a J Makes.* Another early one was, *Why Kick a Moo Cow?*

Then we had the opportunity to start the Italian operation, with the first six J/24s delivered to Paolo Vitelli of Azimut Yachts. An evening spent in his wine cellar consuming bottles of exquisite Italian reds was a real treat. Amazingly, the next day, there was no hangover. That has to be the sign of good wines.

Ultimately, Paolo Boido became J/Boats of Italy to do a good job building strong classes of J/24s and, more recently, promoting J/70s.

This international licensing push contributed greatly to J/Boats becoming a world brand because we had dealer and builder representatives who could promote newer designs.

Presently J/Boats has more designs approved as an international class, eligible for world championships or selection for the Olympics or Pan American Games, than any other builder-designer: J/24, J/22, J/80, J/111, and J/70.

By 1992, there were active National J/24 Class Associations (NJCA) in 22 countries.

Of course, international dealings involve some risk produced by bizarre financial transactions. The first was receiving a brown paper bag full of small-denomination bills from a Caribbean yachtsman in New-port to pay for J/36 #1. Word came about six months later that the Drug Enforcement Administration had impounded the boat in the islands.

The second involved my having to open a personal, numbered Swiss bank account to receive payment for an order for half a dozen J/24s. I went out of my way to explain this to Rod so he wouldn't think I was somehow making off with company funds.

(21) Creating Events

Brand success is more than just selling boats for people to own. It's how that boat impacts the family's lifestyle. To succeed, one has to paint a picture that promises fun, adventure, and even exotic things they can do with the boat and the many new, like-minded friends they'll meet beyond their local harbor.

That lesson was driven home by my experience with the US Youth Championship. A good regatta can play a major role in bringing people together for the first time from around the country.

Time to Get Creative. What events could promote our new J/24 design?

1978 Key West Race Week This was the first of what most people associate with the major multiclass event. It started with J/24s.

My plot was to get new J/24 owners, dealers, and sailmakers togeth-er for "fun in the sun," thus generating lots of free publicity.

Here's the story. Storm Trysail Club (STC) ran its Annual Fort Lau-derdale-Key West Race every January. Top sailmakers and active off-shore sailors all showed up. It was the first major sailing event of the new year. STC put up a large party tent. The yachting press was there. Who wouldn't want to be in the Keys at that time of year? It was just a matter of J/Boats getting STC to leave their tent up for the rest of the week. We sent out our notice of race and arranged for a local race committee, some judges, and prizes.

As mentioned, 20 J/24s showed up, with the country's top sailors attending. This first J/24 one-design event was followed in the summer by a J/24 North American Championship in Newport, Rhode Island. Numerous other regional, national, and world events started to build class strength.

1985 Women's Keelboat Champs When the opportunity arose at USYRU annual meetings to help committee heads conduct their events, I was always ready to step in with our boats, as we had at Noroton and Saint Petersburg Yacht Clubs.

The late Helen Ingerson^ of the Rochester Yacht Club got support for a Women's International Keelboat Regatta. But where, and with what boats?

Time to Get Creative. I was all over it, suggesting we could base it at Sail Newport. There was a sizeable local J/24 Feet that could supply charter boats and maybe even owner-hosted lodging for overseas entries.

The regatta allowed J/Boats to take the lead in the sailing world as being women-friendly.

Commodore Bob Connor of Ida Lewis Yacht Club persuaded his wife, Ann, to run the event. With its key sponsor, this regatta became known as the "Rolex."

Betsy Allison won it that first year, and my daughter Helen was 6th.

There was some unexpected excitement. Halfway through the regatta, Hurricane Gloria targeted New England. We went into action, hauling out all the J/24s onto their trailers, leaving the masts up, then towing the 35 boats into the ammunition dump and parade ground of Fort Adams for protection. They dropped in again when the storm passed to complete the championship.

1996 Down East Race Week We had moved our permanent home to West Boothbay Harbor and still had a summer home on Little Cranberry Island. I liked nothing better than racing around Maine islands in Penobscot, Blue Hill, and Frenchman's Bays.

We started doing this in the 1950s when chartering boats from Bob Hinckley. Later, it was on various J/Boats, up to our J/42 *Gannet* in 1995.

Entering all available races had been a complicated challenge. The Northeast Harbor Fleet had its August Cruise; the North Haven Yacht Club had its West Penobscot Bay Race; the Deer Island Yacht Club, with Bucks Harbor and Center Harbor Yacht Clubs, had their Round Deer Island Race; and Kollegewidgwok Yacht Club of Blue Hill had its Nevin Cup.

The various clubs had done an excellent job scheduling the events on different days during August. But the sailing instructions, when they existed, were all different. Each had "traditional" hand-me-down rules, some from the 1930s, which bore no resemblance to USYRU's prescribed "Racing Rules of Sailing" formats.

It was a nightmare. A good racing result could be nullified by some obscure or unpublished traditional way of doing things.

Time to Get Creative. After two seasons of frustration, I contacted the fleet captains of the clubs involved and persuaded them to agree to a single notice of race and sailing instructions with letter designations for all government marks.

Once it became less complicated for boatowners to enter all the events, as many as 60 entries in three divisions showed up.

DownEast RaceWeek was created. The Rockefeller and Warburg families put up a heavy, oval, granite boulder as the overall race-week trophy in memory of the Warburgs' son, Max. A sterling silver sail adorned the top.

Keeper trophies were unique, small, 5-inch granite boulders from the Maine shoreline etched with "The Max."

We've got the start of a rocky Maine beach right here in our Charleston cottage with seven of those beauties being used as décor and doorstops around the house. They'd also make handy weapons to ward off any home invaders. They were the most decorative and useful trophies imaginable. True keepers!

1999 Charleston Race Week Seems that I get into regatta-creation mode as a way to have more fun sailboat racing and meet new friends wherever we live. It happened in Maine, then Charleston, where we'd moved in 1998, and later in Boston in 2003.

One of my first initiatives as the J/Boats dealer for the Southeast was to start a J/105 fleet based at the Charleston Harbor Marina next to the College of Charleston's sailing facility. We'd built the fleet to six boats. I was looking for ways to create a regatta to attract more J/105s to this fun place to sail. With all the good restaurants and spring garden tours, the city is usually ranked as America's favorite vacation spot.

Time to Get Creative. A fall 1998 meeting of the Charleston Ocean Racing Association (CORA) at the Charleston Yacht Club to plan the 1999 schedule provided the opportunity.

CORA had an event called Charleston Race Week that was held offshore during the July 4 weekend. That wasn't very attractive to this recent resident. Only locals who braved the summer heat attended. We weren't going to lure any out-of-town boats to such a regatta.

The sport of yacht racing has moved to New England at that time of year. Charleston is too hot! Serious racers, like all those J/Boat owners—who travel to Florida for class midwinter championships, Key West Race Week, SORC, etc. between December and March—trailer their boats back north to spring series at the Annapolis and American Yacht Clubs in May. Yup! All my J/105 friends were trailering right past Charleston on the Route 95 "flyway."

So how do we entice them to stop in Charleston on the way home? Maybe free storage on their trailers? Free launch and haul for a Charleston Race Week in April? After much discussion, CORA was persuaded to try it in 1999, advancing their dates from the Fourth of July weekend to April.

Teddy Turner IV, who at the time owned Charleston Boat Works, offered free parking and launching for the traveling contestants. He'd get some bottom and repair jobs in return.

Courses were laid out in the harbor. It's the craziest and most fun place to sail in the Southeast. Currents go up and down and intersect the Ashley and Cooper Rivers. You never have to give up if behind. There's always an angle to play.

Then, there's the appeal to families of garden tours and great restaurants. One visiting J/105 sailor proclaimed, after dining in Charleston, "The restaurants are better than those in San Francisco."

Seems that helping create sailboat regattas has its benefits. The first regatta I organized was the Copa de Ano Nuevo Sunfish regatta in Valencia, Venezuela, in 1965. We had about 30 Sunfish show up and had to build a new floating dock to accommodate them all. I won that one, and now, 34 years later managed to pull this one off at Charleston Race Week. Here's the May 4, 1999, *Sailing Scuttlebutt* #316 report:

CHARLESTON RACE WEEK

Posting a near-perfect record (1-1-2-1-1-1-1-1), Bob Johnstone's J/105 CAMELLIA won the Palmetto Cup and SAYRA (South Atlantic Yacht Racing Association) Offshore Championship as the Overall and Class A winner of Charleston Race Week…Johnstone credits crew members, Round the World Sailor Dave Scully, x-Newporter Dan Dickison and West Coast transplant Patrick Rogers, as being crucial to winning under the trying heavy-air conditions.

With a persistent, concentrated low-pressure center hanging onto the Carolina coastline, temperatures and winds were more like a New England Northeaster with temperatures in the 50's and low 60's (13 degrees below average) and winds in the 20–25 knot range for most of the series. Over 1/3 of the Race Week Fleet suffered equipment damage, retired or elected to DNS due to the rough, rainy conditions in Charleston Harbor.

Charleston Race Week was moved this year from the July 4th week to provide more wind and moderate temperatures for the contestants. Those wishes were more than fulfilled. If these conditions continue for a few more years, Charleston RaceWeek will be right up there with San Francisco's Berkeley Circle in June and could even top Key West Race Week in January for wind.

After 23 years, Charleston Race Week is billed as the "Largest Keelboat Regatta in America"; 259 boats raced in 2019. Of 198 boats racing in 2022, 91 (46 percent) were J/Boats, with five classes sailing one-design: J/24, J/22, J/105, J/88, and J/70. J/70 was the largest fleet, with 48 boats.

2004 Boston Harbor Islands Regatta We moved to Boston in 2003, and I was invited along with Peter Craig, organizer of Key West Race Week, to a meeting of the Boston Harbor Alliance (BHA). Dick Cross, a board member and later chairman, had become a friend and MJM investor and shareholder when he came in with some needed working capital. The buyback of his stock with a 20 percent return was with a good deal on his MJM 34z #62 *Southern Cross*. Nineteen years later, Dick has become a member of the MJM Yachts advisory board with a new MJM 42 on order.

Helping Dick and his BHA get a regatta going was my payback time. The purpose of the initial meeting was to bring focus to the harbor islands by conducting an annual regatta to promote the use of the islands as a recreational area.

Peter Craig described how it was necessary to contact class associations three years in advance to get on their schedules. He further described the need for several racing circles, with at least three mark and race committee boats for each circle. Plus, a professional jury and a paid professional manager and staff were needed to deal with rating certificates and entry forms, etc. He stated, "This was the formula I used to make Key West Race Week a success."

Eyes were rolling. This was way beyond what the group was contemplating. The prospects for hosting a regatta near-term seemed overwhelmingly impossible.

Time to Get Creative. The next morning, I woke up thinking, *Wait a minute! They have a dozen islands to sail around. There's nothing more popular or more fun than "Round the Island Races," whether it's the Maine islands, Conanicut Island in Rhode Island, the Isle of Wight…you name it.*

There are 1,000 or more sailboats sitting in marina slips around Boston and Charlestown and along both the South Shore and the North Shore. Some of those people have never raced but might have fun trying.

To heck with the national classes and people from away. The event's purpose is to have fun and increase local recreational use of the islands.

So let's make this a super-local event. If a boat hasn't raced before or doesn't have a current PHRF rating, no problem; I'll assign them a rating based on a PHRF New England rating for sister ships.

Then we'll make it a pursuit race so the slow boats are out front for most of the race. That makes it exciting for everyone. Crowded starting lines are avoided. You automatically get one-design starts with boats rating the same. The crews can enjoy the scenery.

All we need are two committee boats, one for a spinnaker division and one for a nonspinnaker division. They can be started and finished concurrently if distanced apart.

Two parties can be scheduled: a skippers-meeting cocktail party and dinner the night before and an island picnic and trophy presentation after racing at 3:00 p.m. on Georges Island.

I ran the event as race committee chairman, created the scratch sheets with assigned ratings, scored the results, used one of our MJMs as the RC boat for the spinnaker fleet, and later handed out lots of trophies.

In addition to handing out awards for 1st to 3rd place in six classes, we included the Mayor's Cup for the best performance in either fleet, a Family Crew Trophy, Top Female and Master (65+) in each fleet, Top Classic Yacht (pre-1970), and the President's Bowl for the Top Community Sailing Club performance.

We had one-design trophies if there were three or more of a class. That year there were J/22s, Solings, Catalina 30s, and Thunderbirds.

It was a huge success: 125 boats showed up that first year. Forty percent of them didn't have PHRF rating certificates. Invariably there were four or five skippers that had never raced before. We publicly identified them at the skippers' meeting and warned everyone, "These boats have the right of way no matter what the circumstances."

In the 6th year of running in 2010, there were 98 boats equally divided between spinnaker and nonspinnaker. The J/35 *Black Seal* won the nonspinnaker class, the only J/Boat in that class.

Pictured is the spinnaker division approaching the finish. Left to right in the foreground are the J/30 *Ruffian* (4th); the J/109 *Superstition* (*1st*), the J/46 *Vanish* (3rd), and the S2 7.9 *Club Car* (2nd). There were 14 J/Boats in that class.

Those results reveal my diabolical strategy of promoting pursuit races. Being some of the fastest-rated boats in the event, J/Boats had to start close to last. Then, to win, they had to impress all the other boats in the race by passing them over the course of 12 miles. Couldn't ask for better advertising.

There's a big potential problem with pursuit races. "What happens if the wind dies and the race committee has to shorten the race?" Suddenly, the simplest race to administer becomes a nightmare to score… particularly if it's holding up a postrace awards party.

Time to Get Creative. Fortunately, PHRF provides a solution that has worked with no complaints. Sailing instructions are written with this provision (time must be adjusted for a race of different length): "Shortening Course: Since the cross-over time between PHRF TOD (Time-on-Distance) and PHRF TOT (Time-on-Time) scoring is approximately 3 hours in 12 miles: The Race Committee may shorten the course any time after 3 hours have elapsed from the start of the first boat, by making two sound signals and announcing on VHF that the finish shall be between the RC Boat and the next turning mark, or a nearby floating mark."

(22) Taking Risks

Significant departures from market norms involve risk, particularly in sailboat design, which is slow to change.

In 1977, the J/24 was a considerable departure. Its target category of offshore-capable racing and cruising boats consisted of voluminous, heavy-displacement IOR or CCA rule–influenced designs with big, overlapping genoas and small mainsails. The tooling cost for those designs, first created as custom boats to win races, was amortized by volume production builders who sold cruising boats with a "racing pedigree." The fact that they were slow for their length was unimportant. Being large and voluminous was a plus when selling bunks-to-length ratios for the cruising market.

By eschewing handicap-rating rules that handicapped, as in "slowed," a sailboat's speed potential, J/Boats ushered in a new era of planing offshore keelboats with dinghy-like hulls and easily adjusted rigs that were fast for their length.

Perhaps British journalist Jack Knights summed it up best in *Yachts & Yachting.* He visited us in New Haven. After a wild spinnaker reach in a race, passing 40-footers on our J/24 *Summer Breeze*, he wrote in his Y&Y column, "The J/24 is the Laser with a Lid."

J/Boat owners get a better boat and better long-term "resale" value. When enlightened handicap-rule administrators close ridiculous loopholes, it's back to stability for safety and speed for length, displacement, and sail area.

Courtesy of J Boats, Inc.

Designs unencumbered by distorted hulls, bumps, and other rule tweaks look better and better over the years. Designed to the rule of the sea, "classic" J/Boats, more than 25 years old, still win race weeks and dominate offshore events. J/Boats were 25 percent of entries in the 2022 Newport Bermuda Race and 34 percent of the 2022 Block Island Race...four times that of the nearest competitor, which, in the Bermuda Race, was Nautor Swan.

The next radical J/Boats move changed modern offshore keelboat design forever: the introduction of the J/105, 14 years later, in 1991.

The conventional parachute spinnaker flown from a removable pole and controlled by sheets, guys, foreguys, and topping lift, and by as many as eight crew on a 44-footer, was replaced by an asymmetric spinnaker flown from a retractable (or fixed) bowsprit, managed by as few as one crew member from the cockpit.

This downwind system was featured on Australian 18s with fixed bowsprits and huge asymmetric spinnakers. Then Jay Cross and my son

Peter's One-Design 14 combined a retractable bowsprit with a huge asymmetric chute.

When J/Boats put this innovative system on the J/105, sailors realized it was easier to sail a large racer-cruiser off the wind with less crew. That simpler system gave rise to an increase in double-handed racing events.

(23) Giving Back to the Sport

My involvement with the North American Yacht Racing Union (now US Sailing) started in 1973, four years before J/Boats, when trying to get the US Youth Championship off the ground as the 470 representative on the US Olympic Yachting Committee.

I worked with Bill Bentsen*, Larry Johnson, and Gregg Bemis* of the Racing Rules Committee on improving large-fleet race management. A center-of-the-starting-line mark boat was one of the innovations.

With the advent of the J/24, my involvement with administering the sport of sailing grew dramatically. There was the process of seeking international class status with trips to the IYRU in London, representing the J/24 Class on the USYRU One-Design Class Council, the interface with handicap-racing groups like the Offshore Committee that managed International Ocean Racing (IOR) and International Measurement System (IMS) rules, the Performance Handicap Racing Formula (PHRF) Committee, and the Midget Ocean Racing Class (MORC) Committee.

Being oriented toward promoting "One-Design," I soon became chairman of the One-Design Class Council (ODCC) and a member of the USYRU Board of Directors.

Probably the most significant contribution at the time was an effort to have exemplary one-design accomplishments recognized by the USYRU. We created the annual One-Design Awards for Leadership, Best Club, Creativity, and Best Regatta. Then in 1990, being in the business, I pushed for creation and became chairman of a USYRU Industry

Council to encourage the industry and USYRU to cooperate in further pursuit of common goals.

The first meeting was in Seattle in October 1990, with Dave Irish, Dick Rose*, Chip Johns, Peter Harken*, Dave Dellenbaugh^, Mike Segerbloom, Greg Fisher^, Tony Wilson (Hobie Cat), and John Marshall (North Sails) in attendance.

We concluded that neither the industry nor USYRU was effectively promoting the sport. USYRU's 15 percent share of the racing market at the time was unacceptably low.

Time to Get Creative. A brainstorming session produced several ideas. Six months later, in March 1991, the Industry Council submitted a recommendation to the USYRU Board, responding to the request of the ASAP Industry Group to change the name of the national governing body from USYRU to "Sail US."

At the annual USYRU meeting in October, the name finally decided upon was "US Sailing."

It was gratifying to be involved in that change and creating the President's Club with President Bill Martin* to boost US Sailing's finances. At the time, offshore sail numbers were five digits long. The concept was to approach owners of large racing yachts and offer them one-to-three-digit offshore racing numbers that were inactive.

I had my eyes on sail number USA-24. Dues of $1,000 per year for ten years was the entry fee for membership in the President's Club. When approved, I remember Bill saying, "I know just the guy who will come up with $10,000 right away to get #1." And that's how Jim Kilroy's* *Kialoa* had sail USA-1.

Bill later became chairman of the United States Olympic Committee and Michigan University director of athletics. He and his wife Sally now own an MJM 40z they plan to truck seasonally between homes in Harbor Springs and Punta Gorda.

(24) Newport—Total Immersion

Where one lives can add to or detract from business success. We had moved to Woodbridge, Connecticut, in 1975 for the commute to AMF Alcort in Waterbury. That's where we lived when starting J/Boats in 1977.

The older three kids were at Amity Regional High School. Stu and Drake played in the Connecticut State Hockey Championship. They helped organize an Amity High School sailing team, then went on to win the 1976 Clifford D. Mallory Trophy for the Interscholastic (ISSA) National Championship. Drake founded the SAIL 76 New Haven community sailing program before entering Yale.

We moved to Newport in 1978 to become more accessible to others in the sport of yacht racing. We made that decision during a cold, sleepless night on our J/24, on the Connecticut River during the Essex Yacht Club's Spring Regatta.

We barely had enough blankets. Between tunes on the stereo, we asked ourselves, "Why are we in Woodbridge trying to run J/Boats from there? We should be in a 'nautical' town if this new company is going to go anywhere in the yachting world. Where would that be? Marblehead, Newport, Larchmont, or Annapolis?"

Newport was voted number one, with proximity to Warren, Rhode Island, where Tillotson-Pearson was building J/24s.

"OK, I'll call my friend Herb Finley when we return home on Monday." Herb was a real estate agent and J/24 owner I'd met at the Newport Boat Show.

I called Herb. He said, "I've got the perfect place right on the harbor. Tell me you sent a $100 deposit and get here before Friday. There's another couple scheduled to visit from Philadelphia. If you like it, we'll sign the contract, and it's yours."

We did and lived there for 14 years. This harborside condo had a dock with three moorings. Stu and Drake had a J/24 on one, and we'd put our latest J/Boats design on the other, leaving one open for guests.

It was total immersion in the world of sailing. Newport is now the site of the Sailing Museum, home of the National Sailing Hall of Fame and America's Cup Hall of Fame. Shown below is that happy crew in 1980 on our porch at Beechbound.

CHAPTER 14

After J/24

J/Boats went through several design phases after the J/24. The first of these was typical of boat builders: design and build a bigger boat. You could have predicted it. Within a year, we were designing a J/30...then, right after that, a J/36.

Design editing and restraint did not characterize this period. The designs did not come from consumer research. Rod and I were responding to J/24 owner and dealer requests. By fulfilling the wish list of others, we were beginning to show symptoms of *featuritis*. Nevertheless, we stuck to our offshore one-design strategy.

J/30

J/24 owners asked, "When are you coming out with a 30-footer? Don't get us wrong. We love our J/24, the adjustable fractional rig, the performance, friends we meet. But please understand, we want to spend a month or so every summer cruising with our family of five. It's been a bit tight on the J/24."

Rod started with a red, cold-molded prototype that looked like a J/24 on steroids, with the same sloped deck and no cabin trunk or portlights.

Time to Get Creative. Rod's approach wasn't being received very well by our target market. So, contrary to Rod's inclination to avoid slowing the boat down with a lot of cruising gear, we decided to go for a proper cruising interior, with a cabin trunk having portlights (windows).

Everett hired Peter Van Lanker, a Rhode Island School of Design graduate and now the president of Hunt Yachts. Peter was assigned to work one-on-one with me to design the cruising interior.

How elegant was the result? Princeton classmate and my crew on the Princeton sailing team, Delaware Governor Pierre S. "Pete" du Pont IV, ordered a J/30 and requested that his galley cabinets accommodate the du Pont family china from his father's 72-foot schooner, *Barlovento*. His chauffeur drove the Governor's limo from Wilmington to Warren, Rhode Island, with the set of china, to be sure we got it right.

Comfortable living aboard was important to six families from the Macatawa Bay Yacht Club in Holland, Michigan. They formed J/30 Fleet #1, lived on their boats for the summer, raced one-design, and cruised the North Channel.

The J/30 initiated our practice of sailing the first boat off the line to address the inevitable hit list of issues needing correction. This policy avoided the saying in the boat business, "Never buy a new boat with a lower hull number than 10, by which time the builder will have solved all the problems."

Rod was on Hull #1, *Warhoop*, in extreme conditions at night in the 1979 Southern Ocean Racing Circuit (SORC). Dropping off a 15-foot wave with a crash in the Gulf Stream, skipper John Kolius^ turned to Rod and asked, "How does this boat handle waves like this?"

Rod answered, "I don't know. I've never sailed the boat when it's been this rough."

That prompted flashlights to come out. Kolius^ and navigator By Baldridge searched for cracks, leaks, or signs of stress around the mast step, rudder gudgeons, and chainplates. Fortunately, no problems.

Mary and I were on J/30 *Sleighride* that summer between Cape Ann and Portland, Maine, when the radio reported the '79 Fastnet storm disaster, saying, "Twenty-four crews have abandoned ship, 15 people are dead, 5-boats sank, 136 sailors have been rescued, and Ted Turner* is missing."

Bill Wallace was sailing his J/30 alone across the Atlantic during the storm. Approaching the English Channel, he was knocked flat, recovered, and arrived safely in the UK. The J/30 had withstood a severe test others had failed.

While maybe carrying excessive cruising amenities, the J/30 still outperformed all but a few other custom 30-footers, had the promise of one-design racing and was backed by a reputable builder and national dealer network.

Ultimately, 546 J/30s were sold, and by 1984 there were more J/30s registered under PHRF and more USYRU members who sailed them than any design over 27 feet.

J/36

The J/30 led to the next size up...a J/36. Initiating design work on this larger design took a nudge from a friend and 1964 America's Cup–winning helmsman, Bob Bavier*.

Bob wasn't pleased with the performance of his J/30 in light air. He sailed out of the Noroton Yacht Club on Long Island Sound. He told Rod and me, "I'm having a tough time winning races with my boat. You guys need to develop a boat that performs better in the light air we get here on the Sound. Think about a tall fractional rig, like a 12 meter. That's the best sailing boat in light air I know of."

Time to Get Creative. We took his input seriously. Bob Bavier was one of my heroes. During my sophomore year at Glen Ridge High School, in 1949, as part of an English assignment, I entered a short story contest sponsored by the Women's Club of Glen Ridge.

My short story, "The Battle of Stonington, August 9, 1814," described how *HMS Ramillies*—under Captain Thomas Hardy of Trafalgar fame—bombarded the town and was repulsed. The 1st place prize was a book of my choice. I picked Bob Bavier's recently published *Sailing to Win*. The 10th edition, in 1983, had a J/24 on the cover.

Mary and I cruised with Bob and Charlotte in Maine on the J/40 *Shibui*.

In 1998, our son Peter persuaded us to move to Charleston. Bob found the house we purchased on 7 Church Street (of Sally Carrington fame) when walking his dog.

Sadly, three years later, I bid him farewell in the hospital and was moved to write his obituary, which appeared in *Scuttlebutt* and *Yachting* (May 2001). Bob is buried in Charleston's Magnolia Cemetery.

The J/36 had a tall fractional rig with jumper struts and performed very well in light-to-moderate air and smooth water conditions. Its tall rig would catch the upper strata of higher-velocity air from a building sea breeze. Perhaps the best example was sailing our J/36 *Aja* in a race off Newport on a smooth light-air day with Tom Whidden*, later North Sails president, aboard as tactician. After opening up a huge lead, he looked aft at our competition in the distance and said, "Just like sailing on Kialoa!"

The J/36 racing record was exceptional. Rod won the 1981 ECYRA Offshore Circuit Overall with *Jazz*, the last time being in 1976 with the J/24 prototype *Ragtime.*

Mark Spitz, who'd won seven gold medals in the 1972 Munich Olympics, breaking seven world records, sailed his J/36 *Sumark* to a respectable 3rd in class and 10th overall out of 73 entrants in the TransPac.

Bill Menninger described breaking their speed record twice:

As we entered the channel the wind let up slightly but the waves became steeper and more confused. At the top of one of these waves, I began to question whether the boat would make it to the bottom of the wave in one piece. Surfers turn their boards at the top of such waves so that they can track a more gradual course to the bottom. Sailboats are not so fortunate because of their sails and mast wanting to pull them over on such maneuvers. As we stood at the top of one of these monsters we had just enough wind to accelerate us into the point of no return. I aimed the boat straight down the face and hoped that it would continue that way. We began to surf wildly down the wave and curtains of water rushed up both sides of the boat. Mark Spitz looked in awe at the speedo as we burst over the top and down the net one at 19.6 knots.

Antigua Race Week

My favorite time on a J/36 was when Mary and I sailed with Everett and Ginny Pearson and the boat's owners, plus Quino Sanchez, our Puerto Rican dealer, on *Melissa* to win Division II and finish 2nd overall at Antigua Race Week.

That had to be the biggest trophy haul ever for a single regatta; count 'em: 12 in all. Overall, we were behind St. Thomas bobsled Olympian John Foster in his J/24 *Antidote,* which won for the 2nd time in a row. Not a bad J/Boats result!

We were the smallest boat in a fleet of 22, mostly 41-to-45-foot IOR boats like the DuBois 41 *Immigrant,* Peterson 43 *Goodbye Girl,* and Swan 431 *Crackerjack II.*

Mary and I had an ideal arrangement. Generously forsaking a nice berth on the boat (that's a joke), we rented a beach cottage from the Inn at English Harbor for the week and slept there every night, with the lapping of waves on the beach, after a relaxing seafood dinner with rum punches at the inn's hilltop main dining room.

Since each race day during the week ended at a different harbor or beach, we decided to skip the debauchery of après-race beach parties and steel drums.

We'd hop a prearranged cab back to English Harbor for a romantic, under-the-stars evening at the inn. The following morning, we'd pick up a picnic lunch basket for the entire crew, prepared by the inn's dining room, then take another taxi ride back to where the boat was moored. It was the perfect regatta program.

The J/36 was not easy to sail consistently fast upwind in heavy air and waves. Ideally, sails can be trimmed so the boat can sail up the face of a wave, go over the top, then bear off slightly down the back side in a scalloping course without losing speed.

The large J/36 mainsail and tall, heavy mast with jumper strut made it difficult to manage that type of course without getting blown over excessively as you bore off on the top of a wave and had to ease the mainsail. Too much of a start-stop motion.

Even in light air and slop, the boat had difficulty holding a high line going to windward or accelerating after a tack without bearing off, easing the main with excessive twist. Smooth water was a different story.

Time to Get Creative. John Marshall sailed *Aja* with us on the 1981 Northeast Harbor Fleet August Cruise, distinguishing himself with an early-morning dip in the 55-degree water and helping us win the Y-O-Y-O, twice around windward, leeward course, up and down the protected Somes Sound fjord. Between racing marks Y and O. The fog was too dense to race outside.

John, involved in several custom IOR designs, suggested we take a look at keel design to improve heavy-weather performance. For the subsequent J/35, using the same hull, Rod added about six inches to the tip and made the chord width percentage thicker at the bottom than the top, more of a constant chord thickness, which moved the weight and center of lateral resistance lower and further aft.

When the keel design change was implemented on the J/29 and J/35, with the center of effort of their masthead sailplans located further forward, the improvement became evident in their all-around performance, particularly in heavy air.

CHAPTER 15

J/Boats Reboot

W hen navigational or engine electronics fail or start behaving er-
ratically, the first and often best cure is to turn everything off for
30 seconds, then turn it on again to reboot. When the severe 1981–82
"double dip" recession whacked P/E ratios down to 6s and 7s, J/Boat
sales came to a screeching halt, and we couldn't pay ourselves a salary.

The 1980 launch of the J/36 was a great but short-lived success.
Only 75 were sold by July 1981. We poured the coals into advertising
that fall: $100,000 ($325,000 in 2021). Bad timing! We didn't sell another J/36, nor were we selling any J/24s or J/30s at the time, either.

Time to Get Creative. What that recession did was propel J/Boats into
its 3rd phase of designing even better-performing, race-winning, larger
sailboats by taking away the weight and cost of cruising accouterments,
our own *featuritis* shortcoming. We'd also taken away potential performance from Rod's initial J/30 and J/36 designs when trying to broaden
their appeal to cruisers.

J/29

Rod often commented that all the cruising amenities made the J/30
heavier than the designed weight, slowing it down, although a livable
cruising interior contributed. Before the economy went sour in 1981, the
J/30 sold for $50,000 fully equipped.

Time to Get Creative. "OK, Rod, sales of the J/30 have stopped.
You've wanted a stripped-out, fast MORC boat to beat the Olson 30?
How cheap, minimalist, and fast can we make it?"

His answer was, "Strip out the interior, leaving just four bunks and a head, and put an outboard on a bracket to get rid of the diesel engine weight."

"OK, Rod. But I'm worried about killing off the J/30 in dealer showrooms. To make the J/29 less attractive for cruising, how about going one step further? Lower the freeboard to have just sitting headroom. With the same rig and lowered gooseneck, we get a bigger mainsail."

If you want a fractional rig, fine. Make mine an easier-to-trim masthead. Amazingly, Everett transformed the J/30 into hull #1 of the J/29 in just 90 days, getting the weight down by nearly 1,500 lbs.

J/29 Rabbitt

The standard boat retail price dropped by half, to $24,950. That excited buyers to go back into dealerships for the first time in nearly a year. J/29s started selling like hotcakes. "Twenty-one in the first 21 days!" J/Boats was back in business!

Some customers came to look at the J/29 and said, "That won't do for cruising." The dealer would respond, "No problem. We've got the cruising version, just perfect for you. It's the J/30." So J/30s started selling again.

Five days after the first four J/29s were launched, they finished 1st, 2nd, 3rd, and 5th in Class at the 1982 Block Island Race Week. The J/29 went on to win its Class in the MORC Internationals.

More good news. After we shipped a J/29 to the UK, the Brits were shocked to see it win the IOR Class One Fall Championship on the Solent. It was heavy air. I sailed with legendary UK boatbuilder Jeremy Rogers MBE.

We built 534 over five years, and they keep winning. In 2021, the boats' 40th year, J/29 *Dirty Harry* was named Block Island Race Week's "Boat of the Week" with finishes of 1-1-1-1-1-2 in Class. Another J/29 was runner-up.

Masthead J/35

After its initial 1981 run, we didn't sell another J/36. Its tall fractional rig was a challenge to sail well in heavy air. Putting the J/30 on a diet to create the J/29 worked so well, halving the price, why not do the same with the $84,500 J/36? "We might as well use the tooling for something!"

Time to Get Creative. Following the J/29 success, Everett agreed to go for it!

The J/36 interior was stripped to create the J/35. A simple J/24 type V-berth platform and open head were located forward of the main bulkhead.

As with the J/29, the main cabin had a couple of wide bottom berths on either side, with removable "bundling boards" as backrests to create outboard duffel or sail storage. A minimalist chart table and galley with an Igloo cooler and two quarter-berths completed the picture.

Reduced labor hours and materials dropped the price to $49,500, or nearly half. We learned from the J/29 that a masthead rig was easier to sail fast and consistently in waves. Wanting to do a better job at "one-design" than we had by offering two J/29 rigs, masthead was the decision. We went with our new, thinner, larger-area keel program as with the J/29.

It all worked so well that 330 J/35s were sold over the next nine years. The design was inducted into the American Sailboat Hall of Fame in 1999, following only five other boats over 30 feet: Bermuda 40, Cal 40, Morgan Out Island 40, Freedom 40, and Valiant 40.

By 1998, five years after its introduction, the J/35 had become the fastest-rated and most popular racer-cruiser among the top 100 PHRF designs and all boats rated under IMS.

One of my favorite J/35 stories is about getting a call from a prospective buyer in upstate New York. After he had given me all the particulars to fill out his order, he asked, "Don't you want to know why I'm buying a J/35?"

I answered, "Why, sure."

He said, "There's this guy in our PHRF fleet. Last season, he usually finished last or next-to-last in his C&C. He got a new J/35 this year. This year he wins just about every race, even going in the wrong direction. So I know it's the boat!"

1987 Queen's Cup

My most memorable J/35 race was the 1987 New York Yacht Club (NYYC) Queen's Cup, sailed off Newport, Rhode Island. It's the premier NYYC race of the year. Queen Elizabeth II of England gave the Cup in 1953 to replace the former King's Cup from 1912, which had been retired. Once again, in 2023, it will become the King's Cup.

The New York Yacht Club's annual yearbook lists the winners of its 50+ trophies, the oldest being the Astor Cup, which dates back to 1899. There would be notations to indicate if there was no race winner in a given year, such as "No Race," "Not Awarded," or "Cancelled."

The 1987 Queen's Cup is the only major trophy race recorded in the yearbook as "Race Abandoned."

Tom Leutwiler Photo—STC

There's no mention that the first-to-finish boat and sure winner was in sight five minutes from the finish. That boat was the J/35 *Houqua*.

Here's the story. It was survival racing in 30-to-35-knot winds. Most boats dropped out, many with damage. It was blowing so hard that we sailed Houqua with the heavy-weather jib to an outboard lead and the main on its battens, frequently flogging.

We were on the starboard layline, half a mile from being first to finish!

Crew member Dayton Carr was wincing in great pain, having cracked or broken a rib falling against the leeward cockpit winch. He had to stay in the cockpit.

John Marshall's Hinckley 42C *Dragon Fire* was the only other boat in sight on port tack, about a mile to leeward. He owed us time. We were elated to be winning!

Then, to our astonishment, *boom...boom...boom...*the New York Yacht Club Race Committee (RC) on *Black Knight* fires off three guns to abandon the race, pulls up anchor, and heads back to port.

What? This abandonment had to be the low point in the annals of the Race Committee (RC). At the time, *Houqua* and *Dragon Fire* were in plain sight, about to finish. I couldn't see anyone else.

The seas were rough. *Black Night* was rolling. The RC knew the remaining boats were still a half hour or more from finishing. There may have been injured or very sick RC members aboard. For the RC, this was no longer a yacht race but "survival conditions."

The RC had a viable option to save the race. Since finishes wouldn't be close, they could have left the finishing mark in place, then announced over VHF for boats to take their time when rounding that finish mark and report it over VHF to the RC. *Black Knight* could have returned to port, and saved the race and themselves.

Aboard *Houqua*, survival to the finish was a huge victory. To have overcome such a daunting challenge was one of life's memorable moments, right up there with that two-minute win under similar conditions in the 1972 Soling Olympic Trials.

We felt so bad for Dayton, who had given up a rib for naught. It was a great testimony to the seaworthiness of the J/35.

On the way back in, off Castle Hill, John Marshall's *Dragon Fire* joined Dayton in giving up a part as well: the binnacle with wheel tore entirely out of the deck when John lurched against it in a wipeout. Yes, it was quite a day of sailing!

We made up for it three years later by winning the 1990 NYYC Queen's Cup in J/44 #1 *Iona* to receive a letter of congratulations from HM Queen's office in London. That *Iona* win may have marked a first: a club member who created, built, owned, and helmed the winning Queen's Cup boat.

J/35's extraordinary race record includes the 1984 Chicago-Mackinac Race Overall under MHS and numerous European IMS and CHS championships. A J/35 was the first monohull in Division V of the 1988 Carlsberg Singlehanded Transat.

Ray Demere sailed his J/35 *My Fair Lady* to an IMS Overall win in the 1988 SORC. Houqua won Block Island Race Week and the New England Solo-Twin with Tony Lush.

The Miami-Montego Bay race, Antigua Race Week, Seattle Grand Prix, and RORC and Irish Sea Season Championships are among other J/35 wins.

The J/35 is very much alive, about to enter its fortieth year with an active fleet of fourteen racing one-design on Lake St. Clair. They consistently do well in major Great Lakes events like Chicago-Mackinac and Port Huron–Mackinac Races.

US 42121 *Houqua* lives on as part of that fleet and is now named *Dean's List.*

J/22—Under $10,000 Again

The recession continued to cast a pall over the boating industry in late 1982. J/24 sales had dropped off. We also started wondering whether to apply the diet treatment to that boat. But there wasn't much fat to eliminate.

About that time, dealer Howie McMichael pleaded, "Bob, we're having a tough time selling J/24s since they've gotten up to about $15,000. We need another small boat under $10,000 again."

Time to Get Creative. Maybe we could make it different enough from the J/24 to avoid competing with all its established fleets.

We reasoned that a sit-in cockpit for day sailing, a window in the cabin trunk, a deck-stepped mast to avoid using a crane, and an eight-foot beam for legal owner trailering might do the trick.

The J/22 ended up being 1,000 lbs. lighter than a J/24 and towable by a Volvo station wagon.

It was easier to sail consistently fast upwind because of a more balanced underwater canoe body. As the boat heeled over, the feel of the tiller didn't change. It handled more like a classic keelboat, whereas the J/24, when heeled, rolls up on its wider aft underbody. The feel of a J/24 helm changes, making it more of a challenge to sail consistently fast upwind.

It worked. We sold 160 in the first five weeks at $8,950. By 2018, 1,680 boats had been sold worldwide.

As the J/24 can take some credit for opening the eyes of the Harken brothers to the possibilities of moving from dinghy blocks to the offshore big-boat block business, so it was with the J/22. It put another brother act together: Eric and Ben in Hall Spars. Ben Hall at Kenyon Marine had been our spar builder from the outset with the J/24. When selecting a mast for the J/22, Eric, who alone owned Hall Spars, asked to bid on the job. We decided to give both Eric and Ben a shot. Ben from Kenyon would make hull #1, and Eric from Hall would make the spars for #2. We sailed both.

Eric's Hall Spars won the contest. His mast was better-detailed and stiffer. At that point, Ben saw the handwriting on the wall, resigned from Kenyon, and partnered with his brother Eric at Hall Spars.

At one point, to further combat the price issue and establish more yacht club fleets, we halved the dealer margin on six-boat orders of J/22s.

The J/22 had become so ubiquitous within four years that the USY-RU selected the boat for the following national championships: the 1988 Sears, Mallory, and Prince of Wales Cups; the 1989 Mallory Cup; and the 1990 Adams Cup.

When Gary Jobson was asked at the National Junior Sailing Symposium in Fort Worth in 1987, "What's the best small keelboat out there?" Gary replied without hesitation, "The J/22!"

If memory serves me right, Gary owned one of the 25 or more J/22s at the Annapolis Yacht Club.

Several years earlier, my friend Arnie Gay, from the 1967 Rainbow days, had invited me to pitch the J/22 fleet proposal to AYC. I was staying at his house on Spa Creek. As I knocked on his door, a cat rubbed against my leg and darted in when Arnie opened it. "That's a great-looking cat, Arnie."

Arnie explained, "It's an Abyssinian, the only cat I've ever owned that has chased a squirrel up a tree and caught it!"

"Wow, Mary and I will have to get one of those." And we did so from a breeder...a pair of them were named Lady Di and Cleopatra.

IOR is not ROI

This fourth phase can be dangerous for any corporation. Management, spurred on by success, is tempted to show off how good they are by winning somebody else's game. We did, but at what cost? J/Boats departed from its proven design strategy to take on the International Offshore Rule (IOR), the Grand Prix handicap-rating system of the day.

As Jeff Bezos would say, "This is being competition-oriented and taking the eye off the ball from the key focus...being consumer-obsessed."

J/Boats had started with a fast, 24-foot planing sailboat to satisfy the next-fun-boat needs of thousands of Baby Boomers sailing Sunfish, Lasers, and Hobies. Why bother with the mere hundreds populating the IOR offshore racing clique?

Those people had heavy keelboats that were slow for their size, less manageable, and of questionable seaworthiness.

J/Boats followed the J/24 with larger and faster 30-to-36-foot racer-cruisers that offered more cruising comfort. Even if we won the IOR game, where were the sales for continued business growth? What were we thinking?

We upped performance with family-friendly J/29 and J/35 models to dominate the local PHRF racing scene. Repositioning the brand's "racing success" as winning IOR handicap races, as opposed to being the fastest, easiest, most seaworthy boats through the water, was risky.

What about our Baby Boomers and what they want to own as the next J/Boat? Would we allow smoke-filled back rooms of the Offshore Racing Council to determine our future?

IOR was a measurement handicap rule that evolved from the Cruising Club of America (CCA) rule and that of the Royal Ocean Racing Club (RORC). It did not create faster, more seaworthy boats, as evidenced by the loss of life and sinkings in the 1979 Fastnet storm.

It could be argued that J/Boats was in the sailboat-racing game. And brother Rod should have a chance to test his design skills against Farr, Frers, Holland, Peterson, Stephens, et al. But was this the right course for J/Boats?

Rod commented, in a 1984 paper, *The Impact of the IOR Rule on the Design of Offshore Racing Yachts*:

The desire to design an offshore yacht carries with it dreams of glory—winning Gran Prix ocean racing events such as the SORC and Admirals' Cup...A yacht designed specifically to win IOR races is not ideally suited to any other purpose. In terms of performance such a yacht is slow for its size and sail plan, and not easily managed by a shorthanded crew.

Why design a yacht to the rule? Simple: As long the IOR racing game is pursued by the top talents in the sport, it is worth playing.

The yacht designer, in his effort to create the perfect yacht, has just to shed his idealism.

The J/41 was a pretty boat, with a long, sloping reverse transom. The the year 1984 started out strong. The J/41 *Dazzler* finished 3rd overall in the SORC with Bill Shore aboard. J/41's had a 1-2-3 sweep of the One Ton North Americans and Class E of the Newport to Bermuda Race, with John Kolius^ winning.

The following year was even better. Charley Scott won the 1985 SORC Overall with his J/41 *Smiles*, and the J/34 became America's best-selling IOR design, winning the IOR 3/4 Ton Division in the AYC Spring Series and placing 3rd at the 3/4 Ton NAs.

Considering that winning oats under the IOR were mostly custom one-offs to exploit the latest tweak of the IOR rule, J/Boats' IOR success, selling 44 production boats (19-41s and 25-34s), was extraordinary.

Courtesy J/Boats Inc

Merrimac, my second J/41, after *Aja*, had a sad ending, memorialized on the internet. Enter the boat's name and Sable Island.

In 1999, the third owner was sailing transatlantic to the UK. The story is: An aeronautical great-circle chart didn't show Sable Island. *Merrimac* ran right up on it. Everyone survived.

Photos taken years after the top picture (courtesy *Cruising World*) show the boat perfectly vertical, swallowed whole by the sand, with the rig still standing.

Gary Jobson had ventured onto the island to create a video history of this desolate place.

Heady stuff, this IOR. We got some impressive race results to vindicate Rod's design skills and added luster to the brand. But having sold fewer than 25 of either design was not a good return on investment (ROI) or management time. Extending our third phase by introducing the J/27 instead—or embarking earlier on the J/40 cruising design or a no-rule 40-foot racer-cruiser, like the J/120 10 years later—would have been smarter moves. The J/120 rated 22 seconds per mile faster at 48 than the J/41 at 72 (J/35 speed). We'd built a 6-foot-larger boat with no gain in speed for three times the price. Nuts! Ironic that ROI is the opposite of IOR.

J/27—Back to Basics

Getting back to sea-kindly rather than rule-kindly boats was critical in keeping TPI busy. A 27-footer seemed like the best bet to complement our stable of designs under 30 feet.

Returning from sailing my J/41 *Aja* in the 1984 Bermuda Race, I was off to Block Race Week with the just-launched prototype J/27. My job was to evaluate its performance. It was subpar.

Time to Get Creative. A bigger mainsail seemed to be the solution. Rod came up with a 3-foot-taller mast and a 1-foot-longer boom.

With that change, J/27 came alive to become the "fastest boat under 29 feet or for less than $30,000 in America." Its PHRF Rating of 132 was 42 seconds per mile faster than a J/24.

The proof was 1st overall in the 1984 MORC International Championship among 53 boats under 30 feet, with the fastest elapsed time in three of the five races.

Mission accomplished! We sold 150 J/27s in the first two years and ultimately 189 after an eight-year run. That was four times the total of our IOR designs combined. Total sales revenue was about the same, but at a fraction of the investment we quadrupled the number of happy owners.

J/33

Three years after the J/27, we introduced a baby version of the J/35, the J/33, to capitalize on our sweet spot under 40 feet.

The J/33 was a great all-around performer. Fifty-one boats were sold. The Chatains in Daybreak won the 1993 Chicago-Mac Trophy Overall.

Friend and Chesapeake Bay legend Arnie Gay said about his J/33 *Babe,* "The J/33 is tough to beat. It's the best all-round sailing boat that J/Boats ever designed."

Courtesy J Boats, Inc.

A J/33 owner from Narragansett Bay summed it up: "My boat is unbeatable in a series. Over a summer of weekends with different wind and sea conditions from light to heavy air, my J/33 will always place in the top five and win when sailed smart. The J's are better all-round, manageable boats with no bad habits."

CHAPTER 16

Satellite Navigation

While creating good boat designs for J/Boats was my primary focus, success on the racecourse depended upon good performance data. So I looked for electronics to help me and our owners win more races.

This quest led to a captivating 29-year parallel activity that helped win races and produced a high six-figure supplement to family income.

I was on the verge of marketing a satellite communication and navigation device, not unlike the iPhone, back in 1982.

In 1999 I was granted a US Patent for a handheld GPS and communication system. Such prescience makes for a good story.

So let's take a momentary break from boats to track this sideline adventure to its conclusion.

KVH—SailComp

In 1982, Martin Kits van Heyningen dropped into my J/Boats office on 24 Mill Street in Newport. He had just graduated from Yale and wanted to show me a large black 5" x 10" instrument box with multiple buttons and dials. Martin claimed it to be the first fluxgate digital compass in the world.

His father and brother had designed it in their garage. Besides Apple, J/Boats, and Amazon, here was another garage creation: KVH Industries.

Martin then proceeded to demonstrate five or more unique functions. It was impressive. But this was way more information than one could use in the fast-moving tactical situation of a sailboat race.

Quick decisions must be made. There's no time for analysis or more than a glance at an instrument.

Here was a classic case of engineering *featuritis*. It did all the stuff his father and brother conceived a digital compass could do.

Martin asked, "Would you be interested in trying one on your J/24 *Top of the World*...and maybe consider being the initial nonfamily investor in our new company, KVH Industries?"

I had just helped another Yale grad, my son Drake, get started with J/World Sailing School. So, here was another promising start-up venture.

Time to Get Creative. Putting your head down into the boat and trying to read a needle within five degrees on a conventional compass is a challenge.

"Martin, your idea of the skipper or crew being able to instantly read a compass direction when racing is fabulous. But your instrument box is too big.

"Where would I put it? We need only one big digital number showing compass direction, nothing more. And the best place for that would be where crew on the rail and skipper can all see it: mounted on the aft face of the mast, under the boom. "Martin, if you can come up with a unit about half that size, just showing compass direction in one big number, with no buttons to push, that I can bolt on the mast, I'll personally invest $5,000 in your new company and put this new tactical device on my J/24.

"But there's a caveat. With me being more than a stockholder, you'd have a testimonial. Don't you think my $5,000 investment could double my shares?"

That's how the SailComp 103 Compass came about and how I became the first nonfamily investor in KVH Industries.

KVH products are on more than 50 J/Boat models, and KVH satellite TV domes are on MJM Yachts.

When KVH went public 14 years later, my investment had grown by a 78x multiple...not to mention having helped me win a bunch of races, knowing where I was headed.

Geostar

KVH wasn't the end of my quest for better navigation and tactical data. Knowing where we were headed on a compass was helpful. But knowing where we were and our course (COG) and speed (SOG) over the ground would be even better. Tidal currents have a dramatic influence on position. Loran was state-of-the-art at the time, but rapid updates weren't possible.

Within a year, I'd read an article in *Popular Science* about a technology called Geostar. I called the founder, Princeton professor Gerard O'Neill, to learn more about his navigation system, designed primarily for aircraft. He had been motivated by a 1978 in-air collision between PSA Flight 182 and a Cessna in San Diego. As a pilot, he wanted to do something about it.

Like Loran, the Geostar system also involved triangulation, using three satellites plus radio communications to determine one's exact location more accurately.

With Geostar still under development in February 1983, I became an initial investor again. Another Martin was CEO: Martin Rothblatt, an impressive FCC lawyer.

I shared a vision with Professor O'Neill of a handheld personal transceiver for marine and recreational use with a market potential of more than 5 million units.

At the time, his plan was for a base station to keep approximate track of mobile units like trucks roaming through cell areas using AT&T's Advanced Mobile Phone Service.

Geostar didn't integrate positioning with mapping at the time. Being an early Apple Computer and portable mobile phone user, I envisioned a handheld or boat-installed device that was two way and location specific, incorporating Geostar.

I wrote Apple earlier, suggesting they consider a handheld computing, positioning, and communicating device. But I got no response. The idea was sufficiently "pie in the sky" that keeping copies of correspondence with patents in mind didn't occur to me. The iPhone appeared 24 years later, in 2007.

Eventually, I asked Professor O'Neill, "How frequently could a Geostar position fix be obtained when navigating a tricky channel into a harbor?"

He answered, "About every 30 seconds or so."

Oops! That wasn't a fast enough update for our purposes. Six knots translates to 8.8 feet per second—284 feet, or almost the length of a football field. In the fog, there could be a few rocks and missed channel markers in that space. I was looking for a display showing a boat moving across a map, not hopping all around.

Navstar had been operational for the military since 1979 and, in 1983, was authorized for use on commercial airliners by President Reagan for improved safety. In 1988, Magellan Corporation introduced the NAV 1000 handheld, and the US military had a more accurate satellite Global Positioning System (GPS).

The handwriting was on the wall. Geostar would soon be outdated by a civilian version of GPS.

Rothblatt asked if I'd become Geostar's chairman. I politely declined, as that would have been too much of a distraction from J/Boats. Former Secretary of the US Treasury William E. Simon accepted the role.

I sold out in 1989 for six times the original investment. The timing was good. In February 1991, Geostar filed for bankruptcy, selling its licenses to Motorola for the Iridium project.

Although GPS eventually upstaged Geostar, O'Neill made significant advances in position determination.

Satellite CD Radio—Sirius XM

Martin Rothblatt left Geostar in 1990 to start up his next FCC-related project. He didn't wait long to reach out to a past investor.

"Bob, I left Geostar to become the founding CEO of an incredible system called Satellite CD Radio. It's the first time I've gotten my mother to invest in anything. So I know you won't be disappointed. It's going places."

Here we go again, being an initial investor in a satellite technology company.

Time to Get Creative. This system might play a part in an integrated GPS mapping and digital communication device.

So on August 31, 1990, I agreed to make a $50,000 investment, conditional upon having the first option on channel #1. In so doing, I became one of the original investors in what morphed from Satellite CD Radio to XM Satellite Radio and then to Sirius XM Satellite Radio.

I should have held onto my 5 percent stake longer. When attending one of the initial marketing strategy meetings in Martin's offices in Washington, DC, I was not impressed by the marketing input of the major investor who was focusing solely on the new automobile market. I was pushing for a versatile, removable device for the larger used car market: a radio to plug into the dashboard, removable for a picnic or a boat. Tired of my badgering, that major investor offered to buy me out with a 4x multiple. Funds were welcome back in that 1991–'92 luxury tax era when J/Boats' income was suffering. So on November 14, 1992, I sold my shares and relinquished my option for channel #1.

Selling out was a colossal blunder, considering where Sirius XM Satellite Radio is today.

A year later, on December 26, 1993, a *New York Times* article, "The Next Wave in Radio," described CD Radio's initial test run of the system with a cartop antenna and signals emanating from rooftops to replicate future satellites. The National Association of Broadcasters warned, "This is the single greatest threat to the radio industry. Satellite broadcasting will let you drive cross-country listening to the same channel without interruption."

Worldspace

Ninety days later, I recovered my senses. On February 23, 1993, Martin was on the phone again.

"Bob, I've got my latest great satellite company for you to consider…a global version of CD Radio called Worldspace. Their system covers digital radio in the rest of the world, outside the United States."

CD Radio had licenses for just US frequencies. Worldspace was founded in 1990 to establish a global digital audio and video broadcasting (DAVB) system, providing dozens of audio programming channels to portable and mobile receivers worldwide.

The International Telecommunications Union authorized use of 1467–1492 MHz frequencies. Realizing Worldspace frequencies were close to those of GPS at 1575,42 MHz, my vision of an integrated system seemed closer.

I agreed to invest $50,000 in return for exclusive worldwide rights to manufacture an integrated GPS/Worldspace radio.

Meanwhile, my satellite company sponsor of the previous 11 years, Martin Rothblatt, informed me I should address her as "Martine" and no longer "Martin." In 1994, at age 40, with full support from her wife and children, she'd come out as a transgender woman. She became one of the highest-paid women in America as the founding chairman of United Therapeutics.

US Patent 5,898,680

My 1994 correspondence with Patent Attorney John Holmes described applications and marketing potential associated with my invention of

a closed, handheld case, or communicating network, having a Digital Radio Receiver and position location receiver such as GPS with connected/related plotter of data output and display, which may also include paging, AM, FM VHF, CB, SSB, Weatherfax, shortwave, CD player, and tape deck or any combination of these or other entertainment-information-data sources.

The product has particular application for updated and safe navigation and mapping data and/or graphics in land vehicles, aircraft and watercraft as well as carried by people engaged in outdoor sporting activities such as hiking, x-country skiing, backpacking, snowmobiling, hunting, and fishing. Commercially, there is application in surveying, organizational control, logging & forestry, fishing, and collision avoidance. Governmental interest would include military, geological, political and exploration activities.

Rather than dedicated GPS receivers, integrated digital radio permits data to be updated automatically rather than using CD discs, cards, cartridges and other portable data devices. This invention/concept may also be utilized by networking together a digital radio and GPS/plotter.

The New York Times (3/6/96) reported that AmeriSpace, the Air Force GPS system with 24 satellites, would make the post–Gulf War release of a more accurate GPS available to civilians.

Time to Get Creative. Sixty days later, I advised Worldspace of my intention to file for a patent.

On May 2, an agreement was reached whereby Worldspace would cover the cost of patent applications worldwide and provide the technical patent-writing of Joe Campanella, who would be recognized as coinventor.

I would split royalty income 50-50 with Worldspace or receive 100 percent of income from non-Worldspace radios.

The patent application was filed on November 5, 1996, for a "System for Providing Location-Specific Data to a User."

Finally, after much discussion regarding prior art, United States Patent Number 5,898,680 was granted on April 27, 1999.

A patent application was filed in 13 countries, including China, South Korea, Israel, and Japan, as well as the European Patent Office (EPO).

Satellink

In January 2002, Worldspace/RLJ licensed the patent to Satellink Technologies for use in their aircraft instrumentation systems. I invested $50,000 in Satellink.

Unfortunately, this project was closed out, and my $50,000 was returned as part of a guarantee under the licensing agreement.

On February 27, 2011, I paid the maintenance fee on the patent, having begun investigations on whether to bring suit against major electronics firms that may have infringed the invention.

Campanella had previously assigned his 50 percent interest in the patent to Worldspace. Then, having failed to pay the patent-maintenance fee and selling the business to Yazmi without my prior approval, Worldspace forfeited its 50 percent rights to the invention. So I became the sole owner of the patent rights.

After talking with several leading patent litigators in October 2011 about taking on the likes of Apple, Garmin, Google, et al. for patent infringement, I concluded the time and expense involved were so daunting that I just dropped it.

Nevertheless, I derived a great deal of nonremunerative satisfaction from being an early pioneer in satellite navigation.

1570 Compass

In late 1991, I must have imagined myself navigating at sea four centuries earlier as I became enamored with the beauty of a 1570 Italian gimbaled compass in an ivory case. This is the oldest known compass of European origin at the National Maritime Museum of the Royal Museum in Greenwich, England.

Was this the compass used by Francis Drake on his 1577–1580 circumnavigation, by Pierre LeGrand in the early 1600s, or on the Mayflower in 1620?

I wrote up a marketing plan for a replica, got Ritchie Navigation to quote on some compass parts, and visited the Royal Museum in Greenwich to discuss a licensing agreement, paying the museum a royalty on sales.

But competitors were looking to challenge J/Boats' revival of another bit of 17th-century technology: retractable bowsprits that flew flying headsails on boats called "sprit-boomers" in England. Pictured below is an old fishing boat in St. Malo, France, with the bowsprit retracted along the deck.

I concluded that it was better and more profitable for me to remain in the 21st century to focus energy and resources on our sprit-boomer revival, the J/105, and not get carried away by this 1570 Compass.

CHAPTER 17

Time to Cruise

Having been on the racing circuit for half a dozen years with everything from the J/24 to the J/41, Mary and I were inclined to relax and spend more time cruising together.

It turns out that other J/Boat owners had similar thoughts.

Yacht Racing & Cruising magazine's 1984 brand-loyalty study brought into focus the need for J/Boats to get back in touch with its base...with the needs of Baby Boomers as they were growing older, more experienced, and more dedicated to sailing.

The formula for business growth is simple. The number of new owners coming in the front door has to be greater than the number of owners leaving by the back door.

The *YR&C* study asked owners of J/Boats and 55 other brands, "What brand and size of boat do you now own, and what brand and size of boat are you likely to buy as your next boat?"

J/Boats easily won that contest, with 82 percent of J/Boat owners saying they would buy another J/Boat.

Catalina was 2nd, with 55 percent. J/Boats scored more than double the median percentage of all other sailboat brands.

My immediate response was, "How could 18 percent of our owners possibly think of switching brands? That's terrible!"

So who were we losing out to?

We could discard about half of the respondents who said, "I'm going to buy a Laser for my kids" or "A Grand Banks trawler will be our next boat."

The rest planned to move up to larger, 38-to-44-foot cruising boats, like C&Cs, Pearsons, Hinckleys, Aldens, and Sabres.

J/Boats' young racing audience was growing up. They added to their families and were ready for the next phase of their sailing life.

Time to Get Creative. We zeroed in on 40 feet, the size most sailors aspired to own, whether sail or power. *YR&C* consumer research bore that out.

J/40

J/Boats needed to grow up with and serve its loyal Boomer franchise with the ultimate 40-foot cruising boat.

The first step was to learn what these sailors looked for in the perfect 40-foot cruising design. A questionnaire was sent to over 100 experienced cruisers and J/Boat owners, listing all possible features and asking them to rank them in terms of importance and to list any we may have missed.

Our friend Bob Bavier was one of those invited.

Features of particular interest were:

✓ An aft head to be a dedicated shower, day-head, and location to hang foul-weather gear.

✓ A General Ecology Sea Gull IV water purifier. This is the best water-purifying device available and has been installed on all J/Boats and MJM powerboats with pressurized water systems and icemakers, as well as in all of our personal homes since the J/40. Public water supplies simply can't be trusted.

✓ Dorade vents for ventilation.

✓ A jackline trolley system for safety going forward on deck.

✓ Articulated backrests on cockpit seats for comfort.

✓ A molded lip on the inboard edge of cockpit seats to signal the edge of the seat when stepping off sidedecks at night.

In the fall of 1985, I called Bob Bavier to say we'd finally come up with the 40-foot cruising boat we'd discussed and wanted to give the boat a good test.

"Would you and Charlotte like to take the J/40 *Shibui* for a month in Maine, which includes the New York Yacht Club Annual Cruise... no charge?"

He responded enthusiastically, saying, "That would be great! We were just about to line up a charter."

Mary and I joined them for a couple of days cruising. Then Stu joined us for two days of racing on the club's cruise. Bob took the photo, opposite..

Bavier wrote up the experience in *Yachting* (July '87) in a very complimentary six-page feature, saying in summary: "I liked the J/40 concept on the basis that it would excite an avid racing sailor who turns to cruising and swears on a stack of Bibles never, never again to get caught up in that competitive racing gambit. The rub is that the J/40 tempts you into racing hard once again after years of imagining that was all behind you. Is that all bad?"

Bob Bavier was right. Rodney couldn't design a slow boat. Owners insisted on racing their J/40s.

Hank Bernbaum's J/40 #1 *China Cloud*, with my son Stu calling tactics, won class in the 1986 Chicago-Mackinac Race.

The J/40 became *Sailing World*'s 1986 "Best American-Built Cruiser of the Year."

We've had some wonderful J/40 owners, like Chuck and Adra Kober, past commodores of the Alamitos Bay Yacht Club. Here's how they got involved.

Chuck was presiding over a USYRU annual meeting as president. During a social hour, he confided that he and Adra dreamed of cruising the Maine coast someday.

After seeing plans for the J/40 layout and learning of its success, he asked, "Is hull #21 still available? That was the hull number of my Cal 40. If it is, I might like to own it."

"Yes, Chuck, hull #21 happens to be available. Tell you what. If you buy that boat and let us sail it, other than when you and Adra are using it, J/Boats will take care of maintenance, mooring, and delivery expense to wherever in New England you and Adra want to sail from."

We put the deal together, and the Kobers came out to Newport for *Shibui*'s June 15, 1986, commissioning on the eve of our 30th wedding anniversary. Mary's blessing during the christening is still framed on the bulkhead:

Gracious Lord, you made the seas and all that is in them.
You are the creator and preserver of all mankind.
We ask that you would bless the naming of this boat SHIBUI.
That all who sail upon her may find a sense of your peace and
contentment.
We commend to your protection the Kobers, their family and
friends,
and all those who go down to the sea in ships.
Give them a fair breeze, the joy of shared adventure
and a sense of your abiding mercy and loving kindness.
We thank you for the gift of our lives and of your abundant
blessings.
Help us to increase our faith in the giver of all good things,
Our Lord, Jesus Christ. Amen.

Sadly, 15 years later, on October 22, 2001, Chuck passed away aboard *Shibui* in Bangor, Maine, as he Adra were about to embark on a short Maine cruise.

Adra then sold *Shibui* to their friends US Navy Commander John* and Beth Bonds. John was cited for his leadership contribution to Safety-at-Sea. He was US Sailing's executive director (1988–1994) and owned both a J/24 and a J/35.

The Bonds renamed the boat *Alliance*. Nine years later, on June 8, 2010, Commander Bonds also passed away aboard.

He'd spent the day at the Navy Yacht Club getting the boat ready. He slept aboard and never woke up.

After his memorial service at the New York Yacht Club, I went aboard *Alliance* at the club dock to share a moment in memory.

His notepad was on the chart table with a few scribbled reminders of what he had to do the following day. Like sailors the world over, there's always something.

Then, seeing Mary's blessing from 24 years earlier still framed on the bulkhead below, the tears came.

RIP, dear friend. Beth Bonds carries on as owner of *Alliance*.

Pocket Cruisers

With J/40 success starting in 1985, it's not surprising we'd want to consolidate J/Boats' newfound position in the cruising world by introducing smaller models under 40 feet.

Over the next four years (1986–1989), we introduced five new designs.

Courtesy J/Boats Inc.

The first was the J/28, which did well, with 75 built. It took three designs from each of the following two hull molds to match that number: the J/34c (J/35c+J/110) averaged 30 each, and the J/37 (J/37c+J/39) averaged 25 each.

While good design extensions kept the factory running, these six designs were not particularly innovative, nor, except for the J/39, were they great performers on the racecourse.

Sales weren't better than earlier IOR designs. Prospective J/Boat buyers likely opted for the faster J/29 or J/35, figuring they wouldn't be doing that much cruising anyway.

Camping out on those barebones racer-cruisers wasn't that bad. How long a cruise are you going to take on a 28-footer?

It wasn't until Al Johnstone's first design, the J/32 (below), and a J/40 upgrade, the J/42, was introduced that sales tripled to 85 and 76, respectively.

Courtesy J/Boats Inc.

A serious 45–50 footer would have been a big step. Maybe that's why we lapsed into messing around with dinghies and small cruisers.

Cruising designs under 40 feet were more compatible with the size we'd been building and our coastal cruising habits. They also required less start-up capital.

J/Boats probably should have learned more from that *YR&C* brand loyalty research. J/Boat owners weren't leaving the brand to buy cruising boats under 40 feet. If they were going to get serious about extended family cruising, the research showed they were more likely to move up to a bigger boat.

J/44

J/40's success as the ideal coastal cruising boat led to thoughts of taking the next step up to a larger offshore cruiser.

We were constantly asked, "When is J/Boats coming out with a larger, offshore-capable design?"

The question became, "How big?" Going from 40 to 42 feet would be a typical builder "size creep." But why risk cannibalizing J/40 interest?

Wouldn't a more significant gap between models be better?

Time to Get Creative. One way to determine what people were willing to sail offshore was to analyze the size of the boat they'd be ready to sail 630 miles to Bermuda. In the 1988 Newport-Bermuda Race, the most popular size range was 42–48 feet, 45 feet being the median.

Having chartered boats of all sizes during our summer vacations in New England, I remember how intimidating it was for our young family to step aboard the 43-foot schooner *White Wing*.

The design came out at 44 feet, 10 inches long. We called it a J/44 to seem more manageable than 45 feet. That's the opposite of the practice of rounding up the number to imply the boat was bigger.

The strategy was to design a good, all-around competitive cruising boat that fit the fledgling IMS rule. IMS seemed to be a sensible, seaworthy, and cruise-worthy alternative to IOR. One could always hope! Every J/44 was built under ABS on-site survey to "Class +A1 Offshore Yacht Service."

We must credit Woodbridge friends Mike and Judy Stein for the thoughtful innovation of the "J" galley layout. The scary practice of having the cook strapped inboard of a gimballed stove in rough seas was eliminated.

Courtesy J/Boats Inc.

A secure nook was created in the crook of the "J" shaped counter with sinks amidship. A vertical fireman's pole was an excellent grab post when moving fore and aft in the boat. The galley island also served as an inboard left-foot brace for a navigator seated at the nav station when heeled on starboard tack.

Over drinks, while anchored in Cuttyhunk on the 1988 New York Yacht Club Cruise aboard the J/40 *Shibui*, Nick Brown and I agreed to become co-owners of J/44 hull #1, named *Iona*.

Her hull was being molded on February 14, 1989. I was at TPI that Valentine's Day and had an inspiration. Before the hull's black gelcoat was sprayed, I shouted over the factory din, "Wait a minute, guys! Let's get some red gelcoat and mask off a small, red heart on the transom."

Iona was commissioned at NYYC Harbour Court. Partner Nick Brown, a retired US Navy captain and a protocol officer of the New York Yacht Club, was master of ceremonies. The Reverend Mary Johnstone did the blessing.

Iona had the same color scheme as Nick's father, John Nicholas Brown's, famous 72-foot S&S Yawl, *Bolero*, which Mary had sailed on 36 years earlier in Fishers Island.

Iona got off to a great start in the 1989 season, with the fastest elapsed time in both directions in FIGAWI, the annual pursuit race from Hyannis to Nantucket.

On the return race, we were overlapped with the 12 Meter *American Eagle* after a 20-mile reach.

Then in a light-air Round-the-Island Race during the New York Yacht Club Spring Regatta, *Iona* had a faster elapsed time than two 80-foot maxis.

While it was not an official NYYC one-design, NYYC members formed the J/44 Class Association during a meeting at Harbor Court. Ultimately, the most influential and supportive was Jim Bishop, who became the J/44 fleet captain.

Jim instigated a fleet purchase of one-design sails and was the gracious host for all J/44 crews at numerous events. He was instrumental in having the J/44 become the first design ever given a separate start in the Newport-Bermuda Race.

At a later J/44 class dinner, Jim confessed, "You know why you should buy a J/44? I've done numerous Bermuda Races on custom boats in the past. Gear failures and breakages are par for the course. On my J/44 *Gold Digger*, nothing broke racing down or on the delivery back."

Jim was very generous in supporting sailboat racing. He invested in several International One-Designs to support that class and made them available to Russell Coutts to get him involved.

There were some memorable moments sailing J/44s. Four showed up for the 1989 NYYC Annual Cruise in Maine. On *Iona*, we were joined by Ken Read, Ace Bailey, and Jim Marshall to take the Royal Yacht Squadron Trophy as the overall winner of the squadron runs.

Seven boats showed up for the first J/44 North Americans in Newport that September.

1989 Cadillac Columbus Cup

Next was the 1989 Cadillac Columbus Cup in Baltimore Harbor, organized by Gary Jobson to include top America's Cup skippers from around the world.

Eight J/44 owners lent their boats and provided an owner's rep aboard. Tom Babbitt, from Camden, Maine, who had owned almost as many J/Boats as yours truly, joined me on *Iona*. We drew Russell Coutts and his crew of Kiwis.

My official role was Regatta Measurer, to keep all the boats "one design."

The first problem was Russell Coutts. I went aboard *Iona* for her inspection and couldn't walk through the main cabin. His crew took every loose item on the boat and stacked it almost to the overhead amidships. You name it…all the cushions, anchors, sails, and unhinged doors.

Shocked, I demanded, "Russell! The boats are to be left standard! All this gear has to go back where it was!"

We'd developed a method to equalize displacement: Water tanks would be emptied. Then, a person would move on deck so the tip of the transom was 6 inches above the water, measured from a dinghy. The dinghy crew would then go to the bow to measure the height of the stem from the water. That determined the weight of water needed to equal the displacement of the heaviest boat.

The last challenge was Peter Gilmour. It was down to the match race final for the championship with Coutts. Gilmour had Norwood Davis's *Prima*, the lightest J/44 built. I had come to the harbor early that last morning to recheck the initial weight equalization on the two boats vying for the title.

Prima, which had been weighted with almost full water tanks, seemed to be floating high. J/44s carried 150 gallons of water in two tanks. They'd been emptied. We checked the measurements and proceeded to add about 100 gallons (800 lbs.) of water.

Gilmour arrived and was furious. "What are you guys doing?"

"Peter, we'd equalized the displacement of all the boats at the outset. *Prima* is the lightest of all, so we'd added quite a bit of water. But when we checked her this morning, the tanks were empty."

He responded, "That's impossible. How do you know?"

We described the method. He said, "Show me"

So we went through the process again, measuring the height of the transom tip off the water. When getting to the bow, the measurement was different. It was deeper by 1/16" than the one taken earlier that morning.

We'd had to admit, "Hey, Peter. You were right. Seems we added 42 lbs. more water than needed. Your crew didn't by chance put anything aboard the boat this morning, did they?"

His sheepish answer was, "Yes, a duffel bag."

The visiting Russian crew had drawn *Glory*, owned by presidential candidate Pete du Pont. He wasn't exactly pleased when I sent him a picture of his J/44 flying the red hammer-and-sickle flag of the Soviet Union off her transom.

At the reception, Tom Whidden of North Sails commented, "You know, Bob, one of these days, we should do some business together."

Two years later, I gave Tom a call. "Tom, you remember your comment at the Columbus Cup? Well, my son Peter wants to acquire Sunfish-Laser from Pearson Yachts out of bankruptcy court in Providence, Rhode Island. But he doesn't have the capital. North Sails would seem to be the ideal partner. You could put North Sails on all those first-time sailors' boats. Are you interested?"

Tom agreed. He and Jay Hansen came to our Beechbound condo, and we put the deal together. Peter, age 25, became president and minority partner, along with Gary Jobson and Terry Sutphen.

1990 Key West Race Week

The third major J/44 one-design event was the J/44 Midwinter Championship. Competing was Bill Alcott's *Equation* with Ben Storms steering and sailmaker Mark Ploch and the Declercq brothers aboard. Jay Lutz was driving *Spoiler* for Jack Small and Doug Shaffer. Juan Vich's *Blue Monster* from Spain had Mike Toppa^, Ed Adams*, and my son Drake aboard. *Fair American* was sailed by owners Dooey Isdale^ and Skip Purcell. Jim Stanley's *Capella* and *Iona* were the other two.

Drake had joined me and others of the *Iona* crew for the Fort Lauderdale–Key West Race, which served to deliver the boat for the race week. The race started on January 10. Drake's birthday was January 11. So I hid a cake below in a cabin drawer. At midnight, I was going to surprise him with the cake.

It was a spectacular night. We were beam reaching along the keys, rail down in a westerly breeze of about 17 knots, doing 9–10 knots headed to Key West.

To get out of an adverse Gulf Stream current, we sailed as close to land as possible, in about 15 feet of depth.

The moon was bright enough to light up the bottom, so we could see seagrass clumps passing underneath. At midnight, Drake was at the helm when I came up from below with the cake.

We all sang "Happy Birthday." I asked Drake if he'd like to cut the cake for the crew.

His response was, "No thanks, Dad. The best present you could give me is letting me stay at the helm on this fantastic night."

One disaster during Key West Race Week was when *Capella* hooked *Blue Monster*'s rig in one race, breaking off the upper six feet of the mast. Unbelievably, Ben Hall, who was on *Iona*, managed to get the mast repaired and back in the boat for the following race.

Iona had three other J/44 owners in the crew: Norwood Davis of *Prima*, Pete du Pont of *Glory*, and Jim Bishop of *Gold Digger.*

Mason Chrisman provided lodging for *Iona's* J/44 owners on his DeFever 70 *Wild Goose.* J/44 owners aboard *Iona* also benefitted from a running seminar from crew members: Ken Read, Ben Hall, Ace Bailey, and Chris Bjerregaard.

Each J/44 owner on *Iona* had to host a dinner for the entire crew at one of Key West's better restaurants. I made reservations for a table of 15 at each restaurant two weeks before the event started.

Jim Bishop set the high bar for leadership, welcoming social events and creating pure fun. He chartered a 56-foot Hatteras to operate as an "Open House," with hors d'oeuvres and drinks from docking time onward. He hosted the J/44 class party onboard for nearly 100 guests.

As for fun? Late one night, a runaway horse pulling a carriage with four tourists aboard was careening down the street, with cars honking, several fenders bent, and much shouting. Then, suddenly, the horse stopped and reared up on its hind legs. The four tourists leaped or fell from the back of the carriage and beelined for the shadows of a nearby doorway, obviously experienced in evading inconvenient prosecution by local constables.

The white cap and garb looked familiar. Sure enough. It was Jim Bishop and crew on one of Key West's Wild West horse-drawn carriages.

April Fools?

There were two downers for the week. First, US Sailing's IMS Committee failed to enforce the professed goal of the IMS rule to encourage good all-around offshore cruising boats.

A new Nelson/Marek 46, *Collaboration*, virtually a pure race boat, showed up to win the IMS Class. This rule-beater had a 15-foot-long, shallow IOR racing cockpit with no seatbacks or dodger, an empty fore-peak, and only pipe berths in the aft 40 percent of the interior. There were no privacy bulkheads. Inside, lead ballast equaled 50 percent of the boat's weight, not counting its deep, 9.2-foot draft keel. A combined engine box and main cabin table seated two people.

The IMS rule became an early April Fool's joke. Trial IMS certificates were run on the USYRU computer, reversing displacements, with *Iona* at 19,000 lbs. and *Collaboration* at 22,000 lbs. The computer predicted the J/44 with no interior to be slower…and the NM46 with a full cruising interior to be faster. Go figure!

Stowaway

There was the "cat" problem. After the last race, in preparation for the trip back up to Fort Lauderdale the following day, a crew member inadvertently stuck the diesel nozzle into the holding tank, which quickly filled and overflowed. Quite the odor!

At about that time, a small cat leaped on the boat and ran below. Chris Bjerregaard cornered the cat in the stern locker but couldn't quite reach it behind hoses and wires. So we left all the hatches open so the cat could escape while we went to dinner.

Upon return, there was no sign of the cat. Good!

The following day, as we put the engine in gear, there was a momentary screech, like a slipped belt. But since it didn't persist, we assumed everything was OK.

On the sail north in the Gulf Stream, use of the aft head was unbearable. The stench was worse than spilled diesel. There was a horrid holding-tank odor mixed in. Taking off the side panel of the engine gave us the answer.

The wired coupling was just behind an 8-inch-diameter opening in the engine box for the shaft and coupling. Snared by a securing wire was a mess of catgut and gray fur. When we went to dinner, the cat must have gone through the shaft opening and crawled in on top of the warm engine to spend the night.

And when the engine started in the morning, it tried to get out and got ground up. "Argh! OK, crew, when we get to the slip in Fort Lauderdale, I'll deal with cleaning up this. You go catch your planes."

I asked the owner, whose house we were tied up behind in one of those canals, for some paper towels and a large garbage bag.

Once the mess was all contained and packed up, the next question was what to do with a bag full of dead cat parts. The owner's garbage can was out of the question. The neighbor's beagle was in a pen about five feet away.

Apologetically, I confessed what had happened and asked whether there was a dumpster nearby where we could dispose of the bag. We got into his large, early-model Cadillac and drove to the nearest shopping mall. Being the MLK Monday holiday, it was devoid of cars.

We'd be too conspicuous dropping it into a dumpster in plain sight. But there was one over behind a meat market where we could be more surreptitious about disposing of the bag.

I often wondered how the store owner would have explained that to an FDA inspector if found out.

Fortunately, *Sailing World* magazine judges were not privy to such shenanigans. J/44 became the 1990 Overall Boat of the Year.

IntraCoastal Waterway Cruising

Newport, Rhode Island, March 8, 1990—Mary and I decided to celebrate my 56th birthday with a short Florida cruise on *Iona*.

It was great! The temperatures were between 75 and 85 degrees and clear the first day, but it was a bit choppy outside. So I redid the teak cockpit sole and put another coat of polyurethane on the cabin sole.

The next day, with promoter bravado, we showed locals how easy it was for two people to sail a J/44 under full sail seven miles up the Intracoastal Waterway (ICW). We passed Bahia Mar, then went under three bridges as far as Commercial Boulevard in Lauderdale-by-the Sea. Judging by the reaction from verandas ashore and powerboaters, this was not an everyday practice!

When we'd get to a bridge, I rolled up the #2, and Mary did circles under the mainsail alone.

Berthed at Bahia Mar, we could cross the boulevard bridge to swim in the ocean, get a copy of *The New York Times* and shop in their marine store. We found the perfect teak magazine rack for the main bulkhead.

Day three started with a 2.5-hour beam each way to Miami in 12–14 knots of wind. We were faster, with less rolling than a 60-foot trawler on the same course. Miami Beach Marina was our destination, the site of the Miami International Boat Show.

By coincidence, we encountered our friend Mason Chrisman. A take-out dinner from Joe's Stone Crab ensued on the afterdeck of his 72' motor yacht, *Wild Goose* under the stars.

We had such a relaxed time playing house and reading on *Iona*. That was our only "night out." All other dinners were aboard.

We chartered a 21-foot outboard to explore Biscayne Bay, watching a Star regatta out of Coral Reef YC. We concluded, "One day was enough in a motorboat."

That anyone would own one except for interisland transport was beyond me. It required constant throttle adjustment to stay on a plane at moderate speeds and comfortably get through the relatively light chop.

Who would have guessed MJM Yachts would be in our future?

Queens Cup

Later, the J/44 *Iona* did better under a reworked IMS rule, winning the prestigious 1990 New York Yacht Club Queens Cup off Newport.

Then partner Nick Brown won the 1991 Fastnet Race under IMS.

A total of 68 J/44s were built over eight years.

One of the more ambitious exploits was the postsale delivery of Dewey Isdale^ and Skip Purcell's *Fair American* by a Belgian sailor. The new owner took advantage of the 3,000+-mile Constitution Transatlantic Race in 1991 from Cape May to his home in Nieuwpoort, Belgium.

He claimed a "J/44 record passage," crossing the Atlantic in 16 days, 4 hours to Bishop Rock, averaging 9.5 knots.

Morning Star

An excellent example of how a J/44 lived up to its cruising mission is #19 *Morning Star*, the summer home for 33 years of Dr. Daniel and Sally Benkowski's family in Northeast Harbor, Maine.

Three kids lived aboard in the early years, along with a Labrador retriever and often with visiting grandparents. That's eight living beings, about the same as a Bermuda Race Crew!

But crew capacity exceeded design limits when Sally's sister showed up for one weekend with her four kids. A total of 13 used up "every inch of floor space." You can't get any more dual-purpose racer-cruiser than that.

CHAPTER 18

Family Business

In 2018, with our three sons, Mary and I attended Harvard Business School's "Families in Business" program, a week of case studies under the leadership of Professor David Ager.

My son Peter had been impressed with the HBS "Owner's and Presidents" course he'd taken and thought this family course could help address succession and management issues being dealt with, or not, by J/Boats and MJM Yachts.

We learned that no family business is immune to disputes, disruptions, or potentially the worst-case scenario, dissolution.

It would be disingenuous to gloss over the fact that the "J" family had its share of bumpy roads like the rest.

On the bright side, the eventual solution to some brotherly differences over what the future should be helped keep the family business together and solve the more significant second-generation succession problem.

This challenge is frequently kicked down the road far too long, to the detriment of the next generation's interest in or capability of running a company.

Time to Get Creative. This story has multiple dimensions and subchapters. J/Boats Inc. functioned at three locations: Rod's design office in his house in Stonington, J/Boats' sales and marketing office in Newport, Rhode Island, and the manufacturing plant of Tillotson-Pearson (TPI) in Warren, Rhode Island.

At the outset, when it was just doing the business and selling, my office was in our harborside condo alongside Mary running Naturescapes.

Soon, we added Leslie Ehman, Tom's wife, to help out. Extra phone lines also disrupted normal life at home.

So we rented an 18th-century house at 24 Mill Street, owned by Trinity Episcopal Church. The number of J/Boats employees grew as we added Drake to manage the dealer network and Stuart to handle boat shows and regatta support. We'd invested in a Chevy Suburban as a tow vehicle.

Rod was the only one working alone. Being physically isolated from the Newport office, an hour away in Stonington, he couldn't readily share in the team's camaraderie of accomplishment.

Seven-Year Itch

The depth of Rod's frustration was evident in a memorandum in November 1984, seven years after founding J/Boats. Was this the infamous "seven-year itch"?

Rod was intent on setting up his own yacht design firm, offering to sell me his 50 percent share of J/Boats.

He would grant J/Boats the exclusive right to sell any of "his" designs, but with the caveat that J/Boats couldn't contract a third party to design, sell, or market yachts without his prior approval.

Having my hands tied like that was not motivating, and his asking price was an unaffordable multiple of Earnings before interest, taxes, depreciation, and amortization (EBITDA) at a time when we were still getting out from under the difficult '82 and '83 recession.

Time to Get Creative. Hoping Rod's creative design needs could find other outlets, an addendum to our J/Boats stockholder agreement allowed him to pursue independent design projects as long as they didn't conflict with J/Boats business or its brand of keelboats over 20 feet.

Business returned to normal for almost a year. Then, in August 1985, Fort Adams Sailing Association (now Sail Newport) reported that Rod, doing business as Johnstone Yacht Design, had presented them lines and a sail plan of a plastic 16.5-footer to be produced by O'Neill for delivery two years later, in 1987.

The problem was that J/Boats had already proposed a fleet of J/22s to them, and it was unlikely they could afford both fleets.

Johnstone Yacht Design

Ten months later, Rod resigned as an employee of J/Boats Inc., effective June 15, 1986, to become "Johnstone Yacht Design," an independent company, in return for an equitable allocation of design royalties. This was fine with me. I was willing to help Rod in any way that made sense. I'd even drafted a "press release."

But this was easier said than done. J/Boats was incorporated "to design, build, manufacture, distribute, and otherwise deal in boats and related marine equipment." J/Boats owned the "designs," not Rod.

What would his future role be in boat shows, one-design class administration, customer service, production supervision, dealer relationships, etc.? Those functions built the business and are part of a designer's responsibility under a royalty agreement. Several lawyers tackled this complex set of issues, proposing an array of formulas, none of which held much promise.

Time to Get Creative. This J/Train had to be put back on the rails. If the two founding brothers couldn't sort it out, maybe it was time for the next generation to run the show and shoulder the effort in hopes of continued success.

I approached Edwards & Angell, corporate attorneys in Providence, with an idea: If J/Boats Inc. was a Subchapter S corporation, Rod's and my income as 50 percent owners would come from a split of the profits rather than from a salary as employees. Our sons could be salaried employees. That would let Rod and me step back into "advisory" roles for design and marketing. All the officer roles and board of directors seats would go to the next generation.

The attorneys couldn't believe it. "You serious? We've never heard of such a thing. Usually, the founders at least keep seats on the board of directors."

I replied, "No, the situation has gotten to where Rod and I must step back to keep the family peace. Let the next generation mature into managing the business. I don't even want an office in the building. If I'm there, they'll never learn by having to struggle and make decisions independently. It would be too easy for them to ask me what to do. I'll contribute any marketing input at a distance from a home office like Rod is doing with his design input."

It became official during a stockholder and board of directors meeting on November 5, 1987. Jeff Johnstone, Rod's oldest son, who had been president of J/World's sailing school, became president. Stu became treasurer and VP of marketing. Drake became VP of sales, and Rod's youngest son, Alan, VP of design and production oversight. Rod's third son, Philip, would be the corporate secretary and company lawyer. Management would be compensated equally.

Johnstone One-Design

As the J/Boats corporate structure was being resolved in the summer of 1987, I shared the news with Rod that my son Peter was planning to market a 14-foot dinghy to yacht club junior programs.

After being a sailing instructor at Seawanhaka and Noroton Yacht Clubs, Peter concluded that a high-performance dinghy was needed to stimulate youth interest. He'd sketched out a Taser-like boat with sprit and an asymmetric spinnaker.

Since Rod seemed ready to take on projects outside J/Boats, I asked him if was interested in becoming involved in such a project. He declined, saying, "You can't make money with dinghies." I was inclined to agree with him.

Everett hadn't expressed any interest in having TPI build small boats. So that left Peter free of any family ties or conflict to pursue his 14-footer on his own.

While at Connecticut College, Peter shared a house with Jonathan Pudney, son of Jeremy Pudney, chairman of the International 14 Class in the UK. When "Pud" informed Peter that John Hele in Canada had a boat along the lines of what he was thinking, Peter figured it was worth investigating.

While skeptical of commercial success, I agreed to help Peter. We traveled to Toronto on July 28 to check out builder Dirk Knuelman's Ontario Yachts. That yard also built the Etchells 22, as Everett had before the J/24.

We met Jay Cross, who had designed a Cross-3 International 14 with a retractable bowsprit. John Hele owned the boat. (John later owned a J/130.) Peter liked the boat, the people, and the build quality.

Consequently, Johnstone One-Design Inc. was founded, with Peter as president and majority stockholder. Ontario Yachts was the licensed builder, and Jay Cross was the designer.

In 1987, Peter and Jay thus introduced for the first time the combined system of a retractable bowsprit and asymmetric spinnaker on a production sailboat, the One Design 14.

Retractable bowsprits to fly headsails downwind dated back to 17th-century fishing boats. The English called them "Sprit Boomers." In 1981, Australian Julian Bethwaite introduced fixed bowsprits to 18-foot skiffs to handle huge, asymmetric spinnakers more easily. In 1991, the combined OD14 system was then adopted for larger racer-cruisers by J/Boats for the 35-foot J/105. Thirty years later, there's hardly a new design on the market without that system or its variations.

JY 15

J/Boats did so well with more than a dozen designs before 1989 that we must have felt there was spare time to mess around as hobbyists in the less profitable pursuit of small dinghies.

In 1989, there were 11,963 boats registered nationally under the Performance Handicap Rating Formula (PHRF), which accounted for about 90 percent of all offshore racing boats in America. Forty-two percent of the top 10 new designs introduced between 1976 and 1986 and registered with PHRF were J/Boats. That's four times the nearest competitors.

With time on his hands and possibly motivated by his nephew's OD14 project, Rod erected frames in his Stonington garage to build a 14.5-footer, which became the JY 15.

I wasn't happy with the "JY" on Rod's sail, particularly when he eventually contracted the boat to be built and distributed by Hunter Marine, a brand low on the value scale.

To Rod's credit, however, the JY 15 was introduced in 1989 and succeeded to the tune of about 3,500 boats. He created a family-friendly design and made it available through a high-volume builder to outsell his nephew's One Design 14 by about 10 to 1.

The One Design 14 probably wasn't helped by dual messaging as being the "ultimate" high-performance dinghy with double trapezes, as well as the ideal yacht club junior boat.

Two different rig configurations were offered. Like the Melges 24, it was too much of a hotrod for broader family acceptance.

But we can thank Peter for taking the initiative with the sprit and asymmetric spinnaker system. Ultimately, in 1991, the One Design 14 set the stage for J/Boats to take its innovative leap with the J/105 among racer-cruisers.

It's interesting to note, 30 years later, that the 2021 Sailing World Overall Boat of the Year became the Melges 15, a boat similar to the standard One-Design 14 with a large asymmetric spinnaker but without the trapezes.

Peter acknowledges that this more focused family approach for the One-Design 14 would probably have resulted in much greater success.

Sailing Women

While on family businesses, mention should be made of our daughter Helen's initiative in the sailing world. She was a star, lots of fun to be around, and remarkably coordinated. I remember her falling off the top of a bathroom sink she'd somehow climbed at age 3. In midair, she flipped and landed on her feet! Unbelievable!

Helen was a good figure skater who once easily scored a hat trick in a boy's hockey game. She placed 6th in the International Women's Keelboat Championship.

After I helped Stu and Drake with J/World Sailing School and involvement with J/Boats, then Peter with Johnstone One-Design, I was delighted to help Helen in her quest to create Sailing Women.

Several regional chapters were set up, and the Sailing Women team made some excellent presentations at the 1988 USYRU community boating conference at Lake Arrowhead, California. For one reason or another, the concept never took hold.

While it lasted, this project was a lot of fun, with a team of cousins pictured above (L to R: Louis Rose, Wendy Burkhalter Eck, me, Susan Burkhalter Green, Helen, Mary).

Helen packed more joy and action into her 47 years than most people do in a lifetime. Yes, only 47 years. This chapter in our lives had a sad ending, as described by Mary:

Sadly, the ultimate expression of Helen's love was to profess not to burden the family with her ongoing frustrations and battles with addiction to prescription drugs and repeated need for institutional care by taking her own life on June 4th of 2008 on the Potomac River.

That was a traumatic period for our whole family. With faith and learning and a lot of conversations, we survived. The rest of us: myself, Bob, Stuart, Drake, and our youngest, Peter, all took part in Helen's memorial service at Newport's Trinity Church, full of friends and family.

It was our 52nd wedding anniversary. We all sang our hearts out. The choir concluded the service with John Rutter's beautiful "Gaelic Blessing."

She is memorialized by the perpetual trophy for the top woman skipper in the J/70 World Championship. It's called the "Heli," her nickname in the family and with many friends. One of her best friends, Heather Gregg, won it the first year.

CHAPTER 19

Sprit Revolution

The US Congress was a greater threat to business than the IMS committee. The October 1990 luxury tax was intended to reduce the federal budget deficit during a weak economy. This was a 10 percent added sales tax on all vehicles, boats, and planes costing more than $100,000.

Lawmakers don't get it. It's counterproductive to tax products with high labor content, as massive labor layoffs result. Sales dropped for the marine industry nationwide, putting thousands out of work who might otherwise pay taxes. The state government doesn't get sales tax revenue when no sales exist.

The 1990 J/Boats dealer meeting was at our Beechbound condominium overlooking Newport Harbor. The subject of the economy and lack of boat sales took away from the glorious view of boats and Newport Bridge.

There was consensus: we needed a new boat design to generate excitement and get people back into dealerships.

Time to Get Creative. Sail-away pricing had to be less than $100,000, where the luxury tax kicked in. Would the answer be another '82 recession gambit, stripping down an existing model?

Consistent with our "cruising" emphasis of the previous 14 years, Rod lobbied for a low-priced 30-foot cruising boat with a base price of $70–$75,000 to be a smaller version of the J/34c, or possibly a J/28 with fewer features for a $55,000 base price.

Everett was on board with the idea. Sales were plummeting, and he was anxious to keep the factory humming.

The trouble, however, with a cheap 30-foot cruiser was that first-time younger buyers of such entry-level designs were losing their jobs and unlikely to burden family finances with boat loans.

Wealthier buyers, who could afford to buy a larger boat outright, were also holding back due to sheer cussedness about paying the 10 percent tax and/or not wanting the embarrassment of buying a new yacht while laying off employees. They could afford to downsize but would not likely buy a cheap, 30-foot cruising boat.

J/105 is Born

The idea of installing a One Design 14-type retractable bowsprit and asymmetric spinnaker system on a 30-to-40-foot J/Boat was compelling. Downwind sailing could be made easier and safer for a cruising couple. When racing, there's less need for an experienced foredeck crew.

Mary's and my biggest challenge cruising larger J/Boats was safely sailing fast downwind. We didn't like using the engine. If you turn on the engine to go 7 knots downwind, sailing in a 7-to-10-knot following breeze, the boat and its exhaust will go the same speed in an ever-building cloud of exhaust.

On our J/36, we'd put up a large spinnaker in light-moderate air to avoid that scenario. But if the wind built to 15 knots or more, we had to get it down. Dealing with sheets, guys, topping lift, foreguy, pole, and all that sail was challenging for one person.

A retractable bowsprit with an asymmetric spinnaker that a "snuffer" sock can quickly douse with the pull of a single line would be the answer, although maybe it was too radical for acceptance by reactionary sailors.

Would it work as the primary and only downwind sail on a 35-footer? The concept of using asymmetric spinnakers on larger boats was not new. Team New Zealand had begun using them on America's Cup Designs to be competitive in light air, flying the sail from a mast-mounted spinnaker pole lashed down to the stem at deck level.

The June 1991 promotional brochure for the J/65 design that Rod was developing with Sir Peter Blake at the time, while not showing any bowsprit in the plans and listing two conventional carbon spinnaker poles in the specifications, included running rigging and hardware for use with an asymmetric spinnaker...presumably for light air.

Having sold my interest in the J/44 *Iona* to partner Nick Brown, I was wondering what to sail next. I had dealt with the logistics of managing a crew list of upwards of 30 people to be sure there were 8–10 on a J/35, or more on a J/44 for the next race. It was nearly a full-time job.

Did I want to go back to another J/35? No. I'd given up trying to persuade J/35 owners to change class rules to limit crew numbers and sail purchases. Even so, having another J/35 was tempting. Transatlantic solo sailor Tony Lush and I had won the New England Solo-Twin race in J/35. The boat was easy and fun to sail with two people, particularly upwind, with a 100 percent working jib.

Of course, downwind was a different and dicey matter. Why have 10 sails and a crew of 9 people to have fun on a 35-footer?

A J/35 is noticeably more sea-kindly than a J/30 offshore in waves. I'd gotten to like the wheel on the J/44, being able to stand up while sailing downwind, not worried about the boom hitting me on a jibe.

Would the J/Boats team of designer, dealers, builder, and staff at the meeting buy into a 35-footer with a bowsprit and asymmetric spinnaker? Time to find out.

I asked the group, "OK, team, how about a sporty 35-footer with a modest weekending interior, J/29 headroom, cockpit seats, wheel, retractable carbon-fiber bowsprit, asymmetric spinnaker, three-sail limitation, no overlapping jib, and a crew weight limitation approximating five guys?

"We sold the original J/35 for a $49,500 base seven years ago. That's $65,000 in today's dollars, meaning the new boat can sail away for under $100,000.

"If this boat can get people with money excited, they can tell their employees they're cutting back on their boat expenses."

Predictably, the response was less than enthusiastic. As we learned with the J/24, dealers are the last people you want to ask whether a radical new design will succeed. They generally can't see beyond what some competing dealers sold last year.

Rod and Everett still favored a cheap 30-foot cruiser. But a slim majority of dealers got excited, saying, "Such a boat could sell. It fits the J/Boat performance image. It's different. That huge spinnaker will attract attention.

"The idea of a simple sail plan with a nonoverlapping headsail and a J/24-type crew-weight limitation should be a breath of fresh air to owners of 35-footers, who won't find it so hard to find crew."

The concept was endorsed by my two sons. Peter faxed sketches of an International 14–looking 23-footer labeled a J/7.0 with a 5-foot vertical bulb keel and 7-foot retractable bowsprit. My son Stu had sent a similar drawing from the UK. He had campaigned a One-Design 14 with Cam Lewis in the Darden's Ultimate Yacht Race series.

The next marketing challenge was, "OK, how will we label such a new and different model? We've run out of numbers in feet: 33-34-34c-35-35c-36."

Time to Get Creative. One idea was "J Sport." But that or other names, like "Laser" or "Sonar," were discarded for being a departure from the "J/" with a number strategy for advertising efficiency.

"OK, so how about going metric to be more modern? Wouldn't decimeters make the boat seem larger? There's an *Aphrodite 101* now in Europe. Suppose we use decimeters for this boat and any future sprit boats? That distinguishes them from our nonsprit designs in feet. Besides, there are many more decimeters than feet or meters, so we could keep launching boats for a lifetime and not run out of three-digit numbers."

A majority vote carried the day. J/105 was chosen. It was fun to imagine a new owner telling friends at a cocktail party, "I just bought a new J/105."

Courtesy J/Boats Inc.

Imagine the reaction. "He bought a 105-foot J/Boat! Where'd he get that sort of dough?"

Some were not persuaded, including the designer. A short-lived, post-meeting uprising among the dealers took some persuasiveness to quell.

But Rod came through with a good hull design. As part of being so new, sailmakers had a new challenge of coming up with the ideal asymmetric spinnaker shapes for downwind sailing. Their initial efforts, evolving from the One-Design 14 and light-air designs for America's Cup boats, produced effective reaching shapes. The leech was more open than the fuller shape needed for deep-running angles on a displacement keelboat.

The initial J/105 class rules required using a "snuffer" sock over a 77-square-meter asymmetric spinnaker. After the first season, owners grumbled about the "snuffer rule" and downwind performance. We dropped the snuffer requirement and successfully lobbied owners to increase chute size by 16 percent to 89 square meters.

At the 1991 Annapolis Boat Show, we put on quite a show with the J/105. Whenever traffic was slow, we hoisted the asymmetric spinnaker, which could be seen all over the show. People flocked to see what those crazy people over at J/Boats were doing. We were using an ATN snuffer sock to gobble it up safely.

At the outset, this system was so different it was looked upon as a novelty instead of a miraculous innovation to make downwind sailing easier.

The J/105 became *Sailing World*'s 1992 Racer-Cruiser Boat of the Year.

Fifteen years later, the 2007 Royal Ocean Racing Club named it Boat of the Year, sailing all events double-handed.

After owning two J/105s in Newport in 1992 and 1993, I was then into campaigning J/80 #1 *Mojo* and J/120 #15 *Tern* in 1994. It's nice having a new boat every year!

In Maine, from 1995 to 1997, we had J/42 #1 *Gannet*, J/42 #15 *Gannet 2*, and J/120 #70 *Gannet 3*. When we moved to Charleston in 1998, it was time to start a J/105 fleet, and while there, we had three more J/105s: #224 *Camelia*, #304 *Tern*, which won Key West Race Week in 1999, and #500 *Tern*, which won both 2000 Key West Race Week and the SORC.

The design's inclusive appeal was highlighted by *Sailing Scuttlebutt*'s August 21 report on the inaugural J/105 Ontario Women's Championship at the Royal Canadian Yacht Club, with 12 J/105s and 96 competitors ranging from Olympians to local sailors aged 15 to 70.

After racing, competitors transformed from sweat and grit to glitz and glamour with long evening gowns for a spectacular island-sunset dinner. It was champagne sailing, with tight racing, a large spectator fleet, and a different winner in each race.

Women's championships are planned for the other large J/105 fleets in Annapolis and San Francisco.

As for J/105 seaworthiness, Christian Repard's *Bigfoot* won Royal Malta Yacht Club's Middle Sea Race around Sicily in 1996, finishing 7th boat-for-boat after sailing for more than 117 hours. He had this to say after rounding Pantelleria:

The wind increased to the point we were doing 16 knots on the GPS…In the pitch darkness, I thought that steering would be difficult in large waves, if not stupid to attempt, but as we increased speed, control improved. The 100-mile fetch back to Malta with reefed main and blade jib was a rough ride. The J/105 was doing 8–8.5 knots. We harnessed ourselves in as large waves swept right over the boat. The "Mistral," the NW howler, had come into force with big seas and 30–35 knots of wind. Even in these conditions, it was very comfortable to sleep below. Once in the bunk, it seemed like it was calm outside. We were sailing faster than the Swan 47 and Beneteau First 42S7.

Cruising a J/105? We've known owners who couldn't resist racing the ultimate 40-foot cruising boat, a J/40. The opposite has occurred with owners converting their J/105 into a cruising boat. Pictured in St. Augustine, Florida, is the J/105 *Eagles' Wings* complete with a wind generator, Bimini, dodger, dinghy on davits, and lazy jacks.

The J/105 has become the most popular one-design racing class over 30 feet in the world with over 700 boats in more than 15 fleets, one as far away as Puerto Montt, Chile.

Melges 24

J/Boats didn't focus on a smaller 23-to-24-foot sprit boat until the J/70 two decades later. Our commitment to strengthening J/22 and J/24 fleets weighed heavily on any decision to drop a new design into that size range.

We focused on building owner loyalty and maximizing the size of J/Boats' racing fleets to ensure long-term resale value. The J/22 had recently (1990) become J/Boats' second IYRU-recognized International Class, and the J/24 was still going strong.

But by staying away from the smaller-boat market, we'd left the barn door open for competition to enter this larger-volume market, which was closer to Australian 18-foot skiffs and One-Design 14s, where the concept originated. A quick, smaller boat with few crew could now handle big, asymmetric spinnakers.

A friend and J/Boats dealer was the first to step in: Melges Boat Works of Zenda, Wisconsin. Buddy was a J/Boats Midwest dealer for 15 years. Mutual Soling friend Jack Van Dyke persuaded him to visit Stonington in 1977 to sea-trial a J/24. His reaction? "This is nothing but a scow with beds." Melges thus became a J/Boats dealer.

Fast forward to the 1990 USYRU Championship of Champions Regatta at the Rush Creek Yacht Club in Texas in One-Design 14s. Buddy's sons, Hans and Harry, were competing. My son Peter had arranged through his dealer, John Kolius^, to supply the fleet of OD14s for the event.

At one point, Hans Melges said to Peter, "It would be minting gold if this sprit and A-sail system were put on a keelboat." Harry and Steve Rosenberg, overhearing the comment, agreed. So I wasn't the only one in 1990 thinking along those lines.

Following the J/105 in 1991, we introduced the "J/92 for '92." Melges Boat Works ordered a stock J/92 named *Zenda Express* for Hans and Harry to campaign on Lake Michigan.

They were so impressed that they talked the old man into adapting the system for E-Scows and had Reichel/Pugh design the Melges 24.

To get started, their project got a little help from my son Stuart, who was in England running J/Europe.

Melges, our Midwest dealer, had taken two J/39s as trade-ins upon selling a J/44 and a J/47 (a customized J/44). The resulting inventory burden of $350,000 for the two trade-ins prevented Melges from sourcing funds for the 24-foot project.

Stu solved their problem. He brought in two customers from Ireland, the O'Reilly brothers. They'd become interested in J/39s after J/35s and J/39s had swept CHS (1-2-3-4) at the 1991 Cowes Week.

After flying to the US with the prospects and getting them signed up, Stu called the bank, saying, "Sale of the two J/39s is confirmed." Funds were released for Melges to proceed with their lift-keel, carbon-rigged 24-footer.

The Melges 24 was launched for the 1993 summer season to become *Sailing World*'s 1994 Overall Boat of the Year, the same year J/Boats got the hat trick for its third sprit design. The J/130 was named *Sailing World*'s 1994 Best Multipurpose Club Racer of the Year.

My initial reaction to Melges Boat Works becoming a direct competitor was to cancel them as a J/Boats dealer. But this wasn't all bad news. Having Buddy and Reichel/Pugh also promote a sprit design contributed to broader acceptance of the concept than if it were being promoted by J/Boats alone.

The sailboat market is very reactionary and slow to adopt new ideas, even when they make sense, so the more reputable sources pushing the use of a new system, the better.

Sailing World helped. The first four sprit boats introduced to the market all won accolades as Boat of the Year.

J/24—US-5000

The 1992 J/24 World Championship was scheduled for Annapolis, and I was psyched to sail US-5000 in the event. Rod and I, as founders, were automatic entries. I named the boat *5000* with a large graphic on each side. The zeroes were maps of hemispheres where J/24 fleets existed.

I may have been runner-up to Ed Baird* at the 1983 Worlds in Malmo, Sweden, nine years earlier, but I was under no illusion regarding my current J/24 skills. They would need work, and who better to help than the local world champ?

I called Kenny Read*. "Ken, you must get me up to speed driving a J/24 again. Can I join you on for a sail one day?"

He replied, "Sure, we've got to check some sails. Bill Shore is driving a coach boat. Josh Belsky is doing bow with Betsy Allison* in the cockpit. You can start as the middle man."

Translated, "This 58-year-old could flop back and forth over the hump of the deck under the vang."

It was a windy, 15-to-20-knot NW breeze. We'd been at it for about an hour. I was getting beat up pretty badly, flopping like a seal on a rock, trying not to slide overboard. Josh went around the mast on tacks. Betsy had the easy route through the cockpit. Still no helm time for me.

Finally, Ken turned over the helm to me for the sail back to Sail Newport's hoist. I didn't learn much about making US-5000 go fast at the Worlds.

But I gained an appreciation for how the J/24 had abused the crew for the past 15 years. My first thought was, "Apologies for all the black and blue it may have caused. How could we have perpetrated such a monstrosity on the world...let alone have it become the most popular one-design racing keelboat ever?"

J/80

Time to Get Creative. The second thought was, "Never again! The next small boat for J/Boats will have rolled side tanks, a long cockpit, and no cabin trunk to crawl over. The entire crew can simply stroll across the cockpit to the other side on a tack."

About a day later, I asked the J/Boats team, "Why not introduce a new, smaller sprit boat under 30 feet? And do it ASAP, before the Melges 24 gets too much of a head start?"

Melges 24 interest was high, but we had doubts it would get traction with local fleet formation. The boat seemed too extreme in terms of athleticism for all family members to comfortably handle it...like a One-Design 14 with a keel. Melges owners must travel to regional or national regattas to get good racing.

A more inclusive, family-friendly design from J/Boats could give the Melges 24 a run for its money worldwide. The J/80 was thus born and became the first production sailboat to be SCRIMP-built (Seemann Composites Resin Infusion Molding Process).

Everett arranged with Bill Seeman for TPI to be the licensee to develop the process further. Woven cloth/mat fiber and core materials are placed in the mold dry. A bag is placed over it all. Then the resin is drawn in by a vacuum through many tubes to create a void-free and tough laminate.

Sailing World commented, "The J/80 is easier to handle, less intimidating, safer, and better suited for sailing offshore than other modern sport boats tested." Two Swedes must have read the article. They crossed the Atlantic in a J/80.

I remember sailing a J/80 single handed under spinnaker back 20 miles from Block Island Race Week to Newport in 1993. The boat is so user friendly it has become the design of choice of J/World Sailing School to attract first-time sailors.

Courtesy J/Boats Inc.

In Europe, where it was also built (and before the introduction of the J/70 20 years later), the J/80 became the largest one-design fleet at events such as Spi Oeste in France. There were 117 boats at the 2013 World Championships in Marseilles.

The Spanish J/80 Class has more than 145 boats. The Real Club Nautico de Barcelona, site of the 2024 America's Cup, alone has a fleet of close to 30 boats.

Courtesy J/Boats Inc.

There's something to be said for the importance of an all-round, easy-to-handle, fast, family design with offshore capability. J/Boats' design philosophy has resulted in 1,675 J/80s worldwide. Add to that 1,705 of the newer, 23-foot J/70s, with close to 100 more on order.

The total J/Boats delivered in the 23-26-foot sport boat category is 3,480. That's four times the number of Melges 24s, the latest being #866 *Zenda Express.*

J/Boats took 20 years (until 2012) to introduce that smaller sprit boat. But it was worth the wait. At the 2022 Charleston Race Week, J/70s outnumbered Melges 24s by a wide margin of 78 to 14.

J/120

The J/120 is arguably the most successful 40-foot one-design racer-cruiser ever built. With 230 launched, that's nearly double the number of Farr 40s, triple that of the J/40, and more than the 144 Cal 40s or the 200 venerable Hinckley Bermuda 40s.

J/120 was born of a defensive strategy: "Let's not lose a large market segment by waiting too long to introduce a 40-foot sprit boat, a size many people aspire to own."

Time to Get Creative. We'd overshot the mark coming out with the J/130 first. We built only 43.

We learned our lesson when scooped by the Melges 24 with the smaller boat. Regarding a 40-footer, J/Boats lost no time in getting the first J/120 launched in January 1994 for the Miami International Boat Show. We offered a carbon rig option for the first time.

As a measure of performance progress among 40-footers with cruising interiors, going back through the decades: the J/120 rates 54 seconds per mile (s/m). That's 30 s/m faster than the J/40 (84 s/m), 66 s/m faster than the Cal 40 (120 s/m), and 90 s/m faster than the Bermuda 40 (144 s/m).

A boat going 6 knots travels 10.2 feet per second. The J/120 would be three football fields (918 feet) ahead of a Bermuda 40 after sailing a mile. Pretty dramatic! No wonder she outsold our J/40 nearly 3 to 1.

One of the most enjoyable experiences Mary and I had was working with the Moorings Charter Company to set up a fleet of ten J/120s at the Moorings in Tortola. This joint venture, including J/World Sailing School and North Sails, promoted "Round-the-Islands Race Weeks in a Virgin Island Paradise."

The 1998 schedule offered one-design racing at five major Caribbean regattas, including Antiqua Race Week, and six BVI Round-the-Islands Race Weeks. Putting the program together involved a couple of trips to Tortola and working with an outstanding Moorings staff. The yacht clubs that took advantage of the program came away thrilled and signed up for a repeat the following year.

The program was discontinued when not enough clubs participated. Most likely, racing against people you see all year was not appealing to those wanting relaxed fun in the sun.

People frequently ask me, "What's your favorite J/Boat?" My standard answer is, "Since I have a choice of all of them, it must be the one I'm sailing now." The fun of this business is creating a better boat for ourselves that doesn't exist in the market.

That was certainly true of the J/120. I went from J/120 #15 *Tern* in 1994 to J/42 #1 *Gannet* in 1995. Then, after owning a pair of J/42s, I returned to J/120 #73 *Gannet 3*. My third J/120 was #9 *Gannet 4* in 2002, followed by three J/105s in Charleston, then J/125 #1 *Wings of the Wind* in Maine, plus another J/42 #61 *Iona*.

David Janes's J/120 came as close to a "clean sweep" as anyone could expect of a 40-foot sailboat. His *J-Bird* corrected out to 1st in fleet in the Puerto Vallarta Race, more than half a day ahead of the other 22 boats in the racing division.

Part of that margin was due to a staggered start over two days. But in the 15 races since the event began in 1971, only three other boats have managed this feat. All were 70-footers. Janes followed his strong performance with *J-Bird* in the MEXORC with a 1-1-2-2-1 series to earn the Copa Rolex Trophy watch.

J/120s went 1-2-3 in the 1998 Ensenada Race. The fleet in Southern California numbers 28 boats. Other accolades include the 1995 *Cruising World* Overall Boat of the Year and Best Value in a Full-Size Cruiser.

Chuck Townsend won the New York Yacht Club's Queens Cup in 2002 with his J/120 *T-Squared,* and Ben Hall and I won the New England Solo-Twin overnight race in *Tern.*

I had taken J/120 #9 as a trade-in on a J/32 from friend Cesar Rojas from Cartagena, Colombia. He wanted to do some cruising in Florida with his grandchildren. We won many races with that latest *Gannet,* including DownEast RaceWeek and Charleston Race Week. Ultimately, #9 became *Crosswave* and was sold to its fourth owner, Wayne Zittel, who ran J/World Performance Sailing School in San Francisco.

Excerpts from an article by Eugenie Russell, entitled "Suddenly Gone," in the August 2020 *SAIL* describe its fate:

In the annual Baja-Ha-Ha race from San Diego to Cabo San Lucas...At 1000, Ray shouted, 'Whale ahead!'...We tried to steer slowly to windward to sail clear of them...Seconds later, there was a loud BANG! amidships. The boat stopped. Another BANG followed further aft, pushing the stern up and to starboard with a CRACK and RRRIP of tearing fiberglass. Lifting the lazarette hatch, the rudderpost swayed back and forth with water pouring in through a large hole in the bottom where the bearing used to be. A large wave crashed over us. Stuffing sail bags and the manual pump were not enough. It was time to inflate the liferaft...it got jammed under the lifeline.

The cockpit suddenly disappeared under my feet. Seconds later, the Windex at the top of the mast went past my face. The boat was gone, along with the liferaft! We were all swimming. Suddenly the liferaft pops back up. The painter had broken free from the pressure valve on the hydrostatic release. We all climbed aboard and made a Mayday call on the handheld VHF. After an hour, we heard the Coast Guard helicopter, which confirmed on Channel 16 they saw us. A rescue swimmer dropped into the water. He explained the procedure for us all to be lifted into the chopper. It took about 45 minutes...

J/120s continued their winning ways 28 years after their introduction. Michael Fozo and Robin Kendrick's J/120 *Proof*, with Wally Cross aboard, smoked the 2022 Chicago-Mackinac Race overall by 1.5 hours. Runner-up was Bill McKinley in his Ker 46 *Denali^3*. Bill is a J/70 owner and former MJM 50z owner.

In 3rd third place was Mitchell Padnos in his Club Swan 42 *Sufficient Reason*. The last time a J/Boat won was Mitch and Tracy Brand's J/122 *Sufficient Reason* in 2013. So you could say the top three finishers are/ were J/Boat owners.

J/160—World Beater

Photos courtesy of J/Boats Inc.

Following the success of the J/120, a larger oceangoing cruiser seemed to make sense. Since the mid-40s were addressed with the J/130 and J/44, a larger 50+ footer was decided upon. The resulting J/160 (52.5 feet), with its well-appointed interior, became the 1997 *Sailing World* "Big" Boat of the Year.

Miami owner Dr. William "Scott" Piper III traded in his J/40 *Pipe Dream VIII* for J/160 *Pipe Dream IX* to record thousands of miles on multiple globe-circling voyages.

Pipe Dream hit 55-knot gales off the Cape of Good Hope in the Agulhas Current, where huge, square waves are known to crack freighters in half. He motor-sailed with feathered reefed mainsail at 10 degrees apparent, doing 7–8 knots right into the seas. He was awarded the 2008 Cruising Club of America Blue Water Medal, having logged over 180,000 miles. On three separate occasions, he logged 1,000 miles over four days to win a division of the Expo '98 Round the World Rally.

Among 35 built, *Kativa* was the first to finish the 1996 Isla Mujeres Race. *Bushwhacker* won the 1997 Puerto Vallarta Race.

J/160s continue to do well in offshore races. Howard Hodgson had moved up from his J/42 *True* to his J/160 *True* to take 3rd in class in the 2022 Newport to Bermuda Race

As an aside, Howard now owns the "lobsteryacht" *Java*, which was an inspiration for modifying my Dyer 29 and the styling of MJM Yachts 20 years ago.

CHAPTER 20

Down Easters

M ary had a higher calling than being CEO of Naturescapes Inc.
After serving as deacon and hospital chaplain in the Diocese
of Rhode Island; she believed being a priest would better fulfill her
pastoral mission.

The standing committee and Bishop Hunt supported her calling and enrollment in Berkeley Divinity School at Yale.

What would happen to our marriage and family life if Mary was going to spend most of the next two years away in New Haven?

Time to Get Creative….on the home front once again.

An "every day but Monday" solution evolved. We rented married-student quarters on the Yale Divinity School campus. Mary drove the two hours back to Newport from New Haven on Friday after classes. We'd spend weekends together, and she served as a deacon at Trinity Church on Sundays. Then, Sunday afternoon, Mary drove back to New Haven. I'd drive to New Haven for dinner with Mary on Tuesdays after work and stay Tuesday and Wednesday nights. With a briefcase full of work, I had the serenity of our divinity school apartment all day Wednesday to get caught up.

After breakfast Thursday, I'd drive back to J/Boats in Newport for a full day's work. So the only day of the week we didn't see each other for a meal was Monday. Who wants to see anyone on a Monday? I only missed a single weekday at J/Boats.

We did this for two years. Mary graduated in 1989 with a master of arts in religion and was ordained as an Episcopal Priest at Trinity Church on June 24, where she became assistant rector.

Upon the departure of Rector Lorne Coyle, the vestry called Mary to be the interim rector.

Episcopal canons dictate that no matter how talented or popular she might be, a priest cannot be called as rector by the vestry in the same church where she has served as assistant or interim.

In 1994, Mary had been on the shortlist for rector at St. Gabriel's in Marion, Massachusetts, and St. John's, Lafayette Square, the "Church of the Presidents," in Washington, DC. That's the church made famous in 2020 by then-President Trump holding the Bible upside down.

Ultimately, Mary was called by the Bishop of Maine to become the "Vicar of Boothbay" in 1994. If that sounds like a new TV show…it could have been.

It was time for me to go into the support role. After all, Mary had been supporting me in my professional moves for the previous 38 years.

I was still functioning as the strategic marketing partner and 50 percent owner of J/Boats Inc. Having a phone, fax, and computer in Maine, I could fulfill my role at J/Boats, figuring out what the next "J" should be. No need to be physically present in Newport.

With the second generation managing the J/Boats office in Newport, my moving to another seaport town was another opportunity to give them further independence.

From our remodeled waterfront Maine "farmhouse," we looked down onto the Boothbay Harbor Yacht Club (BHYC) anchorage.

It didn't take long after hearing BHYC was considering the purchase of a fleet of Ideal 18s for me to swing into action to promote the six-boat fleet of J/22s described earlier.

J/42

As a new Downeast Mainer, one of my goals was to create a "proper" cruiser for J/Boats. We'd designed some excellent cruising boats in the prior nine years, starting with the J/40. But with its IOR-type reverse transom, people would pass our J/Boats display at shows, lift their noses, and say, "Oooh, forget it! Those are just race boats."

Time to Get Creative. To overcome this stigma, sailors at the Boothbay Harbor Monday Men's Luncheon became my sounding board. I'd present them each Monday with the latest plans or sketches of J/40 variants, a different deck, keel, transom, cabin trunk, mast, interior layout, etc. Then I'd pester them the following week. "OK, how about this one? Is this more what you'd expect of a proper Downeast Cruiser?" J/42 became a product approved by a committee, not designed by one…an important distinction.

Our J/42 #1 *Gannet* was launched in June 1995, named after the beautiful steamboat first used to seed the Maine Coast with baby lobsters in the early 1900s.

J/42 is arguably the best "couples" cruiser ever. With carbon mast and modern low CG keel, it handles like a 35-footer with the stability of a 50-footer.

Onne van der Wal Photo

J/42 is what modern cruising boats should be. Her stability index of 139 degrees and righting moment of 1,792 foot-pounds is only approached by the Navy 44s. The vertical center of gravity (VCG) is 1.4 feet below the waterline. Her modest keel draft was only 6.6 feet.

J/42 ranks first on that important indicator for control in large waves and heavy wind offshore: a length-to-beam ratio of 3.4. vs. the 3.0 or less on designs that fared poorly in the '79 Fastnet Storm.

Princeton '56 college classmate, fellow Sears Cup finalist, and founder of the Hurricane Outward Bound School Peter Willauer purchased a J/42, *Eight Bells,* and lived aboard for eight years, doing several transatlantic crossings.

I love that boat (I owned three) and remember one voyage aboard *Gannet* en route to the Annapolis Boat Show:

September 30—Offshore, Newport to Cape May, New Jersey. The wind was ENE gusting to 25 knots, clear, shimmering sea. It must be what heaven is like! Surfing down waves was such fun driving that we turned off the autopilot. With full main and small jib wing-'n-wing, we consistently exceeded 12 knots, hitting a high of 14.6 knots. The average speed over 20 hours was 9+ knots. That bettered our prior 8+ knot average in 16 hours from Boothbay to the Cape Cod Canal. There was never water on deck—very smooth motion. I took a shower and toweled off in the main cabin without holding on. Oriental throw rugs were still on the floor from the Newport Boat Show. The flower arrangement from the show, on the shelf over the port settee, never tipped over.

After a successful summer season racing in Maine, we sold J/42 #1 and ordered #15 *Gannet II* to be launched in June 1996. The family powerboat saga began that month. More later.

Ultimately, we sold 77 J/42s, almost as many as the 86 J/40s. That combined total of 162 is ten times that of IOR J/41s sold.

But first, to allay any impression my sailboat racing DNA and search for speed had faded into the sunset or been overcome by laid-back cruising: there was the J/Boats' business of larger and faster sailboats to attend to.

CHAPTER 21

More Speed & Comfort

K nowing Everett Pearson's high-tech building capability and not wanting J/Boats to play second fiddle to anyone regarding performance, Rod was intent on designing a 30-foot rocket ship. The pursuit of fast, carbon-hulled racers, however, is not a proven path to business success—not, that is, unless combined with or complemented by the family comforts sought by our expanding customer base.

J/90

The J/90 became *Sailing World*'s 1998 Best Sportboat of the Year. Was that accolade the nautical equivalent of the *Sports Illustrated* cover jinx? We sold only five boats!

Courtesy of J/Boats Inc.

More than likely motivated by his nephew Peter's success getting the high-performance 49er dinghy into the Olympic Games, knowing Everett Pearson's high-tech building capability, and believing the J/Boat design team didn't have to play second fiddle to anyone, Rod wanted to design his own rocket ship.

At the project's outset, my son Peter had offered to leverage his International 49er Team of Bethwaite's technical know-how and Ovington's high-tech building capability in the UK behind a two-boat program, a J/65er and J/95er, with Rod and Al as principal designers. Ovington and Bethwaite were confident in exceeding Melges/Farr design speeds with "the 35 percent performance gains of the 49er."

The plan was to achieve ISAF International Status, with a high-visibility Grand Prix racing circuit established 18 months after launch, similar to what the Dardens had done for "Ultimate Yacht Race with the One-Design 14 and Ultimate 30."

As tempting as such a program was, we already had the J/125 program underway. So the decision was made to give Rod the green light without outside help.

The J/90 hull and deck were an epoxy composite of carbon fiber biaxial and unidirectional inner skins, premolded Corecell A-500 foam core, and a Kevlar/E-glass hybrid outer skin, molded using TPI's SCRIMP technology.

Hull and deck, weighing less than 900 lbs., were postcured to 140 degrees in a closed oven. Longitudinal hull stringers and transverse keel floors were also infused with the primary hull structure (not tabbed later as a secondary bond) to achieve optimum strength.

Net, net: like the IOR program 12 years earlier, this was a departure from the proven J/Boats design strategy of a versatile and forgiving family one-design. J/90 was a racing machine at too high a price tag for a 29-foot, 6-inch boat. It had two lightweight pipe berths, no head, no galley, no sink, no running water, no cabinets, etc.

Eleven years later, a Seattle sailor acquired the hull, deck, mast, and boom from TPI for J/90 #6, which never got built. He wanted a boat that could sail to its PHRF rating in light air. This Johnny-come-lately owner recruited International 14 whiz and America's Cup foil designer

Paul Bieker to apply his magic in putting the boat together. Bieker used a taller, deck-stepped, triple-spreader Melges 30 mast with a rocker bottom and PBO shrouds anchored by carbon fiber chainplates molded to the edge of the hull.

The owner was thrilled. "We love this boat. It is the easiest, most stable and fun boat we have ever sailed or raced."

J/125

My sailboat racing DNA and search for speed had not faded into the sunset or been short-circuited by the cruising lifestyle.

The business of large, faster sailboats needed attention. To grow, J/Boats had to attract more first-time owners coming in the front door than departing out the back door. Why were any owners seeking other brands, and what could we do about it?

Time to Get Creative. A comprehensive survey was conducted with *SAIL Magazine* in 1997 using the entire database of J/Boat owners plus all recent inquirers/prospects.

One revelation was that the new Farr 40 was attracting some J/Boat owners. The Farr was introduced in 1996, built by Carroll Marine in Bristol, Rhode Island, and had become a popular offshore one-design, not as successful as the J/120 but with a leg up on J/Boats among the serious racing crowd.

IOR designs had become passé. "Performance" had become the name of the game. Right up our alley. So why not introduce a flat-out, narrow, carbon fiber 41-footer to overwhelm handicap rules with pure speed?

Here we go again, reacting to and trying to beat the competition at its game without putting our imprimatur on an innovative new design to address our core market.

The *SAILING* survey showed that the top choice for the "Boat of Dreams," with a 19.6 percent preference, was the "J/125 concept" described as "The Hinckley Picnic Boat of Sailing...Pure Beauty and Speed-Less Cruising."

Runner-up, with 12.9 percent, was the "J/42...Stable, Shorthanded Performance Cruiser." Since we had the J/42 project well underway, it seemed there was a clear mandate for the J/125.

But the J/Boats design team, including yours truly, wasn't paying close attention to the consumer feedback. We were too focused on trying to outdo the Farr 40, the race boat, and ignored the "Hinckley Picnic Boat" part of the research's description. Our design had an open foot well with seating on the deck rather than a J/105 or J/120 cockpit with backrests.

Peter tried to set us straight, sending us ex-ISAF president Paul Henderson's prophetic email on the subject, dated October 19, 1997, which supported J/Boats' focus on family performance rather than flat-out racing machines.

The Farr one-designs are transition boats for the sport. They got rid of overlapping headsails and runners but are exclusive "race-boats," not inclusive dual-purpose boats. Top performance boats will become dual-purpose again with reduced crews and sails with yacht appearance and comfort like smaller Wallys with proper coamings, cockpit, and decent simple interiors, not requiring a weekend transformation from family use to racer...with a broadened appeal.

Peter asked, "Why we would directly take on Farr race-oriented boats instead of doing an end run à la J/105, J/44, or J/120? Keep the speed of the J/90 or a J/125 but make them special."

That was an astute observation. We sold fewer J/90s (5) and J/125s (16) than we did J/34s (25) and J/41s (19).

The closest we'd get to a "Picnic Boat of Sailing" concept was later, with the J/100 and J/124. While yacht-like, neither had the speed of epoxy-carbon-Corecell construction, which could have kicked acceptance up a notch. But both were acclaimed as the prettiest J/Boats ever built. We sold 160 J/100s and 35 J/124s between 2005 and 2007. The J/100 is J/Boats' most successful design over 23 feet in the past ten years. Maybe there's still a future for a carbon-built J/12 "Superboat" to realize the concept's ultimate potential.

Courtesy of J/Boats Inc.

There always seems to be a silver lining under even the darkest J/Boats cloud. The J/41 won the SORC and the One-Ton North Americans. The J/125 became the 1999 *Sailing World* Boat of the Year among "Sportboat/Racers."

J/125 has become a rare cult boat on the West Coast, now fetching $350,000 on the used market, comparable to the price a new boat would become 12 years later.

On a screaming reach, this boat is a hoot! I loved winning with hull #1 *Wings of the Wind* with a minus 15 sec/m PHRF. If you saw another boat behind you at the finish, you'd lost.

In 2019, during the 50th anniversary running of the 2,225-mile Transpac Race to Hawaii, four boats from a production one-design class—the J/125s *Hamachi*, *Velvet Hammer*, *Snoopy*, and *Reinrag*—finished 1-2-4-5 overall, frequently reaching 20+knot speeds. That's 25 percent of all the J/125s ever built! Crazy! It sure added to the J/Boats mystique as "The World's Best Performance Sailboats!"

The year 2022 has been an excellent one for J/125s. James Nichols and Shawn Dougherty's *Hamachi* and James Andrews' *Velvet Hammer* came close to repeating their 1-2 finish in the 2019 Transpac, with a 3-6 finish overall in the 2022 Pacific Cup. Roy Disney's* Volvo 70 *Pyewacket* won, and the Santa Cruz 70 *Westerly* was 2nd. Between J/125s were the Wylie 70 *Rage* in 4th and RP55 *Zwi* in 5th. That is some fast company!

Standish Fleming's J/125 *Nereid,* in a windy 125-mile Newport to Ensenada Race, took home the President of USA Trophy for 1st overall in PHRF, the City of Newport Beach trophy for UL-B Class, and the Amigo Cup for a "1st Time Skipper."

There's a fun six-minute sequence in the 2022 movie *Top Gun: Maverick* with Jennifer Connelly (as Penny Benjamin) driving a J/125 upwind. It's blowing. Tom Cruise is awkward, hanging onto the backstay when Jennifer commands, "Tighten the backstay to depower the main!"

Confused, he asks, "What's that?"

Jennifer, "You're Navy, aren't you?"

Tom responds, "Penny, I don't sail ships. I land on them!"

Then when blasting downwind under the asymmetric chute with Tom on the wheel, she sweetly says to him, "Now you are Navy!"

J/145

We thought we were on to something with carbon-boat performance but also believed there was merit in Peter and Paul's dual-purpose yacht approach. We didn't want the competition to scoop us with a larger offshore boat.

Time to Get Creative. Not having introduced a new sprit design over 44 feet for four years, a high-tech 48-footer equipped with a proper cruising cockpit and livable interior seemed to be the answer to capture some of those J/Boat owners departing the franchise.

Here's the response from one owner indicating that we'd created a "special" boat: "This is the first boat I've seen since buying my J/105 nine years ago that has really got me excited."

Courtesy of J/Boats Inc.

The J/145 was the fastest J/Boat yet, with a -18 PHRF Rating. The boat would slice to windward at 8 knots and regularly did more than 10 knots on a reach. Hull and deck were SCRIMP-built using Toray biaxial carbon and E-glass skins with a Baltek Superlight 45 core.

I had a great time sailing hull #1 to win the Detroit Sailing World NOOD regatta with Wally Cross and friends.

The publisher of *SAILING Magazine*, Bill Schanen, has raced extensively on Lake Michigan with his family on the J/145 *Main Street*. As you might imagine, the awards piled up among the 18 boats built:

2001 Sailing World Best Racer-Cruiser of the Year
and Class Winner at Key West and Detroit NOOD
2003 Rolex Fastnet Race—1st & 2nd in IRC 0
2003 St. Malo Race—1st overall
2003 UK Overall IRC Season Championship
2012 San Diego YC "Boat of the Year"

J/46

In parallel with the "Sprit" designs, J/Boats pursued its more classic cruising models. Having upgraded the J/40 to the J/42 in 1994, we did a similar upgrade five years later to the J/44.

A carbon rig, extended transom, and lower CG keel created the J/46. This modification made a very stable, manageable cruising boat.

Courtesy of J/Boats Inc.

I remember sailing #1 *Hawke* with Mary on its shakedown voyage—the New York Yacht Club's Cruise on the Chesapeake. We sailed downwind, wing-and-wing, with the reefed main and working jib in a 30-knot northerly with huge waves.

It was like being on a train. Mary took over after an hour of sketching to effortlessly drive the boat when surfing down waves at 12+ knots,

Ultimately 67 J/44s were sold, along with 43 J/46s, 110 of that hull design. The J/46 became the *Sailing World* Boat of the Year 2000 among offshore cruisers and was a *SAIL Magazine* "Top Ten Design of the Year."

J/100 Beauty

At the 2003 Annapolis International Sailboat Show, I was thinking, wouldn't it be time for J/Boats to capitalize on demographic trends, as with MJM Yachts?

There appeared to be consumer demand for luxury day boats. Our J/Boats builder, Tillotson-Pearson (TPI), had built some 400 of the Garry Hoyt*–designed Alerion 28s over the previous ten years. They had self-tacking jib booms and cockpit seats with cushions.

The idea for a luxury day boat harked back to the 1997 *SAIL Magazine* research that referenced a "Hinckley Picnic Boat of sailing."

Time to Get Creative. I bounced the concept of a J/100 off Rod's son Alan, who had taken over many of J/Boats' design responsibilities.

"Al, what would you think about J/Boats designing a luxury dayboat to compete with the Alerion in the market?"

His response was, "Be difficult. We're spending so much time on the new J/65 project, there's no chance of working on another design right now."

Al was right. The J/65 project was draining a lot of time from our small four-person staff, delaying the introduction of two or more designs in the 22-to-50-foot core business area.

A 65-footer was also a departure from designing boats we wanted to own personally but couldn't find on the market.

The annual dealer meeting was coming up in Newport to discuss future new product directions. That was a timely opportunity to test the level of interest in this luxury dayboat concept.

I'd learned from the J/105 experience that it would be wise to lay the groundwork with a few dealers beforehand. So I called some of our elder statesmen among dealers, like Dave Irish and Howie McMichael, to ensure their support at the meeting.

The J/100 project got approved and, when launched, was acclaimed as the "prettiest J/Boat yet."

It became the 2005 *Sailing World* Overall Boat of the Year. More have been sold (168) in the past ten years than any subsequent J/Boat design over 30 feet.

With a self-tacking Hoyt jib boom, the boat certainly met the easy-handling needs of the aging Boomers.

Incredibly, it was fast and seaworthy enough to win the 3,300-mile 2007 Double-Handed Transpac Race to Hawaii. I loved this boat and owned four of them. All were based where we spent summers in Northeast Harbor, Maine.

On #1 *Tern* in 2004, we won DownEast RaceWeek overall and were the fastest boat in winning the Maine Retired Skippers Race with my son, Drake.

With #50 *Tern* in 2005, we won the Maine Hospice Regatta and raced #111 *Tern* successfully in 2006. On #132 *Tern* in 2007, we again won DownEast RaceWeek with an asymmetric spinnaker tacked to the stem-head fitting without a sprit.

And for the third time, we won the Maine Retired Skippers Race with Ginger Miller and daughter Helen as crew. Interesting story:

The forecast was 20–22 mph, gusting to 30 out of the NW. We didn't exactly have a heavyweight crew. It was a pursuit race where the handicap was applied at the start, with the slowest boats first.

We were one of the last boats to start, about 40 minutes after the first. There was a flood tide. The start/finish line was at the entrance of Castine Harbor. The first leg was a 2-mile, starboard broad reach South to Islesboro Ledge. Then it was a 5-mile slog upwind, north to Turtle Head, the northern tip of Islesboro. The last leg was a 3-mile run to the finish.

Upon rounding that first mark, the fleet ahead of us had tacked immediately onto port to stay in deep water and take advantage of what they thought would be a push from the flood tide going upwind.

We did the same. But something wasn't right. The girls were hiking out. It was blowing. We were heeling more than I would have liked. Boat speed was right at 7+ knots. But our on-deck GPS readout showed a speed over the ground (SOG) of only about 5.5 knots. What?

Were the instruments screwed up? If anything, SOG should have been higher than boat speed with a flood tide behind us. The water seemed smoother than you'd expect, with a strong wind against the current. It's like the tide was ebbing.

Maybe the tide tables were wrong. Unlikely.

Time to Get Creative.

I thought. *What can we lose? Let's tack in under the Islesboro shore and see what happens. See if that's better.*

Heli was one-person trimming dervish in the cockpit, with Ginger scrambling across to hike on the weather side. Getting near the shore, we tacked back onto port.

Speedo and COG were a close match at 7+ knots, finally making sense. Amazing! The explanation had to be a unique tidal phenomenon.

The NNW wind was blowing so hard across the northern tip of Islesboro that the incoming flood tide was being bent over the top of the island and down its east side. The whole fleet was inadvertently bucking a "reverse" flood.

It's not surprising they didn't figure it out. Their knotmeters on deck were reading as normal. Navigators were most likely needed on deck to hike in strong winds. Nobody was at the nav stations below to see COG data displayed. Otherwise, short-tacking under the Islesboro shore would have seen more company.

There were also some nice lifting gusts coming off the land. They must have thought we were crazy when, half a mile from the weather mark, emerging from under the island on port tack, we started crossing larger boats on starboard tack coming from the right out of deep water.

They had already powered past smaller boats in the heavy wind. While larger, they were rated slower than *Tern*, and we made pretty quick work of them, rounding the last mark in 1st place! We'd won the pursuit race already, with only a 4-mile run to the finish. You should have heard Helen and Ginger's excited shrieks.

The photo of the elated crew was taken by our host, the Reverend Ed Miller, after tying up at the Castine Yacht Club dock. After this picture, Ginger and Helen took off their sea boots to reveal that both had painted their toenails *pink*! Here I'd thought our secret weapon was the GPS!

It's taken another ten years for J/Boats to focus more on this grow-ing luxury day-boat market with the introduction of the 28-foot J/9 (below) in 2021. Reportedly, 75 boats are already on order, setting it on its way to eclipsing the J/100.

Courtesy of J/Boats Inc.

J/65

In 2005, I was immersed in getting MJM Yachts established and making money. Only one model, the 34z, had been launched.

The J/Boats team, having sold 35 J/160s in nine years, was excited to take the next step in tackling the large, multimillion-dollar yacht market.

Courtesy of J/Boats Inc.

Rod and Al came up with a spectacular design. It was beautiful and fast enough to have won its division in the Bermuda Race. But only two boats were sold.

The project, however, required a marketing strategy and distribution plan significantly different from what J/Boats had in place. This would have been like starting a whole new business.

Unfortunately, I was otherwise committed. My priority had to be the survival of MJM Yachts. J/Boats had become less reliable as the sole source of our future income.

J/95—Triple Crown Winner

Nevertheless, in 2007, I was still strategic marketing partner and 50 percent owner of J/Boats Inc. and could get excited about contributing some time to the company's future with innovative designs that fit our 22-to-55-foot market.

Having spent two years cruising our MJM 34z in southwest Florida, I realized the area was ideal for winter cruising.

Before March, Florida's East Coast and the Bahamas are colder and rougher due to strong, prevailing winter NE breezes. After those winds get warmed and slowed by flowing over the Florida peninsula, they become balmy offshore breezes in the Gulf. Sadly, there's an absence of sailboats in the narrow, shallow inside passages between Sanibel and St. Petersburg.

I thought, *It's too bad; because of the draft, more cruising sailboats can't enjoy these waters.*

While some J/Boats' cruising designs had shoal-draft keel options, five feet was still pretty deep. And even in deep-water harbors, water-front homeowners were often depth-challenged by shallow water close to their docks.

Think of all the shallow bodies of water where a good shoal draft boat would be fun to sail: the ICW, Georgia and Carolina Low Country, the Keys, Chesapeake Bay, Barnegat Bay, Great South Bay, and Cape Cod, among others.

J/Boats are all about performance sailing. Deep-draft J/Boats could have been missing out on half the potential market.

Time to Get Creative. Mary and I visited Salon Nautique de Paris in December 2007. What caught my attention was a pretty boat with twin rudders and a swing keel. It may have been a Joubert-Nivelt-designed Toufinou for the shoal waters on the west coast of France.

My reaction was, "Heck, J/Boats can do better than that." Motivated by MJM Yachts' progress, having sold 50-34zs and a dozen of the new 29zs for the waterfront homes of aging Boomers, on returning home, I recommended J/Boats come out with a 30-footer that could sail upwind in three feet of water.

Rod was psyched, saying, "I've wanted to do a boat like that for the past 20 years." It was like the old days, brainstorming a new design together. Rod seemed pleased to again be the lead designer on this project.

His son Al had been establishing himself as the world's best performance designer of racer-cruisers with his J/109 winning at Spi Ouest, Cowes Week, and the double-handed Round Britain Race. In addition, Al's J/122 design was on the way to becoming the Royal Ocean Racing Club's 2008 Boat of the Year.

The resulting 31-foot shoal draft J/95 was billed as a "luxury day-sailer" to be introduced at the 2009 Miami Boat Show.

This announcement was made to dealers in March 2008, barely 90 days after conception. J/95 had a carbon-fiber mast, wheel steering, 3-foot draft, twin rudders, keel/centerboard, retractable sprit, and asymmetric spinnaker. Like a Sunfish, it could sail upwind in three feet of water. The saildrive is protected by the keel.

I'm not sure why we sold only 36 of them, other than lack of dealer coverage in non-J/Boat shoal-water sailing locales. It's a hidden gem with potential yet.

The experts sure liked it.

Courtesy J/Boats Inc.

The J/95 became the first sailboat design in history to become a Triple Crown Winner:

- *Cruising World* 2009 Boat of the Year and "Best Weekender"
- *Sailing World* 2009 Boat of the Year
- *SAIL* 2009 Best Boats—"Performance-Cruiser"

International J/111

The 2008–2009 recession hit J/Boats hard. We wanted to invigorate the market with a new design, as we had with the J/29 and J/105 in two previous "down" economies. Sales of the J/109 had dropped off after a seven-year run of 278 boats.

The J/Boats sweet spot had been 35-36 feet. We'd built over 1,500 boats in seven models in the 25 years since the J/35. That's better than one per week. We hadn't introduced a new model in that size range in eight years, since the J/109 in 2002. Could we come up with a distinctively different and faster boat to get people excited?

Time to Get Creative. The decimeter model designation of "1-1-1" (36'4") sounded like a winner. The J/111 was 2.2 feet longer on the waterline than a J/109, yet narrower and 1,500 lbs. lighter, with about the same sail area on a 2-foot-higher carbon mast.

There's a minimalist weekend cruising interior and cockpit seats with backrests. The displacement-to-length ratio is only 119 vs. the J/109's 172. PHRF rated the J/111 at 42 sec/m, a whopping 30 sec/m faster than its J/109 predecessor and 12 sec/m faster than the longer J/120. Design progress at J/Boats for sure!

Gerard Sheridan Photo.

With money tight, how could J/Boats fund the $500,000 for tooling to get the project off the ground? Stu bet that by publishing the performance numbers and drawings in *Sailing Anarchy, Scuttlebutt, Seahorse,* and to sailmakers, enough $50,000 deposits would come in to fund the start-up.

Paul Heyes in the UK and Didier le Moal in France got behind the effort. Orders came in from the Netherlands, Germany, Spain, France, and Sweden to supplement those from the US and Canada.

The J/111 was granted World Sailing's International status with boats in the requisite seven countries. Building the boat in the US and France became the icing on the cake. World Sailing liked the prospect of more income in hard times, too.

J/Boats received 20 deposits. The J/111 was off and running. They are still selling 12 years later. The next available hull number is in the 140s. Coincidentally, that compares with the number of MJM 40z hulls sold, which started in the same year. The J/111 is an excellent example of the J/Boats "family performance" concept. I loved that boat and owned #37 *Fleetwing* in partnership with my friend Henry Brauer. On Wednesday nights in Newport, Mary and I could race with however many more showed up.

Scott Sellers and his 14-year-old daughter, Merritt, in his J/111 *No Surprise*, made national news for being the first to finish and the winners of the double-handed division of the 204-mile 2022 Bayview Mackinac Race. While Dad slept at night, Merritt was given credit for going from two miles behind to two miles ahead of *Utah*, another J/111, to secure the win.

The following weekend, with 18-year-old daughter Hannah aboard, Scott won the 12-boat J/111 class in a storm-tossed, 289-mile Chicago-Mac race. J/Boats made up 26 percent of the entire fleet of 239 boats.

Martin Chumiecki photo

Then, how about the husband-wife team of Christina and Justin Wolfe on J/111 *Raku* finishing 2nd by only 1:24:45 after 2,022 miles in the Pacific Cup from San Francisco to Hawaii?

The J/111 was the 2011 *Sailing World* "One-Design Keelboat of the Year," *SAIL Magazine*'s "Best Performance Yacht," *Voile Magazine*'s Boat of the Year in France, and *Yachts & Yachting Magazine*'s "Reader's Yacht of the Year" in the UK.

A J/111 is featured in Christopher Rosow's inaugural novel, *False Assurances*. This must-read thriller has terrorists boarding a J/111 in the middle of the Marblehead-Halifax Race.

J/70—36 Years in the Making

The reader will remember that a lift-keel, easily trailerable 23-footer was a concept called the AMF 7.3 (meter) to appeal to Sunfish, Laser, and Hobie Cat sailors.

The initial J/Boats business plan of February 1977 had a lift-keel J/23 introduced a year after the J/24, with double the sales potential. We had set July 1, 1977, as the "go/no go" for the J/23. By then, we'd sold 50 J/24s, with good momentum to keep us busy. So it was a "no go" on the J/23. Rod's prototype was sold to a friend, who did very well with it on the racecourse.

Courtesy of J/Boats Inc.

The J/70 has a PHRF rating of 117 versus the J/24's 168 or the J/22's 180, or about a minute per mile faster. Even half that difference would have had a major market impact in 1977.

Finally, *Time to Get Creative.* Twenty years later, in September 1997, a ramp-launchable, lift-keel J/70 was identified as one of the top "New Product Ideas" by the *SAIL Magazine* research project.

When asked about the reasons for purchasing a competitive race boat, 31 percent of J/Boat owners and 24 percent of nonowners said, "Need a boat to trailer to regattas." Yet this author recommended we backburner such a design, having written 17 years earlier, in 1995:

> While it may help attract more people into the entry level of the franchise at about the same price as a J/22, we have to ask the question: Is such an entry-level strategy that important?
>
> There are some 2,000 new sailing families acquiring our used one-design models from J/22 to J/30 each year...for less than $30,000?
>
> A J/70 would compete with the J/22 and J/24 as a daysailer/one-design for yacht clubs and YRA starts in order to succeed.

There's a marketing axiom that I might have been smarter to apply earlier: "If you don't do it to yourself, someone else is likely to do it to you!"

It wasn't until 2012 that J/Boats decided it was time to introduce that J/70, 36 years after a 23-foot lift-keel design was identified as having a market potential greater than that of the J/24. "What if..."

The J/70 has taken off as the boat of choice for the European Sailing League. There are active fleets from Moscow to Marstrand, from the Med to Chile.

Courtesy J/Boats Inc. &
YCM-Studio Borlenghi

Much of this excitement stems from my son, Stuart, setting up Didier le Moal as J/Composites in France and publishing J/News with a reach, with the social media multiplier, of close to 1 million readers per week.

The 2022 International J/70 Worlds in Monaco (above) was limited to 90 boats from 23 nations. There were another 90 on the waiting list.

CHAPTER 22

MJM Yachts

I n none of my craziest 1977 dreams did a powerboat ever appear… let alone did starting a powerboat company comes to mind. In earlier years, while competing in crowded harbors and bays in Solings, 470s, Sunfish, and J/24s, powerboats were a nuisance with their disruptive wakes. We disparaged them as "stinkpots."

As a teenager, my fondest memory of powerboats was the thrill of going 20 knots in my step-grandfather Rodney Stuart's 24-foot Sea Beaver *Salt Acres*. The designer, Hubert Scott-Paine (1891–1954), was a Brit who designed the PT-Boat for Electric Boat Company in 1940. The July 1949 *Yachting* ad photo below shows a powder horn sheer and the alignment of the bottom of side openings with the deck, similar to our first MJM 34z. The overall appearance resembles our second design, the MJM 29z Downeast model.

Dad once purchased an old, wooden, raised-foredeck, 1930s-style day launch. I remember seeing it only once. I don't think it had a name. It caught fire before I remember riding on it. That made short work of the Johnstone family foray into motorboat ownership.

But we did spend some time on family friend Ed Moore's beautiful Matthews 40 cruiser *Zinganee*, seen in a Matthews Company ad from the same 1949 *Yachting*. The MJM design influence there was the 360-degree sightlines and large side windows.

But aspirations to own a powerboat, let alone build one, were out of the question.

As I got older, however—age 54 to be exact, in 1988—and was riding high, having created a dozen award-winning sailboats, a pretty water taxi named *Delight* caused a flight of fancy.

It got me thinking, "What about starting up a powerboat company?" Having spent summers at Mary's family cottage on the north shore of Little Cranberry Island, with its town Islesford, facing Mount Desert Island, we saw some classics.

The luxurious way to get around between the islands and towns of Seal Harbor, Northeast Harbor, and Southwest Harbor was to be seated on a wicker chair in the cockpit of John Dwelley's water taxi, *Delight*—a graceful, 32-foot 1947 Bunker & Ellis–designed Picnic Launch.

Delight has a narrow beam, a low freeboard with a nicely sprung sheer, and a long, open cockpit with a blue canvas Bimini top. It was easy to fall in love with such a craft.

But before trying to market such a boat, I wondered whether another design would have more potential. I flew down to Tampa that March to inspect and sea-trial a Bombay Launch and a Wichman 30. These were center-console models with a small cuddy forward for a head and/or berth.

Ultimately, the local "Picnic Launch," upgraded with head and berth, won. I contacted David Stainton of Cranberry Island BoatWorks about building such a boat and got a preliminary tooling quote from North

End Composites in Rockland but later I came to my senses.

There was plenty to do at J/Boats getting our first large offshore design, the J/44, built and launched without the distraction of me starting up another boat company. So much for that powerboat venture!

J. Dwelley photo

Hinckley Picnic Boat

Thoughts of that pretty Bunker & Ellis Picnic Launch hadn't completely died. At the 1992 Annapolis Boat Show, marine businesses selling boats priced over $100,000 still suffered from the impact of the Fed's luxury tax debacle.

Under the *Yachting* hospitality tent, Bob Hinckley, his partner Shep McKenney, and I were bemoaning the sad state of boat sales.

I shared the J/105 "radical new design" strategy to answer the luxury tax sales slump. We then started brainstorming new product ideas for Hinckley.

I told my *Delight* "Picnic Launch" story. Bob, being from Southwest Harbor, was familiar with the boat and had probably ridden on it. So I threw out, "Why wouldn't something like that be a natural for Hinckley?"

Bob recalled, "Well, Hinckley did build 35-foot powerboats back in the 1930s."

The seed was planted. Replace "launch" with "boat," and there it is! Shep took the concept two steps further with a prettier boat designed by Bruce King^ and added the innovation of jet propulsion with joystick controls. The "Picnic Boat" was launched, and the rest is history.

Later, in 1995, I was enlisted as a marine advisor for a powerboat project by my son, Drake, on behalf of his friend Jim Rogers from the Fishing Bay Yacht Club in Deltaville, Virginia. I accompanied Jim on a visit to Duffy & Duffy's yard in Brooklin, Maine, just before their merger with Flye Point to form Atlantic Boat Company. Duffy was reputed to be one of the better-designed Maine lobster-boat brands, which added "lobster yacht" recreational models to its line.

Jim was toying with the idea of getting into the boat business. All I remember is going for a sea trial on a very loud Duffy 35 among the islands of the Eggemoggin Reach. That experience dampened any thoughts I had about recommending an investment to Jim without a lot more research.

Dyer 29 *Grace*

Meanwhile, racing and cruising our J/42 *Gannet* in Maine had been wonderful in July and August. But we wanted to expand our horizons by exploring quaint, near-landlocked harbors up rivers around Booth-bay in spring and fall. That's a challenge for a sailboat. So we started dreaming about a motorboat with an enclosed, heated pilothouse as a nice addition to our fleet. Here's what happened next.

On a Monday, June 10, 1996, I was driving to New England Boat-Works in Portsmouth, Rhode Island, to commission our second J/42, *Gannet II*, which was entered in the New York Yacht Club Annual Regatta starting that Friday.

Our 40th wedding anniversary was Sunday, June 16th. I'd done nothing special in terms of a gift for Mary. After all, this was a major anniversary. I was desperate.

Time to Get Creative. At a stop in Yarmouth, Maine, to pick up new sails for *Gannet II* from Win Fowler, sitting in the yard of our J/Boats dealer, East Coast Yacht Sales, was a beautiful, bright-red Wasque 32 powerboat with a "For Sale" sign. My heart flipped. That's it. Just the type of boat we'd been talking about. I was ready to make the move!

"Sorry, Bob, we just put it under contract, but we've just taken a listing on a very nice 1993 Dyer 29 at Boothbay Region Boatyard near you. How about that boat?" Mary had talked about a Dyer, and we'd seen lots of them on Narragansett Bay, as they are built by The Anchorage in Warren, Rhode Island. That could be perfect.

"How do we put that together? I'm off to Rhode Island to commission my new J/42. I'd like to see the boat and am not sure that Mary will like the idea. I haven't told her I'm buying a powerboat and won't be back until next week."

"No problem, Bob. All you have to do is put in an offer. If it's accepted, we'll write up a contract conditional upon you and Mary visiting the boatyard next week for an inspection and sea trial. If Mary doesn't like the color or the ride, whatever the reason, just say sorry, you can't accept it."

With that assurance, driving south while on the phone, we went back and forth with the owner on an $84,000 purchase agreement.

Our "big" anniversary dinner was to be at the New England Boatyard's Melville Grill with Mary, daughter-in-law Hadley, and our two infant grandkids, Nick (3) and India (3 months). Yours truly was less than dapper for the occasion, wearing grimy khakis and a sweaty polo shirt, emerging from a full workday on *Gannet II*.

Fortunately, I had gotten a card, which, when presented with a description of the gift, brought a flood of tears from Mary. "Oh, Love, that's been my dream boat." Whew! Thank goodness! There was no way we wouldn't accept the boat upon inspection the following week.

A wonderful coincidence: the Dyer 29 design was first launched in 1956, so it was the Dyer 29's 40th anniversary as well. In deference to Mary's profession, our Dyer 29's name became *Grace*.

It's been difficult to separate our boats from the business of boats. *Grace* is hull #292. So The Anchorage had built, on average, seven hulls per year since its inception 40 years earlier. Why not more? If we loved it, why hadn't everyone else?

Sharing my marine marketing knowledge to help the builder do better seemed a generous bonding thing to do. I asked Tad Jones, son of The Anchorage's founder, "How many new Dyer 29s are you building each year?"

He answered, "one or two." Surprised it was that few, I asked him to describe the selling process.

"When a prospect calls up with interest, we invite them to Warren to sit down with us for two to three days to go over all the options they can choose from. Of some 300 29s built in 40 years, no two are alike. Professional fishermen and experienced yachtsmen all have different ideas about their ideal boat, and we take pride in building their dream boats."

Shaking my head, I said, "Tad, no wonder you're only selling one or two boats yearly! Let's turn this process around. First, the majority of prospects calling you expect you to be the expert…the very knowledgeable second-generation managing 'guru' of this legendary family company. Impress them with that experience instead of kowtowing to their lesser knowledge of what they imagine they'd like. Tell them that in 40 years of dealing with the most knowledgeable yachtsman, boat captains, and fishermen and having built 300 of them with all sorts of modifications, the consensus 'best' Dyer 29 is the model they should buy. Offer them five or six equipment options. Otherwise, pick your cushion fabrics plus your hull and deck nonskid colors." Anchorage sales of the Dyer 29 started to increase.

Making Boats Better

In the 1960s, our Quaker Oats expatriate benefit plan provided one-month vacations from Colombia and Venezuela with all-expense-paid travel back to our home in the US. We defined that as our vacation home: Little Cranberry Island, including fare for the Islesford Ferry.

During 7 to 10 days of our monthlong vacation, we'd charter a cruising sailboat from Bob Hinckley. These included, over the years, a Sou'wester 30, several H-35 Pilots, an H-36 yawl, and an H-38. That's how our friendship with contemporaries Bob and Tina Hinckley in Southwest Harbor began. At the outset, in 1961, our crew consisted of our three kids, the oldest aged 3. At the end of the charter, I provided Bob Hinckley with a list of a dozen ways he could improve the design. Example: the Pilot 35 had a wicked weather helm. "Why not move the mast forward and/or shorten the boom?"

It was a two-way relationship. I never forgot the lesson Bob taught me on the importance of seaworthiness in marketing. On a couple of occasions, I could overhear his sales pitch to a potential customer, and he'd conclude with, "Eh, yep…one thing for certain about a Hinckley is how it's built…you know you'll always make it back home!"

As I was unable to resist my penchant for wanting to make a boat "better," it wasn't long before ideas for improving our Dyer 29 surfaced.

The soft top was a maintenance headache, cleaning off seagull droppings. There was no transom or deck seating other than collapsible lawn chairs. The radar had to go on a tall pole, which wobbled around. The helmsman had to stoop down to see under the low upper frame of the bass-boat-style windshield.

The boat was "loud" and "wet." Engine noise reverberated through-out a completely open area under the deck. The bow would plunge into a wave and bow steer, veering off to one side or the other. In a moderate beam breeze, bow spray would soak the back of the piloting seat, not to mention anyone seated aft in the transom seat. The rounded stern sections contributed to rolling. The fridge had no space organizers. It was just one large cavity.

Clearly, rather than rebuilding *Grace,* the best way to have our desired improvements was to order a new Dyer 29.

A hard-top pilothouse with side curtains was inspired by the working deck of a Maine lobster boat. The prettiest of those was *Java,* a Stanley 36 lobster yacht. The pilothouse can be enclosed with roll-up canvas and heated during cold spells. You can see the similarities of this functional pilothouse layout with that of all MJM yachts.

Courtesy of John Williams Boat Co.

I'll never forget being in The Anchorage shop during their Christmas party. Tad Jones and I were up in the cockpit of my new boat, tape measures in hand, working out the design dimensions of the pilot house.

Looking back from my MJM perspective, as much as we loved this Dyer 29 at the time, it was too tall and not pretty. Lesson: a small boat with a pilothouse, having standing headroom combined with a sprung sheer and low freeboard, isn't "graceful." In other words, beauty does not always follow function.

With our latest Dyer 29 "optimized," what was left to improve upon? There were faster boats and maybe prettier boats, but not enough to justify making a switch. The Dyer also made sense because it was light enough, at 8,000 lbs. with less than a 12-foot beam, to be easily trucked between Charleston winters and Maine summers.

Mary was able to manage *Grace* alone. Can't beat that! We owned several Dyer 29s, and I functioned as The Anchorage's only dealer.

J/Powerboat?

With the next generation running J/Boats in Newport and my brother Rod not being under the gun to produce a new sailboat design, he had time to design and then build a 30-foot powerboat named *Ripple*. He planned to install an innovative New Zealand jet propulsion system, sent me the plans, and lobbied for making it a J/Boats project. I was not a fan of jet propulsion, its maintenance issues, or its handling, and my experience driving his first powerboat design several years earlier had not stirred up the same level of enthusiasm for marketability as had the J/24.

But to explore whether there was any commonality of vision to enable us to collaborate moving forward, on November 14, 1998, I sent Rod and the J/Boats staff a five-page "memorandum" outlining seven business/marketing concerns and suggesting 30 ways the design could be improved.

I was trying to rationalize my support of Rod's project. But he was pretty set on doing it his way. Arriving at a joint vision for a new design had been fundamental to our most successful J/Boat designs.

This was different. Like Fred Astaire singing "Let's Call the Whole Thing Off," this was a "You like "to-may-to", and I like to-*mah*-to" moment. We concluded that it was best not to muddle or dilute the world's leading performance sailing brand: J/Boats.

Consequently, we'd go our separate ways with powerboats and not include any under the J/Boats brand.

Create a New Powerboat?

It wasn't until the summer of 2002, inspired by my son Peter's innovative Gunboat Catamaran venture in South Africa and after owning several Dyer 29s, that the inevitable brainstorm happened: "The world does need a better powerboat!"

The evolution of what that ideal powerboat would be, for us personally and for 70 million Baby Boomers soon to follow, had been percolating for six years.

I had more time available, having transferred my J/Boats Southeast dealership in Charleston to Teddy Turner Jr. Little did I realize that this new powerboat company would become a 14/7 job: 14 hours for 7 days a week. It wasn't "work." I'd be having too much fun!

Peter had a parallel train of thought and had preliminary conversations with Doug Zurn about building a 34-foot powerboat alongside his Gunboats in South Africa. That caused my latent entrepreneur DNA to bubble to the surface. But was this crazy? Any powerboat thinking was still adjunct to my focus on J/Boats and sailboat racing. But something had been happening to us. Mary and I were starting to spend more time together on that Dyer 29 *Grace* than on our latest, 40-foot J/120 *Gannet*—even for cruising.

Sailing had evolved for me into mostly racing with the guys. Mary was happy to run *Grace* herself to bring friends out to spectate and take photos. At 68, I wasn't getting any more agile. Cruising under sail together on our J/120 was becoming more of a challenge: climbing over lifelines to get aboard, hauling up the mainsail, grinding winches, and carefully flaking the mainsail on the boom at day's end. Keep in mind, Mary was no slouch when it came to sailing. As my crew in the Olympic 470, hanging out over the water on a trapeze, we were ranked #5 in the US, having qualified twice for the World Championships in 1973 and 1974. Mary also droop-hiked over the side of a Soling, secured by ankle hobbles, in placing 6th in the 1971 World Championships. We also raced numerous Js together over 20+ years.

There was a sense of our going through a life-changing phase in our boating. Was it time for our boats to switch roles? Should a powerboat become our larger, properly equipped cruising boat and the sailboat a smaller racing and day-sailing vessel? Standing watch alone at night at the wheel of a 40-foot sailboat in foul weather gear while the other slept below when passage-making from Northeast Harbor to Boston had lost its charm. Be nice to cover that distance in daylight.

"OK, to implement such a plan, what are the options? Is there a powerboat on the market we can get excited about?" There were some pretty boats like the Hinckley Picnic Boat or two later "me-too" jet-powered designs, the Doug Zurn-designed Shelter Island 38 and the Mark Fitzgerald-designed York 36. These weren't very functional or practical to own.

In terms of functionality, there was always something like a Stanley 36, a bigger version of the Dyer, but it was too heavy and slow. As much as we hated to admit it, our wish list of what we now wanted in a powerboat, after owning several Dyer 29s, backed us into a corner.

No other boat on the market excited us, yet we weren't totally happy with the Dyer 29.

Yes, we'd be crazy to own another boat company, and the world certainly didn't need any more motorboats. That is unless we came up with a breakthrough design. But that could be rolling the dice.

Securing Our Future

Thoughts of investing in a new boat company raised questions about our finances. What was the source of future income? Life insurance premiums are ridiculous after age 75. Was it wise to have all our nest eggs in the J/Boats basket? Lately, I'd been feeling a bit sidelined at J/Boats. While I still owned 50 percent of the company, not being CEO and in operational control had become a frustrating challenge. There were limits on the next generation's willingness or capability to take risks, be more aggressive with new product introductions, and upgrade the dealer network. Granted, some of my frustration was self-inflicted. I didn't have the energy or heart to be disruptive in pushing family members beyond the status quo...better to leave that to the 2nd-generation officers and board members of J/Boats Inc.

I fantasized that it might be fun to manage my own boat company, unencumbered by those more averse to risk-taking. I'd never before, not even at J/Boats, had that freedom. This could be fun, kicking up my heels, doing what comes naturally ♫...tra-la-la! Plus, if successful, it would secure our financial future. The keys to success would not differ from those I'd employed at J/Boats: capitalize on management and marketing skills to introduce new, innovative designs.

Why wouldn't a new powerboat design be successful if it was prettier, faster, more fuel efficient, more seaworthy, more functional, quieter, more comfortable, more versatile in use, and more fun to drive? With that many targets of opportunity identified, it seems like it would be easy...like shooting fish in a barrel.

But I was under no illusions. Creating a new brand in the powerboat market wouldn't be as easy as in the sailboat market. The networking of sailboat racing aficionados in *Sailing World Magazine* (65 percent of J owners read it) and among sailmakers just didn't exist among powerboat owners, any more than it did among car buyers. Was there a market niche for a high-end, high-tech, "best-performing" brand of powerboat? And how would that term be defined? Speed? Fuel efficiency? Handling? Functionality? A combination of those qualities? You'd think that performance would be a much easier sell for powerboats than for sailboats. Because what brings joy in sailing is the act of being one with the boat, water, and wind—the wind in your hair and the sun on your face. Not so with powerboating, which had more functional objectives—it was more like driving a car. Getting from Point A to Point B: to fishing grounds, to a rafting party, to the beach; exploring a harbor and getting there fast enough to beat weather systems or the roughed-up seas from an afternoon sea breeze, etc. Come to think of it, there were thousands of open, uncomfortable, outboard-powered center consoles running around, and there weren't many "yacht-like," comfortable powerboats that cruised faster than the 16-knot displacement hull of our Dyer 29. A planing powerboat hull would provide far more crew comfort than a planing sailboat hull. Being able to go 25 knots to run faster, under control in 6-to-8-foot waves offshore, or to have lifting strakes and chine flats redirect wave energy for greater stability in a cross sea: these were relatively unknown benefits in the powerboat world. Going that fast in a sailboat can be pretty scary and not relaxing at all. Demographics indicate that we were not crazy in thinking this way. We were just getting older. I was an excitable 68 at the time and once again in market strategy mode. Surely, all those Boomers would soon be thinking the same way we did about the ideal powerboat. They are the same people who followed us from Sunfish in the 1960s to J/24s in the 1970s to J/44s in the 1990s...or, if in power, from 14-foot Whalers to express cruisers to Grand Banks trawlers.

Wouldn't all those Boomers soon be looking for a fun, pretty, functional, easier-to-own-and-operate powerboat? J/Boats grew along with their Boomer market in their changing preference for sailboats. Why not now with a powerboat? The right design could appeal to the emerging Baby Boomer market, ensuring another 10 years of solid growth and another 10–20 years of sustained business beyond.

What Would It Be?

Since it didn't exist, we'd have to create it. "If we were going to spend more time on a powerboat, what would it be?" Mary and I started listing features we'd like. I sketched out a Downeast-type craft. It was a stretched version of our Dyer 29 hard-top but on a hull with the sprung sheer of the prettier Stanley 36.

Before sitting down with a naval architect, we made a list of what we sought in this "ideal" next boat. This was a six-page "Guidelines for Grace—Bob & Mary J's Next Boat" (9/3/02). Our fundamental premise was that there were five ways to improve on the leading Downeast-style boats, like a Hinckley Picnic Boat, Stanley 36, York 36, Shelter Island 38, Sabre, or an East Bay. The five ways were:

A Pretty Boat—Priority #1 was a knock-'em-dead beautiful boat that promised great functionality and versatility with a signature brand look. When rowing away from your boat on a mooring, you had to keep falling in love with her repeatedly. When entering harbor, heads had to turn. Upon arrival at the marina, admirers had to approach and comment, "What a beautiful boat; what is it?"

Faster and Fuel-Efficient—25-knot cruising speed with s 35-knot top speed having superior fuel efficiency. Speed gets you further, makes it faster to reach cruising destinations, takes advantage of smaller weather windows, and enables outrunning of large seas.

Less Wake—It would be nice to go 10 knots instead of 5 knots where "No Wake" restrictions exist and readily get up on a plane to go at posted 25 mph speed limits while complying with 15" wake height limits on the ICW.

Higher Comfort Index—That's a function of both physical comfort and the absence of anxiety or fear: slicing through rather than *umph-umph* colliding with 2–3 foot waves, with less than 80 decibels of sound at 25-knot cruise, minimum roll at rest or at slow speeds, predictable control when exiting or entering narrow inlets in large waves, certification at the highest level of construction, and seaworthiness.

Easier to Operate—A quick response wheel, 360-degree sight-lines from the helm, and the ability for a non-boating spouse to dock the boat as easily as parking the family car.

I failed that last requirement on MJM 34z hull #1 *Grace* by not specifying a bow thruster or bow and stern thruster My sin was pride in my ability to maneuver the single-screw Dyer 29 after six years of practice. This probably cost many sales, starting right at our first Rockland Boat Show, when it took me three tries to make a landing, witnessed by all the competition.

Needless to say, hull #1 *Grace* was the only 34z without a bow thruster. Yet it took this dummy another three years, until 2006, for our hull #36 *Grace* to reach that magical "like parking the family car" moment... by adding a stern thruster. Fortunately, the error didn't turn out to be fatal.

That ease-of-docking lesson was so well ingrained we didn't hesitate in 2007 when designing the MJM 40z to take the next step in maneuverability: Volvo IPS "Joystick Docking."

Design Brief for *Grace*

Having spent six years trying to upgrade the Dyer 29 and being involved with creating 33 designs for J/Boats, we didn't need a "designer" to create our dream boat. We were the creators. We needed a good naval architect to implement our creation by engineering how it went together, collaborating on making it look pretty, and getting the weight study right so she'd float on her lines.

So who would this naval architect be who had an eye for creating beautiful lines? It took Peter and me all of about 15 seconds to both say, "Doug Zurn." He'd done the Shelter Island 38 for Billy Joel, which was prettier than the Hinckley Picnic Boat. Peter was already talking to him about a building in South Africa.

I called Doug and told him, "I'm thinking of doing a powerboat of 33–35 feet and wanted to find out whether you are available, what it might cost to come up with a preliminary profile that I could get excited about, and when we might be able to review it."

Doug replied, "I am available and want to become involved with the project. Figure about $3,500 to develop a preliminary profile, and we could meet just before the Newport Boat Show." I agreed and sent him a rough sketch.

In preparation for that meeting, Mary and I came up with five pages of a "Guideline" (9/2/02) that, in addition to the performance-and-handling goals described to Doug, meant finding a high-tech builder. It laid out 32 features sought in this new wonder boat to solve our and others' problems with powerboats. Here are 15 of them:

(1) Length & Seaworthiness—A length of 32–34 feet, the latter being prettier, was desirable, with a relatively narrow 10–10.5 foot beam for a seaworthy waterline length-to-beam ratio more than 3:1.

(2) Trucking Dimensions—Less than 13.5 feet in height on a trailer and 12-foot max beam to permit seasonal trucking with only a "Wide Load" sign between Maine and Florida.

(3) Co-Pilot Seat—For shared adventure. Both of us wanted to be involved in navigation, sightseeing, and safety…two pairs of eyes are prudent in today's crowded waterways when going 25+ knots.

(4) Fresh Air and Visibility—Fully opening windshields for un-obstructed visibility at night, avoiding lobster pots when returning from a dock-'n'-dine or navigating in the fog.

(5) Spotlight on Bowrail—Above the helmsman's line of sight and not reflecting on the foredeck or stainless fittings.

(6) Fast Response Destroyer Wheel—A 24" varnished, teak-rimmed wheel for function, "yacht-like" image, and natural steering motion…rather than a slanted stainless bus wheel.

(7) All-Weather Pilothouse—Heating, ventilation, and air-conditioning to seat three couples and sleep two with center roll-up plexi/screen and roll-up side Strataglass sides.

(8) Solo Docking and Mooring—The helmsman must be able to dock or moor the boat singlehandedly by leaning out the side opening to loop a line over a dock cleat or use the "Lobsterman's Trick" of picking up the wand from the side-opening window next to the helm. Then let the bight of the mooring line slide forward on a line, having been previously run from the bow cleat aft to the midship cleat.

(9) Summer Porch Sociability—An airy "summer porch" that opens up to combine pilothouse and cockpit space for the party.

Billy Black Photo

(10) Safe Foredeck and Boarding Access—12–14" sidedecks with an *intermediate step* from the cockpit sole. Grab rails running the length of the pilothouse roof to allow a person's grip to be transferred to a 30" bow rail when going forward. Narrow the deck width adjacent to the *step up* from the cockpit so it's possible to step over the gunwale from the dock right onto that interim step without stepping up on the deck, then back down into the cockpit.

(11) Grab Rails Everywhere—There are 18 total: on cabin trunk forward, verticals outside and inside corner posts adjacent to piloting seats, on the aft corner posts for boarding, over/under hardtop, outside/inside companionway, outboard of helm seats on the dash, and over the galley. This was born of our sailing experience.

(12) Transom Door and Swim Platform—For boarding when docked "stern-to," swimming; to include telescoping swim ladder operable by someone who has fallen overboard

(13) Varnished Teak Transom Seat—Mary's favorite on nice, sunny days. An Adirondack-style seat I designed for the Dyer 29. This would add a touch of elegance to an area devoid of high-maintenance teak.

(14) Lifting and Spray Strakes—Critical to avoid bow steer plunging down steep waves and rolling in a four-to-six-foot beam sea. Lifting strakes redirect wake energy out and down when planing over 20 knots... almost like stabilizers.

(15) Functional Styling—Sheer can be beautiful with hull flare, but too much flare can cause a fendering problem. Same with excessive tumble-home. An aesthetic and functional balance is needed with a vertical radiused transom.

The idea of tumblehome as an added mark of beauty was derived from classic Hacker craft and other Adirondack runabouts. Thinking retro, the proposed MJM 34z layout dates back to the 1930s. Look at the tumblehome and large opening side windows of the Wheeler 38-foot Playmate as seen in the *Yachting* ad photo below.

The design of the side window and large openings was critical to developing a distinctive signature look. The overall graphic design depicted a parabolic shape with the nose, or curve, facing forward, with the open end aft. Hinckley and its copiers had it backward, with the open end of the parabolic shape facing forward.

Signature Look

The look had to be unique, like none other, to qualify for a design patent and signature brand appearance, extendable to other sizes as we grew. Not easy! I did not want to fall into the trap that Hinckley did when several boat companies copied their look, resulting in numerous lawsuits.

Doug Zurn showed up the day before the 2002 Newport Boat Show with his first drawing. See below.

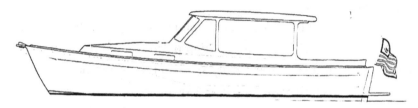

It had the tall pilothouse, sprung sheer and low freeboard amidships of our Dyer 29. "Not quite what I had in mind, Doug."

But he had a good eye, and I was enjoying the process. So we kept at it, exchanging 14 emails and faxes over the next month. We'd gone back and forth on all the details of the look, layouts, piloting console, propulsion, bow shape, tumblehome, transom curve, bow flare, sheer line, headroom, head, galley, ergonomics, etc., to come up with the *distinctive signature look* below.

While in this process, I conveyed to Doug my preference for elements reminiscent of my favorite powerboat designs: the reverse ("powderhorn") sheer of the Scott Paine-designed Elco PT (and Sea Beaver) or a Carolina sportfish with its bow flare for added buoyancy to deal with rough inlets; the flush working deck and open sides of a Maine lobster boat; and the tumblehome and curved transom of an Adirondack speedboat.

Having agreed upon the "look," the next step before sharing plans with a potential builder was to contact MJM's patent and trademark attorney, John Holmes in Washington, DC, to apply for a design patent from the United States Patent Office (USPO), with Doug and me as coinventors.

A design patent provides unique protection for the "Ornamental Look of a Product." Infringing a design patent can be very expensive. The earnings of an entire company are put at risk since the overall design of a boat is a signature trademark of the brand, not just earnings from a unique widget produced by the company. In this case, it was not just the look of the 34z but a unique look that could be applied to boats of any length. Drawings included a Sportfish with tower, Bass Boat Express with sloped side windshields, and 50-foot versions, which could be introduced by MJM.

Brand Name

OK, once we have the design scoped out, what will the company be called? What's the brand name going to be? Who will build it?

Needless to say, it would be helpful to have a "J" in the brand name and to use that umbrella brand name in combination with model designations in length for marketing efficiencies, similar to J/Boats. Several options with the words "motor" and "power" were considered. But what narrowed the options was the goal of creating a balanced brand symbol that would be distinctive at the end of a gold cove stripe on either side of the hull, near the transom, as we were doing with the "J" over a bar.

Another challenge was to use the "J" in such a way that it would not look like or be used like the "J" of J/Boats.

Ideally, that cove stripe symbol would also be the company's name to provide instant recognition without cluttering up the side of the cabin trunk with some other logo or writing, like Tiara, Sabre, or Hinckley. The latter has a winged foot design at the end of its cove stripes. When fiddling around with cove stripe graphics using a "J" for Johnstone and "Ms" for motors, it occurred that the "Ms" looked like waves. So, what if we put a wave on either side of a "J" to create "MJM?" Bingo! For the brand logo and company name.

Company Name

For the full company name, MJM, what? Boats? BoatWorks? Industries? Craft? Marine? Just plain MJM was too much like MGM. This would be a high-end, luxury product built of epoxy and state-of-the-art technology. "Yachts" seemed the most logical high-end moniker. And recent design trends outside the marine industry supported that direction.

In today's technology-saturated age, the definition of "luxury" is shifting, according to Laura Entis, lead author of *Entrepreneur Magazine,* and Glenn Entis, Academy Award Winner, creator of *Shrek* movies, and past CEO of DreamWorks Interactive. Here are excerpts from their article in the upscale *2016 Social Register Observer,* which underlined the MJM Yachts market positioning:

> In the past, luxury design was tethered to the twin peaks of exclusivity and timelessness. A Hermes Birkin bag. A Patek Philippe watch. A Bulgari ring. What elevates these items above mere commodities into the rarified atmosphere of "luxury" is their high price points, yes, but also the artisan skill that doubles as a guarantee against irrelevancy...But this is analog luxury... Apple has set the precedent for what luxury design, in the digital age, should feel like by creating products that are at once

beautifully engineered and provide a "seamless experience that extends from the hardware to the software."...It's no longer just about aesthetics, but about the entire user experience that aligns design with value beyond appearances, status and logos...technology's influence on luxury design has shifted the definition from rare, timeless items to products that combine beauty and functionality.

Companies and products that manage to hit all three notes—beauty, status and extreme functionality—are emerging as luxury designs' next frontier. Perhaps the best example of this? Tesla.

The battery-powered cars are at once extraordinarily expensive, a clear-cut status symbol and roundly praised for the exquisite beauty of their design. In functionality, Tesla is also second to none. Its Model S P85D received an unprecedented score of 103 out of 100 from *Consumer Reports*, which praised the car for its safety features, fuel efficiency and ability to accelerate from 0 to 60 miles in 3.5 seconds.

"If you are doing something different that solves a legitimate problem, consumers are going to be excited about it." Digital luxury then has its own rules, ones that value clean design. Clarity is paramount and can contribute to something feeling luxurious. "While ornamentation reads as luxury in the analog world, in the digital world it too easily registers as clunky and crowded. Simplicity reigns supreme."

MJM Yachts is a close parallel in the world of yachting: MJMs have sleek, classic styling, uncluttered layouts, industry-leading technology, exceptional performance, stability, comfort underway, offshore safety, fuel efficiency, and fingertip handling.

MJM's investment in technologically advanced yachts put the brand at the forefront of "digital luxury" at a price level comparable to the benchmark of "analog luxury," jet-powered Hinckley Yachts.

Licensed Builder?

I left Venezuela to join Quaker Oats in Chicago to become more proficient at marketing, believing that production, accounting, and selling skills were more readily sourced. Key to corporate growth was innovative marketing strategies and products. Marketing includes distribution, sales, advertising, new product development, consumer research, and pricing. I wanted to direct my energies toward the consumer and new exciting boat designs rather than dealing with who's coming to work today, a shortage of resin, or other distracting daily manufacturing issues. Perhaps the most challenging aspect of business success is "risk-taking"—the timely placement of multimillion-dollar bets on promising but unproven new designs. And as Jeff Bezos said, "Being obsessively consumer-focused."

A licensed builder, as an independent business entity and legal "seller" of record, can be responsible for quality, efficiency, and customer service with its profit and management rewards for a job well done.

Warranty can be a real sore point. Boats are boats. Every so often, a frustrated owner would call J/Boats, griping how they'd been or not been treated by the builder, dealer, or supplier in resolving a warranty issue or some other problem. While such complaints are not always justified, and while the builder may have provided exemplary support service, timely and fair solutions to such challenges are critical for the long-term strength of the brand. As an ombudsman, I sometimes sided with the owner, and sometimes with the builder. Such an impartial court of appeals diffused numerous disputes and enhanced the brand's goodwill.

Also, there are enough horror stories in the marine industry to make buyers nervous about advancing $100,000 or more to a dealer or builder before taking legal possession of their finished boat. But MJM and I personally had a Triple-A credit reference from MJM's bank, plus we held a UCC lien on funds advanced to the builder. This double level of buyer protection facilitates sales while providing the builder with interest-free working capital funds to reduce the cost of operations.

The big question was, "Who is going to build this new dream boat?" To be more agile and easier to handle, it had to be lighter and narrower than conventional powerboats. Mary could then push off from a dock or a piling without dislocating her shoulder and operate the boat solo without me aboard. Many 34-foot boats were beasts weighing upward of 20,000 lbs. To go light meant to go high-tech to have the structural strength, performance, and fuel efficiency that we needed. Who among larger, production-oriented powerboat companies had experience building such a boat and could be our licensed builder? I wasn't about to start up my own production operation and didn't have the capital to do so.

Having built the Rampage line of sport-fish powerboats, Everett Pearson at TPI could have been ideal. In retrospect, that might have been my smartest move for the epoxy composite molding and production efficiencies he was capable of. At the time, however, I didn't want to create a direct conflict of interest with my 50 percent J/Boats partner-brother…imagining what could happen during customer plant visits, mixing up the Johnstone image between powerboats and sail.

Not anticipating the enormity of what the building challenge would become has to be chalked up to a bit of hubris. With a primary focus on marketing, I was convinced that the ideal business structure was via contracting manufacturing with a licensee. After all, it had worked for Naturescapes and had gotten J/Boats up and running. Here I go again with MJM Yachts.

I'd inadvertently been a disciple of Jeff Bezos's philosophy of "True Customer Obsession," described in his book *The Collected Writings of Jeff Bezos*: "There are many ways to center a business. You can be competitor focused, you can be product-focused, you can be technology focused, you can be business model-focused, etc. But…obsessive customer focus is by far the most protective of Day 1 vitality…Customers are always beautifully, wonderfully dissatisfied, even when they report being happy and business is great. Even when they don't yet know it, customers want something better, and your desire to delight customers will drive you to invent on their behalf."

Even Harvard Business School Professor Frank Cespedes, at MJM's 2019 dealer meeting 17 years later, commented, "The business structure that MJM has set up, with itself spearheading the marketing and new product development, with the licensed builder focusing on efficient, quality production and a design firm handling the naval architecture and engineering, where each party is responsible for their performance in meeting agreed upon business goals…rather than having multiple, overlapping daily meetings to get things done…is arguably the ideal business structure, as it rewards each partner's contribution accordingly."

But he said, "There's a caveat. The key to the success of such an enterprise is trust. Without that trust, where one party is investing for the future, and another is milking it for short-term gain, it becomes a highly stressful business to manage."

High-Tech Construction

Was "High-Tech Production Efficiency" an oxymoron when it came to powerboats? My son Stuart was cofounder of Boats.com, which acquired YachtWorld. He had daily contact with leading powerboat manufacturers like Brunswick (SeaRay and Boston Whaler), Hatteras, and Genmar. He agreed to poll the technical departments of these builders to learn whether they had a production facility experienced in building high-tech boats with epoxy. The answer came back a couple of weeks later. "Dad, I talked with all of them. Not only did they not have such a capability, but they didn't know of anyone else who did." So much for a Naturescapes or J/Boats efficient production start-up scenario!

Powerboat molding was not as sophisticated as sailboats. Sailboats are powered by a finite amount of energy—the wind. It's a greater design challenge to create a better-performing sailboat. A balance must be struck between light weight, stability, and structural strength. With powerboats, there's little performance incentive to make high-tech boats. It's cheaper just to add bigger engines. After all, you can make a barn door go 50 miles per hour (mph) with six 400-hp outboards. But that's a vicious cycle. More horsepower meant bigger engines, adding more weight and the need for larger fuel tanks. The powerboat industry was producing heavy, inefficient, cheap hulls powered by bigger and bigger engines.

At J/Boats in 1992, for the J/80, we were the first to use SCRIMP infusion and cored laminates with vinyl ester or epoxy to build higher-quality production boats. SCRIMP is a vacuum-infusion process in which a vacuum pump draws resin into a covered mold where the dry woven/mat glass fiber has already been taped into place. The powerboat industry was far behind the sailboat industry in taking advantage of new construction methods and materials. There hadn't been much progress since the late 1950s.

The door was thus open for innovation. Create "the World's Best-Performing Powerboat" if, as with wind for sailboats, "performance" can be defined as the speed generated by a fixed amount of engine horsepower rather than having the wide-open throttle (WOT) highest speed afloat. The best line we came up with was "Twice the Fun, Half the Fuel," a boat that could cruise 25 knots, getting 2 nautical miles per gallon (nmpg) instead of 1 nmpg.

When Stu couldn't find a production powerboat builder, I called my son Peter, past president of Sunfish-Laser and partner with North Sails in Edgewater Powerboats. This was 2002. Peter advised me to call Bob Dougherty, "an old geezer like you, Dad." Dougherty was the technical whiz behind the original Boston Whaler, the founder of Edgewater Boats, later Everglades Boats.

I called Dougherty. "Bob, my son Peter suggested that with your knowledge of powerboat builders, you could help me. I'm planning to introduce a better-performing, fuel-efficient, Downeast-style express cruiser. The goal requires advanced epoxy composite construction, so it's strong, light, and more manageable. Is anyone capable of building such a boat on a production basis that you know of? For instance, what about the Sportfish builders in North Carolina that claim high-tech?"

After a moment of contemplative silence, Dougherty replied, "Well, Bob, sorry to say it, but you're looking for something that doesn't exist. There's nobody I know who's building a high-tech boat on a production basis. Those doing high-tech are for custom, one-off race boats like Outer Limits or Fountain. Forget the Carolina Sportfish. Those are heavy and claim high-tech, but not the kind of high-tech you're looking for."

A Sailboat Builder?

A change of strategy? I interpreted these two setbacks from Stu and Dougherty as meaning there was no hope of dealing with a powerboat company. So my focus was redirected to a builder in the sailboat industry.

In retrospect, I may have given up too soon. What I failed to consider and investigate further was the willingness of Fountain, Donzi, Magnum, or ex-AMF friends at Wellcraft to partner on a line of luxury express cruisers to compete with the likes of Hinckley and Sabre. These builders, apart from a custom high-tech race-boat sideline, had production facilities for popular recreational designs and, presumably, capital to invest in good projects. Such a strategy would have been no different from that pursued with Naturescapes: going with the most efficient printer of a lower-tech outdoor billboard business that had the capability of upgrading its process to higher-resolution printing to enter new markets.

But I wasn't that smart. I fell back on what was more personally familiar, accessible, and seemingly easier to pull off rather than taking on an unknown, larger challenge.

One such candidate was Sabre Yachts owner Daniel Zilka, a Princeton classmate of my brother Rod and a friend. We met and cheered on the Tigers together when the Princeton hockey team played the University of Maine in Orono. In addition to his main Sabre Yachts facility in Raymond, Maine, Zilka owned the custom shop North End Composites in Rockland, the same people that quoted on my flight-of-fancy "Picnic Launch" project 12 years earlier.

Daniel could build MJMs in Rockport without a direct conflict with Sabre in Raymond, right? All seemed good and positive. We shared detailed drawings, marketing strategy, and our plans.

But when it got down to signing the builder licensing agreement, Daniel would not agree to the noncompete clause. Presumably, by then, he'd decided to introduce his low-priced Back Cove line at the North End Composites in Rockland in 2003…about the same timing as the MJM 34z.

Boston BoatWorks

We had approached custom boatbuilders: Bennett Brothers in Wilmington, North Carolina; Turner Yachts in Ontario, Canada; Eric Goetz in Bristol, Rhode Island; and Morris Yachts in Trenton, Maine. Bennett and Turner's quotes were not competitive in terms of initial investment, pricing, and technical experience with our eventual builder, Boston BoatWorks (BBW). Goetz and Cuyler Morris couldn't start for a year and would require new building space.

We'd saved mutual sailing friend Mark Lindsay of BBW as a last resort. Mark had 40 years of experience building high-tech epoxy boats. He was a legend among Olympic sailors for his craftsmanship, building gold-medal and world-championship designs, and worked with Bill Koch to build an America's Cup boat in the Nevada desert. Doug Zurn had apprenticed at BBW as a fledgling designer to learn more about what was needed on the building side of the business. But we were also aware of BBW's shortcomings as a one-off custom builder, at the time, with nothing to build. In fact, with a partner and ex-banker Scott Smith, BBW was in debt, having given a note in lieu of final payments on a custom 46' sailboat to a Seattle client.

BBW was in the old, 9,000-square-foot navy power plant in East Boston. They were available to start work right away with the tooling.

And I was more concerned with becoming the guinea pig for a production builder that didn't have high-tech experience than I was with the risk of taking on a custom builder learning how to build boats efficiently. So BBW and Eric Goetz emerged as the two top candidates. But Eric had his TP52 race-boat project underway and couldn't get to MJM for a year. That did it. We signed a builder licensing agreement with BBW on December 12, 2002.

The late Mark Lindsay (1944–2019) was a wonderful, gangly (6'5"), bearded and gentle, Zen-like character. He was both idealistic and technically oriented. He had his own 30-foot sloop, was a longtime member of the Appalachian Mountain Club, was Chairman of Courageous Sailing, and raced a Rhodes 19 year round on Boston Harbor.

At the time, I couldn't have imagined how much of a struggle the effort would become for Boston BoatWorks to transition from a one-off custom shop to that of an aspiring production builder, or 17 years later, after Mark's death, a smoldering lack of trust and an absence of common goals would finally disrupt arguably one of the more successful partnerships in the marine industry…to the point that MJM was obliged to set up its manufacturing facility in Washington, North Carolina.

Thinking back, had MJM gone with TPI, it would have met the same fate J/Boats experienced when Everett Pearson sold TPI to Walton (Walmart) family interests, which put in place an incompatible, self-serving management team in lieu of an enthusiastic, forward-looking business partner excited about investing behind growth.

Again, to quote Bezos, "Do you want mercenaries or missionaries" as partners? Everett was a fellow missionary. BBW started that way but lapsed into mercenary mode upon Mark's passing. Shades of AMF!

What I did take away from Everett and his Rampage experience were his scary stories of builder-liability suits he'd had to deal with. It seemed powerboat owners were more litigious than sailors.

Working with a custom builder in debt, with an empty order book, a builder who had gone through Chapter 11 bankruptcy, and a new designer who had never done the laminate and structural calculations to qualify for International Standards Organization (ISO) certification for seaworthiness, made me nervous.

Doug's response was, "We don't need it. I can attest to the quality."

"Sorry, Doug, but I'm not willing to risk being sued for an inadequate design. No jury will buy you as a 'designer' testifying on your behalf. We need the highest authority possible."

"Well, I've never gone through that exercise and all the calculations to get ISO approval for certification. You'll have to get someone else to do that."

I had the perfect source, Steve Burke of Burke Design, a composite and structural-design engineer who had been an expert witness in several court cases. I worked with Steve at TPI in creating the J/125 and J/145 carbon-fiber sailboats. He had the technical background that would be critical in producing a high-quality, high-tech powerboat. Steve did the computational work for ISO on all the J/Boats. He was added to the MJM team to design the composite laminates and structure.

MJM 34z #1 *Grace*

They say boats live up to their names—maybe, eventually, as it didn't happen with *Grace* until later in her life. One of the shortcomings of a custom boat shop like BBW was that if every boat is different, the workers building the boat don't have the experience of having learned by making previous errors to avoid repeating them.

Boston BoatWorks used the onsite wet-prepreg method, extolled by *Professional Boatbuilder* magazine, where epoxy resin is squeezed into and excess squeezed out of the fabric by high-pressure rollers before the impregnated fabric material is laid bow-to-stern inside the boat so fiberglass strands ran the full length of the boat.

The first 34z never got close to "production" status. Molding the tooling for the first design, then building 34z #1, occurred in a small, WWII US Navy concrete, power-generation building. Molded parts and boats had to be shuffled in and out of the space as several boats under construction were moved from one station to the next or from the floor slab down into an assembly well by overhead crane and truck. It was all catch-as-catch-can. Independent craftsmen seemed to come and go on their own time schedules instead of a well-trained workforce punching the clock at an established shift start time. It was self-training by trial and error.

It was a bit scary to ship *Grace* to the Maine Boats & Harbors Boat Show in Rockland on Monday, August 4, 2003. Four tradesmen worked aboard through the night with the boat still on the trailer.

I couldn't wait to drive our beautiful, newly created *Grace* into the show. It was a disaster! It was me, the company owner, who put on the wrong kind of show, much to the kicks and grins of competitors Hinckley and Sabre. You could just hear them saying, "That's one boat company we're not going to have to worry about."

Having learned to operate a single-engine power boat sans bow thrusters on the Dyer 29, I was proud of my waterman skills. Well, there are limits, and this was one of them. The wind was blowing about 25 knots from off the boat-show float, and there were only about 40 feet to move sideways into the dock space...upwind...between two boats already positioned in the show. After about three tries, having to go out and circle back each time, my deckhand and I got close enough that we could throw some lines and be pulled in sideways. I was mortified. This was a publicly witnessed debacle for the brand and boat, almost as bad as losing those first four J/24 rudders in their inaugural 1977 race.

MJM's company owner was not the worst of the boat's problems. When Mary and I finally got *Grace* to Northeast Harbor, the building process continued. Our hit list was over 100 items long. The electronics were a particular challenge. The BBW "electrician" detached multiple single-color wires from a navigation display without making notes. I asked him, "How do you know where to put them all back again?" He pointed to his head and claimed it was in his "memory." Of course, never having dealt with these particular systems, it wasn't, in fact, in his memory. Things went from bad to worse. BBW had nearly 100 percent turnover among its building crew that first year.

Slow Start-up

How do we dial up the sales of 34zs? I'd estimate greater than 50 percent of the reason people first consider buying a boat is, "A friend recommended it," and nobody had seen one yet. Or another 30 percent say, "I saw it on the water," and there weren't any floating. With all other factors, such as advertising, dealer reputation, builder reputation, magazine articles, and boat shows adding up to 25 percent, there's not much going for a start-up boat company with no powerboat history and only one boat on the water for people to see. As mentioned earlier, this is a much tougher nut to crack than the sailboat market.

We'd run ads for six months, declaring, "34z—Twice the Fun! Half the Fuel," extolling the benefits of high-tech construction and a superbly designed and engineered planing hull. With all the fuss about automobile fuel efficiency, MJM phones should have been ringing off the hook. No such luck. There's a total disconnect between the fuel efficiency of powerboats and that of the family car. Amazing! A 35-foot express cruiser typically consumes nearly triple the fuel of an auto. MJM got that number down to 1.5 times, with half the number of fuel-dock stops.

An 11,500 lb. MJM 34z got 2 nautical miles per gallon (nmpg) at 25 knots, or 12.5 gallons per hour (gph). Say it averaged 6 gph over 200 hours of annual use. That's 1,200 gallons costing $3/gallon, or $3,600 per year.

Many 34-foot sport cruisers burn twice that. The family car going 12,000 miles/year at 30 mpg would burn 400 gallons or $1,200 per year.

It was like pulling teeth to get those first boats sold. Two of our loyal and most successful J/Boat dealers were the first to step up. Paul Mikulski in Annapolis for hull #2, which went to Dave Gallitano, and #4 went to Howie McMichael's sister, Joan, and fellow sailor Bill Kelly. #3 went to a new dealer, Dan Howland, in Florida for Frank and Jewel Benson. More on that boat later. We installed a custom marlin tower on #5 for an Ocean Reef couple, the wife of which would greet me at boat shows with a big, enthusiastic hug, then explain to astounded onlookers with a big grin, "I'm number five."

The next, #6, *Zephyr* went to Gerald "Jed" Hendricks to cement a wonderful 18-year attorney-client relationship, right through the transfer of MJM Yachts LLC ownership to my son Peter and to this day. On my first visit to establish a corporate attorney in Boston, Jed walked into the conference room and exclaimed, "That's a great-looking boat! When can I get one?"

At the time, I was desperate for orders and replied, "How about #6 in June for the coming summer?"

Needless to say, he became my personal and corporate attorney.

MJM Goes National

After the Rockland Boat Show and its summer in Northeast Harbor, *Grace* went on the boat show circuit: Newport, Norwalk, and Annapolis, then south to Fort Lauderdale, then to watch the grandkids sailing Optimist dinghies with hundreds of others in the Orange Bowl Regatta under the watchful eyes of sons Peter and Stuart. MJMs are the perfect grandparents' boat. The kids would raft up alongside to use the head or catch a bottle of water.

To get the boat around the tip of Florida after the regatta, I had worked it out with a friend and buyer prospect from Naples for him to drive to Miami in his Porsche Cayenne and hop on *Grace* to join me. Mary would then drive his Porsche back to Naples. We spent the first night at Plantation Key, then rounded Everglades National Park the next day on the way to Naples. We met long-term friend and MJM boat captain Mike Hall for the first time. He caught our lines at the Naples Yacht Club Dock.

After a week of cruising, we shipped *Grace* to Southern California for the San Diego show in hopes that our West Coast J/24 builder, Don Trask, and his son, Jeff, of Performance Sailcraft, could stir up some sales. The boat would then be trucked up to Bob Ross of Sail North-West, the J/Boats dealer, for the Seattle Boat Show.

We would have been much smarter to demo and display the boat for the winter in the much higher-potential South Florida market. How MJM Yachts ever survived as a business for the first six months is a miracle. The wheels started to fall off on both coasts. While Mary and I were enjoying scenic Highway 101 up the California coast, stopping at Hearst Castle and walking the beach at Carmel, I got a call from our initial dealer in Florida saying the owner of 34z #3 was so upset he wanted MJM to take the boat back. He had gone boating with his family several times. Each time he went out, something went wrong—electronics, steering, etc.—the latest being that the engine overheated, and SeaTow had to pull *Jewel* back to port.

The 34z raw-water intake had an unusual three-way valve. The handle at a right angle to the intake was *on*, not *off*, as is usually the case. He inadvertently put the tricky valve for the engine in the wrong "closed" position, toasting the impeller. Needless to say, it was the owner who was fried, smoking mad, and frightened to expose his family to another such adventure. "Take it back!" This was a serious blow financially, but we worked it out, and he agreed to take the next available hull in exchange. Mary and I took #3 back in trade to be our next *Grace* for a wonderful, trouble-free summer of cruising in Maine.

The second disaster occurred, unbeknownst to us until later. For the trip from San Diego, the trucker loaded #1 *Grace* stern-first for the trip to Seattle, and it rained. Well, a 34z towed in reverse at 60 mph is like a huge wind scoop. In every nook and cranny—through the louvered companionway doors, up into the seams of the beautiful vinyl foam backed/plywood overhead panels, into the instrument panel even with covers on—it was brutal for 1,255 miles, like being blasted with a pressure hose. You can imagine the mess to clean up before the show. That pretty much eliminated being able to earn any margin on that boat.

Fortunately, a home for the boat was found. Carol, Sail Northwest's office manager, persuaded her father, a past J/35 and J/40 owner from the San Francisco Bay, to come to the rescue. Bill and Nancy Headden of Friday Harbor were given a great deal after MJM covered the cost of repairs to the boat. They enjoyed a couple of years of great cruising among the San Juan Islands until Nancy passed away in 2006.

Two years later, the widower captain was at his dock when the fleet chaplain of the Seattle Yacht Club, the Reverend Meg Lewis, an Episcopal priest, stopped by to admire *Grace*. Upon stepping below, she saw Mary's framed commissioning prayer:

Blessing of *"GRACE"*—August 15, 2003

Oh God, we give you thanks for this occasion—
The launching of "Grace," the first "34z."
We thank you for the uplifting spirit of this
Beautiful craft for all the creative minds,
Hands & hearts that dreamed her into being.
We ask your loving protection upon her in
Weather fair & foul. Bless all who sail upon
Her, that these may be "Times of Refreshment."
Bless her from bow to stern, port to
Starboard, above decks and below.
And now may God, Father, Son & Holy
Spirit bless, preserve & keep "Grace," her
Captain & crew, this day & evermore.
Amen

Chuck Guildner Photo of #59 *Encore*

Then she discovered the boat's name, *Grace*, was a reference to God's grace and glory and that the brand "MJM" was an acronym for another female Episcopal priest. At that point, Meg couldn't deny that this was a match "made in heaven" with both the vessel and its captain. They were married shortly thereafter.

When the Headdens retired to Arizona, *Grace* was sold to a couple in Southern California, who owned it briefly before reversing her original journey back to Newport, Rhode Island. She is now owned by a member of the New York Yacht Club Race Committee who volunteers use of the boat for local regattas.

The Reverend Mary had the opportunity to rechristen *Grace* after 15 years, during the commissioning ceremony at New York Yacht Club's Harbour Court of the newest MJM, the quad 400 hp Mercury Verado–powered 53z *Zing* on July 18, 2018. We'd come a long way in those 15 years since that first launching in Maine.

Midwinter Cruise

For the first 15 years or so, Mary and I would take our latest MJM for a month's cruise, generally starting in Naples, Florida, then visiting Sanibel and Boca Grande before cruising across the Okeechobee Waterway to Stuart, then down to the Jupiter Island Club, Palm Harbor, Bahia

Mar, and then delivering the boat into the Miami International Boat Show. At this point, Mary would fly home instead of doing the show.

After the show, I'd generally park the MJM for about five weeks inside at a Loggerhead Marina high-stack facility until the Palm Beach show in late March.

After the Palm Beach show, Boston BoatWorks principals Mark Lindsay, Scott Smith, and I would cruise the boat north to the Isle of Hope Marina in Savannah, drive them to Savannah airport, and pick up Mary.

We would spend another several weeks seeing friends and college classmates between Hilton Head and Charleston.

Having lived in Charleston between 1998 and 2003 and been involved with the start of Charleston Race Week, we enjoyed going back for a few weeks to visit with friends and spectate at Race Week.

That routine continued through the spring of 2018. Later that October, we'd moved from 39 Washington Street in Newport to our cottage at Bishop Gadsden in Charleston. Our midwinter cruises have since ended up where MJM Yachts was born in 2002.

MJM 29z—Deck Yacht

It wasn't long after introducing the MJM 34z—about a year—before the product innovation wheels started turning again.

Mary and I noticed how many outboard- or inboard/outboard-powered deck boats populated Florida waterways…usually with four to six people comfortably seated, having fun in the shade under a Bimini top.

The sociability of a boat is a major factor in its enjoyment, and those deck boats had it figured out way ahead of express cruisers and motor yachts. Was there some way to incorporate that concept in an MJM?

Time to Get Creative. A deterrent to the look of the Dyer 29 with a hard top is the height of a person standing on top of an engine. Our hardtop Dyer, with the engine under the bridge deck, was not a pretty boat.

Two ways around the problem were (1) using a large engine box as a seat in the pilot house or (2) installing a Volvo I/O (inboard/outboard) engine under a transom seat. There, the engine would make less noise, and the pilothouse and cockpit decks could be on the same level, lowered to just above the drainable height near the waterline.

MJM was still struggling in 2016 to gain momentum in the marketplace. Our top dealer at the time, East Coast Yacht Sales in Yarmouth, Maine, wasn't willing to take on the first 29z in inventory, so my friend, the former commodore of the Northeast Harbor Fleet, and my partner in J/111 *Fleetwing*, Henry Brauer, stepped up to the plate, naming her *Corsair.*

Like that Bunker & Ellis 32, *Delight,* which almost got me into the powerboat business 28 years earlier, we developed a 29z water-taxi model with a Bimini over the cockpit that had zip-in removable sides. See the photo at the Cannes Boat Show.

When 34z and 29z sales slowed during the 2008–2009 recession, it seemed time to introduce Europe to these fantastic designs. I arranged with our bank, Bath Savings Institution, for a working-capital loan increase, justified by export potential, to cover a 34z going into the HISWA Amsterdam Boat Show…and a 29z to Cannes.

The fun part of the Netherlands was the postshow delivery of the 34z, with J/Boats dealer Robin Verloop, to Rotterdam, on the elevated Dutch canals, looking down on fields of flowers.

Cannes was impressive, with its boat manufacturers' two-story glass display buildings. We got great press features in French and British boating magazines but didn't sell a single boat. The timing couldn't have been worse. Within 90 days, we decided to bring both boats home. Fortunately, the 40z had begun to take off, putting MJM business back onto a solid footing.

40z—IPS Joystick Docking

Onne van der Wal photo

Several 34z owners were enthusiastic about owning a larger boat to spend more time aboard. I wasn't quite ready or financially capable of doing so. The late Ed Palm of Grosse Pointe, Michigan, and Naples, Florida, was one of them. He was the owner of a J/105 and 34z. He started hounding me about coming out with a 40-footer.

I remember staying at his house during the 2006 US Youth Championship event at the Grosse Pointe Yacht Club. We were sitting on his patio around a firepit, having a drink, when he put it to me in unmerciful terms. "Well, Bob, are you going to come out with an MJM 40z, or am I going to buy a Hinckley?"

Time to Get Creative. With those fighting words, the project got into gear. "OK, Ed, I'll take hull #1 if you commit to me now to take hull #2."

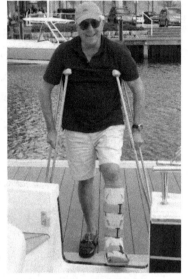

He agreed and requested a custom Paul Luke soapstone fireplace for those cold nights in the North Channel.

We had Sheepscot River Pottery in Maine create the custom tiles portraying Ed's J/105 to decorate the face of his fireplace.

I'll never forget the *Bert & I*–type comment by Paul's son, Frank Luke, when he delivered the beautiful, stainless, framed fireplace to Boston BoatWorks.

When asked how the stove would do if the boat were cruising at 30 knots, Frank replied, "Well, we'd been doin' 70 miles p'hour on Route 95 comin' down heah, and it did jes' fine."

The 40z was designed to take advantage of the latest Volvo "Integrated Propulsion System" (IPS). This was joystick docking, first introduced at the 2005 London Boat Show. Two inboard engines are connected to forward-facing drives under the boat, which rotate independently to move the boat in any direction dictated by the joystick. When we started development in 2007, Volvo was still concerned about how different hulls would respond to the system.

They wanted a completed 40z hull with nothing but the engines mounted sent to Chesapeake City, Maryland. We declined but sent them the lines to show our hull shape was close enough to the hull forms they'd already approved.

Boarding the 34z or 29z from a floating dock was a challenge. One had to climb from the dock up onto the deck, then step down into the cockpit. A two-level boarding step on the dock was needed but not always available. Stepping down onto a low swim platform and entering through a transom door was no easier.

Time to Get Creative. The 40z was to have some new features for a powerboat: the same flush cockpit/pilothouse deck as the 29z but with an innovative feature to deal with aging Boomers, kids, parents, dogs, you name it. There'd also be side-opening hull doors port and starboard, at floating-dock height, 24" over the water. These would eliminate the up-and-down-over-the-deck routine for boarding. We'd learned with our several 34zs that climbing up on deck required a two-level boarding step on the dock. Then one had to take two steps back down into the cockpit.

Another problem of 38-to-40-foot express cruisers is daytime privacy. Who wants to be in a day-long cocktail party where the only place to sit is in a "salon"…because there's nothing but beds and heads below. That scene gets tiresome really quickly when living on the boat for a month.

Time to Get Creative. A dinette/office, convertible to a double berth cabin with dual head entrances, was the answer. I had my private office to run the company. Mary could meet with a friend on deck or do her reading, email, or phoning.

A separate shower with an overhead vent hatch, seat, and toiletries bin, having a view out of an open port to see the sunrise, is a beautiful way to start every day.

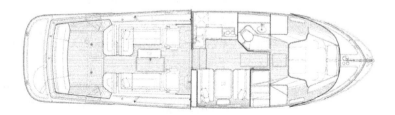

Another feature is the separate shower with a portlight, overhead vent hatch, seat, and toiletries bin. There's nothing quite like taking the morning shower while looking out an open port at the sun coming up in the harbor.

MJM 40z #1 *Grateful*

The New Year's Eve party sale of 40z #1, which became *Grateful*, was quite the story.

We were at the house of friends in Jamestown, Jeff and Cindy Heath, parents of US and Olympian soccer star Tobin Heath. The subject turned to boats. They got excited about owning a 40z. We invited them for coffee at our house on the Point in Newport to talk further.

This was New Year's Day 2009. We made a deal. *Grateful* would be the name, with Jamestown, Rhode Island, as the hailing port. The boat would be shipped to Naples, Florida, at the end of the month. They would own it with the caveat that Mary and I could use it for our mid-winter Florida cruise, an MJM owners' rendezvous in Naples, and both the Miami and Palm Beach Boat Shows.

It wasn't long before Jeff thought, "Wait a minute, it's our boat; can't we come down and spend some time cruising on it with you?" Seemed a reasonable request, but the boat was a bit small for two not-so-close couples to be spending a night or two on together. What to do?

Time to Get Creative. "OK, Jeff, here's a plan. You and Cindy fly down to Sanibel, where we plan an MJM-owner cocktail party on board, then dinner out and a photo shoot with Billy Black the next day. Why don't you rent a beach cottage for two nights, join us for the party and photo shoot the next day, and then we'll cruise together to Boca Grande? You stay at the Gasparilla Hotel. We'll stay on the boat. The next day, we'll cruise back down to Naples, stopping for lunch at South Seas Plantation. You buy the dinners; we'll provide the fuel."

Worked beautifully. Jeff later confessed that it was the best time they'd had together since their honeymoon.

MJM 40z—Just in Time

By December 2007, before the 2008–2009 depression impacted sales, we'd delivered 54-34zs and 23-29zs. From 28 boats in 2007, output dropped to 17 boats in 2008, but we sold only 4 of those initial models in 2009.

Fortunately, the new 40z saved us. We delivered nine to offset the decline, sustaining revenue at $10 million.

The overseas business helped. One 40z went to Stockholm, and two went to Spain.

Loading the boats on a Sevenstar Yacht Transport ship in Newport was a fun adventure. I'd cruise the new boats from Boston through the Cape Cod Canal to Newport, then drive them out to the ship, where they'd be craned up and placed in a cradle.

Ten days after putting #11 *Black Swan* on the ship, I flew to Madrid, then Gibraltar boarded the ship, and rode the 40z down to the water with the owner, Fernando Del Pino.

Next, I flew to Ibiza for a ride on #10 *Shakti* with its owner and saw that island's unique harbors and hills.

Eleven years later, #10 *Shakti* became *Z*, my son Peter's MJM and temporary residence in Washington, North Carolina, where he was managing the new 200,000 sq. ft. MJM production facility…and awaiting completion of his new house.

MJM 40z Handles Rough Seas

Sales were still slow in 2010, and I was looking for some creative way to communicate the seaworthiness of the new 40z.

Remarkably, the MJM 40z and the Nordhavn 40 were the only 40-footers to have been ISO Certified as "Category A Ocean." How could we get that message across?

Time to Get Creative. The answer was to have photographer Billy Black video the 40z from a helicopter on a rough day in the Gulf Stream.

When the opportunity arose, Mary and I were in Palm Beach on our 40z #21 *Zing.* It had been blowing 25–30 knots from the NE against the Gulf Stream all night. Waves were still 6–8 feet high and close together. It was still gusting to 25 knots.

Fortunately, Billy was in the area with helicopter pilots on standby. Mary stayed ashore. I drove the boat (with that broken leg) with one of our MJM brokers.

I narrated a seven-minute video with the 40z going into huge seas at 8–10 knots, running parallel with them at 20 knots, and running down sea at 25 knots, in complete control. This video has had 86,000 hits in six years. Google "MJM 40z Stability in Rough Conditions." The 40z in this video is shown before the installation of Seakeeper gyros four years later, which further reduces roll by 93 percent.

MJM grew 25 percent in 2011 with the introduction of the MJM 36z, then another 30 percent in 2012, thanks to the 40z video. Nobody but Nordhavn dares show a video of their boats in such rough conditions.

One fellow told me, at a boat show, "I bet you got lots of hits from that 40z video in the Gulf Stream. Well, don't get too excited about how many were watching it. I watched it 200 times."

Another, who owned a Hunt 25, said, "Whenever someone asks me what boat they should buy, I tell them, 'Go look at that video of an MJM in 6–8 foot waves.'"

The 40z IPS design, and the later 43z outboard model using the same hull, have been very successful, with 140 sold. They are in such demand they sell on the used brokerage market for close to the original cost.

Weather Windows

The value of speed and seaworthiness in dealing with weather can't be emphasized enough. The experience of two 40zs on the same Tuesday—April 17, 2014—is illustrative.

Walter Teller on 40z _Juno_ was looking for a weather window to cross the Gulf Stream from Old Bahama Bay in the West End to Lake Worth Inlet.

More than 30 boats were held up from crossing the Gulf Stream. They would remain so for another eight days. It had been blowing 25 knots from the NE against the Stream for 36 hours, creating mountainous waves.

Reliable forecasters called for the smallest of windows: the wind would drop to 6–8 knots from the SE with 10-foot seas early the following day. By midday, the wind would increase to 25 knots. That evening, it would come in hard again from the north with the passing of a cold front.

At 7:45 a.m., as many incredulous captains watched, two boats departed for the 55-mile passage across the Gulf Stream to Lake Worth Inlet: a 57-foot Nordhavn and Walter's MJM 40z _Juno_.

Walter tells what happened:

I knew the lull was due to the wind change and wouldn't last. I thought the shift to SE would settle the Stream for a few hours before it built again to 10-footers.

The course was 283, but we headed 265–270 to allow for the set of wind and Gulf Stream currents. We had a nice start, running at 22 knots into moderate seas.

The beauty of our 40z was that we could power up the steep faces of confused waves that rose from nowhere like a random field of steep moguls on a ski slope. Then we could power back, if needed, to avoid burying the bow, going down the backside and up into the next wave.

The anchor frequently skimmed along the surface in the troughs before we headed uphill again. It took some vigilance. There was no regularity or predictability to the seas.

The boat was so responsive that I could adjust to each wave's speed and angle of attack. When down in the troughs, waves seemed to rise over the pilot house, which was quite a sight.

We caught just one sudden steep wave on the stern quarter, which spun and rolled the boat a bit, but recovery was swift—a thrilling ride.

The crossing took 3 hours and 15 minutes, averaging about 17 knots…remarkable in those conditions. We always felt secure, dry, and comfortable, especially knowing the crossing would be fairly brief. And it was.

We had some nice following rollers to surf coming in the Lake Worth Inlet and were at our slip in Old Port Cove before the wind built back up to 25–30 knots.

Bob and Mary Johnstone's 40z *Zing* In North Carolina, on the ICW, we had to deal with the same frontal passage window as *Juno*. But it was one hundred miles longer: 155 miles from Southport Marina on the Wilmington River via the Intracoastal, up Adams Creek, and down the Neuse River to Belhaven on the Pamlico River. Southport Marina had an ex-navy weatherman giving transient boaters a detailed forecast every evening at 6 p.m. His prediction for the next day, that same April 15, a Tuesday, sounded ominous: southerly winds of 25 knots, switching to strong 25+ knots from the NNE that evening after the passage of a well-developed cold front. All other boats, including a Vicem 55, elected to stick it out in Southport to wait out the passage of the cold front the next day.

If we waited also, we'd be facing two added days of slogging to windward into some very steep seas on long stretches of open water in the Wilmington River, Bogue Sound, Neuse River, and Pamlico River, on up the Alligator River and Albemarle Sound.

A second problem was our reservation at City Docks in Beaufort that night. It would be bouncy with strong southerlies in the early evening. Then, after the front went through, we'd have to bash our way against strong northerlies on the Neuse and Pamlico Rivers the next day. Not fun. Could we bypass Beaufort and make it 155 miles to Belhaven before nightfall?

Time to Get Creative. Having a boat that can cruise at 32–33 knots with less than 11 feet of air height meant no worry about being slowed several hours by bridge waiting time

Our downhill skiing strategy was to bypass Beaufort, planning to do the 155 miles to Belhaven before 1700 hours.

We departed Southport at 0830 with a stiff SSW wind at our backs. What a blast! It was a great boating day for an MJM. We covered the first 20 miles down the Cape Fear River and into Myrtle Grove Sound in 40 minutes.

Then endless docks with floats reduced our speed to 7–8 knots in several places. We arrived at industrialized, potash-dominated More-head City at 1:45 p.m. (5 hours and 15 minutes later). The only bouncy part of the remaining trip was 10 minutes of a short beam sea, clearing Winthrop Point as we exited Adams Creek into the Neuse River.

Onne van der Wal photo

It was another sleigh ride, with a tailwind down the Neuse until we turned into Bay River, crossed Pamlico River up the Pungo to Belhaven, and arrived at 4:30 p.m., exactly eight hours later, averaging nearly 20 knots.

MJM 36z—Outdrives

We learned from the 29z and the 40z that a single-level deck from the transom to the companionway was a welcome safety feature. Then, after the enthusiastic reception of the side-opening hull doors on the 40z, we asked ourselves whether we could take advantage of these advances to make further use of MJM 34z tooling.

Time to Get Creative. So, in 2011, with a new deck mold, flush decking, side doors, and Volvo inboard/outboard stern drives, the 34z became the 36z. Some thought it was the prettiest MJM of all.

Mary and I cruised hull #1 from late January until the Miami Boat Show, where she was sold to a husband-wife doctor team in Stuart.

Ed Palm even bought one—his third MJM—to store in the Hamilton Harbor Yacht Club's hurricane-proof building in Naples. He kept his 40z, with a fireplace, in Harbor Springs, Michigan, until realizing it could be trucked to Florida for the winter to avoid ownership of two boats.

Photo courtesy of MJM Yachts

Billy Black photo

The 36z is an excellent sea boat. Some say it's better than the 40z, going through waves. I'm not sure that's verified by Ed Palm's story about coming back the 80 miles from Key West to Naples against a strong norther with mountainous 8-to-10-foot waves on the nose, only to find a sizeable fish in the cockpit.

Northeast Harbor, Maine

My other favorite 36z story happened in 2018, underlining MJM's Downeast legacy and bringing to mind our longtime summer stomping grounds and favorite place to race sailboats.

David Rockefeller Jr. had been honored by the Mystic Seaport Museum with the 2017 America and the Sea Award for his environmental program, Sailors for the Sea. Having been an original board member of Sailors for the Sea and an earlier honoree, I attended the Seaport's gala in New York and offered up for auction an MJM 50z picnic cruise in Naples.

David's wife, Susan, put in the successful bid, and David made good on it for a short cruise with Mary and me into the Gulf, then lunch at the Naples Yacht Club.

Two days later, we were delighted to hear he'd purchased an MJM 36z named *Susanna* to replace a Maine lobster yacht he kept in Seal Harbor, Maine.

Rugged Rocks

Facing Seal Harbor on Mount Desert Island and Cadillac Mountain, the highest peak on the Atlantic Coast north of Brazil, is Rugged Rocks, the shoreside cottage Mary's mother purchased on Little Cranberry Island in 1934. Mary spent her summers there as a girl and learned to sail at age 10 in her Cape Cod dinghy with a red sail.

We were engaged at Rugged Rocks on August 12, 1955, and raced our 15-foot Cape Cod Mercury *Mussel* against our neighbors Jack and Helen Merrill in their Bullseye. Jack was the commodore of the Cruising Club of America.

As our kids approached college age, they were more interested in the social action in Northeast Harbor than in being stuck on an island.

Since Mary and I had become more like building caretakers and less like a carefree vacationing family, we sold Rugged Rocks to island friends and rented for the next ten years in Northeast Harbor.

Northeast Harbor Fleet

That's the unique name of the local yacht club. Sailboat racing in the area is great fun. So much is going on with crazy currents and wind shifts. There are always opportunities to catch up if behind in a race.

It can get a bit dicey in fog. An anecdote describes how old-timers navigated in dense fog. "Put a crew member on the bow with a sack of potatoes to throw ahead of the boat every 20–30 seconds. If you don't hear a splash, *tack*!"

As the NEH Fleet's Cruising Class Captain for several years, I'd worked with past commodore David Rockefeller in creating and running DownEast RaceWeek. David approached me in 2003, saying, "Bob, would you be willing to start on the six-year flag officer path as rear commodore from 2004 to 2005?"

My response was, "David, thank you. I'm honored. But I have a full-time job getting MJM Yachts off the ground and still have my J/Boats marketing role, plus plenty going on here in the cruising class. I don't see being able to do justice to the role."

He can be persuasive. "Bob, look, it's not that difficult, nor does it take much time. How about starting next year as rear commodore?

See how it goes that first year. If it looks overwhelming, you can bow out before the next step of becoming vice commodore or even commodore."

"Wouldn't that be awkward for the fleet to deal with?"

David replied, "No worries. It's happened before. My dad stepped down before becoming commodore. So it's OK."

"Well, David, that's good company if your old man set a precedent. I'll give it a shot and see how it goes."

I stayed the entire six years with the help of some outstanding members and staff.

I was also gratified and greatly relieved to have persuaded my son Stuart's Tufts roommate, Fran Charles, to take a summer break from his full-time MIT sailing master job to become fleet manager.

Franny replaced Greg Wilkinson, the Boston College coach, and former Eastern Yacht Club's sailing director. Greg had been there for nine years.

Fran started in 2009. He was there through 2022. So his tenure thus far is 14 years, an NEH Fleet record dating back to 1923. Congrats to Franny and the fleet!

Powered Windshields

Let's return to the world of MJM Yachts. One of the beauties of sailing is breathing fresh air. Fixed windshields on powerboats take away from that experience.

The solution, opening windshields, isn't a new idea. Our 1956 model Dyer 29 had them, as do all MJM designs starting with the MJM 34z. The manual brackets with twist-knob securing devices are awkward, particularly for short people. We provided a 4-foot stick with a rubber cane tip for greater reach.

Time to Get Creative. We'd wanted since day one to have a push-button electronic method for raising and lowering the windshields.

Bless Mark Lindsay. He applied his MIT training to the challenge of finding the solution. Several companies were contacted over the years. They all tried, but none had a system that worked.

Billy Black photo

Ultimately, we located a Chinese company that made a compact, stainless, self-contained synchronous electronic lift system that worked beautifully.

It was a moment to celebrate. After eight years, "We'd done it!" Another first in the powerboat world. But having just read David Mc-Cullough's *The Wright Brothers*, I couldn't resist.

"Wait a minute, Mark. Let's put this in perspective. We're good, but not quite in the Wright Brothers' league. One hundred years ago, Orville and Wilbur, a couple of bicycle makers, figured out how a man could fly. It only took them three years!"

Who Needs a 50 Footer?

Here we go again. Some of our most dedicated MJM 40z liveaboard cruising couples kept asking, "When will MJM introduce a 50-footer?" I'd heard this refrain for a couple of years. It had been four years since launching the 40z. What was I thinking?

Dragging my heels is what I was doing. Why does anyone need a boat larger than our 40z? I love that boat. It's perfect. Easy enough

351

to handle like a center console, and you truck it anywhere with just a "Wide Load" sign. There are three separate sleeping areas for family cruising, and it's Category A Ocean-rated. Besides, a 50-footer is a significant investment of about $3.5 million for the design, tooling, and the first boat.

@2009 King Features Syndicate, Inc.

Slowly, reality overcame procrastination. More space is desirable for extended cruising. A larger boat will be smoother in a seaway. Our competitors, Hinckley, Sabre, Palm Beach, and Grand Banks, had all launched 48-to-50-footers, accounting for about $100 million in annual sales.

So, Johnstone, if you are going to make anything of this MJM Yachts brand, you better get in the game. I relented. But the challenge remained, "How can MJM come up with a 50-foot design that's better than what's on the market already? A 'me too' won't get very far."

Time to Get Creative. If the reason for owning a 50-footer is liveaboard comfort, how did competing brands stack up? I laid their interior layouts side-by-side to compare. It was a *eureka!* moment. "Holy smokes!" They don't get it.

Their designers never lived on these boats. Otherwise, a critical aspect of extended time aboard would have been addressed: daytime privacy. There's no place below to read, be on the phone, or work at a computer in privacy away from a "salon."

Mary and I learned on the 40z that I could conduct MJM business at the dinette while she met friends, read, and did emails up on the bridgedeck.

A 50z could have two private spaces below: an owner's cabin with an easy chair and a desk and a convertible second guest cabin with seating and a table.

Proof of the "daytime privacy" concept was two couples we'd befriended. After two years of having lived on their 48-footers for a month or two, they'd become frustrated by the lack of privacy and sold them "before we killed each other."

Onne van der Wal photo

A *New York Times* article described "Dual Master Suites" as the latest Baby Boomer home trend. Older couples have learned it's easier to get a good sleep if each has their own "master bedroom" with an ensuite head and shower.

Arguably, it's even harder to get an uninterrupted night's sleep on a boat. This issue may explain the interest in 2nd-stateroom layouts. Research reveals that very few owners cruise with overnight guests. So the 2nd stateroom must be for the owners.

The 50z dining-lounge area converts to create the 2nd master suite with either twin foot-to-foot berths or a double with table lowered. A heavy privacy curtain is standard. A portable bulkhead and entry door is available as an option.

Either way, the 50z becomes the most "luxurious" yacht in its category by featuring "Dual Master Suites," each with a head, a glassed-in shower, a desk/table, a reading chair, and a pouf to double as a footrest or desk chair.

Onne van der Wal photo

The shot above shows the original, rolled-up vinyl Strataglass siding. We offered sliding glass at a later date.

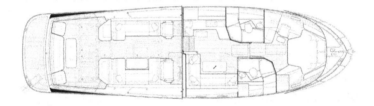

Coup de Grace

Doug's preliminary 50z design was constrained by having to install a pair of D8 or D9 Volvo 500 HP IPS diesels that were 9" taller than the D6s of the 40z. We had to choose between two equally bad layouts: Do we (1) raise the cockpit deck and lose our sleek, low profile and side opening doors at floating dock height, or (2), like Sabre and Hinckley, move the engines forward under the bridge deck, with jackshafts running aft to the IPS drives, putting the noise and vibration under the guests and losing our huge storage areas and the flush deck between cockpit and bridge deck?

We'd be back to the 34z tripping problems. Even worse, to get head-room in the "saloon," we'd have had to raise the boat's profile by 9", and bridge-clearance height by the same amount. Yikes!

Time to Get Creative. "So, Doug, now that the boat will have a beam of 15 feet instead of the road limit of 12 feet, what about three smaller D6 435 HP diesels side-by-side instead of those two big D9 500s? Less weight and 30 percent more horsepower. Will they fit so we can keep our flush deck layout, have a lower profile, and maybe have a 35-knot cruising speed, 10 knots faster than Hinckley, Sabre, Palm Beach, and Grand Banks 48–50 footers?"

Triple engines with 35-knot cruising speed reinforced MJM's "Best Performing Brand" status, particularly in powerboats where "perfor-mance" meant "speed." But so as not to scare away our Maine dealer, nervous about losing the Downeast "traditionalists" he claimed never cruised over 20 knots, we offered the "standard" 50z with twin D6 435s. Triples were a $160,000 option.

Only two of the first 20 owners elected twins, and that was for shallow water. Twins had a 10" shallower draft: one boat for the Chesapeake and the other to avoid a rock next to the owner's private dock in Marblehead.

There was a nagging concern people would think three engines would burn 50 percent more fuel than two, hurting MJM's twelve-year claim, "Twice the Fun, Half the Fuel—The World's Most Fuel-Efficient Powerboats." Volvo technicians allayed that concern. "No worries, Bob. Fuel consumed is a function of horsepower applied to go a given speed, say 25 knots, whether it's one, two, or three engines. Total fuel burn will be the same."

The MJM 50z is a very fuel-efficient design for its size, burning at 35 knots, what the competition burns at 25 knots. I'll never forget driv-ing hull #1 *Zing* to the Annapolis Boat Show. We'd been at McMichael Yacht Brokers in Mamaroneck, New York, for a couple of days, taking customers out for sea trials. I was joined by two others for the run from

American Yacht Club in Rye, 262 miles to the Annapolis Yacht Club. From AYC to AYC.

Billy Black photo

We started down Long Island Sound at 6:45 a.m. and went down the East River with a rising sun shining off the buildings, with early commuter boats zipping back and forth. It was a beautiful sight! We had the speedo pretty well pegged at 35 knots.

We cleared New York Harbor, went under the Verrazano Bridge, and rounded Sandy Hook at 8:00 a.m. By 10:00 a.m., we'd passed Atlantic City, then rounded Cape May by 11:00 a.m., went up Delaware Bay, and entered the Chesapeake and Delaware Canal by noon, pulling into the Annapolis Sailboat Show at 1:15 p.m. The total time was 7.5 hours for an average of 34.93 knots. That may be a recreational yacht record. Breakfast in Rye...lunch in Annapolis.

Friends arriving later for the weekend show said, "Wow! That's faster than we made it by car on the Jersey Turnpike from New York City!"

No Roll, Seakeeper Gyro

Ten knots faster, dual master suites, greater stability. That's three legs up on the competition. Throw another log on the fire: the greater the competitive advantage, the better. Recognition for another World First would be icing on the cake. Reduce investment risk!

That unique opportunity presented itself at the 2013 Fort Lauderdale Boat Show. There was excitement about a new "Seakeeper" technology. Seakeeper was founded by Shep McKinney after he and Bob Hinckley sold Hinckley Yachts. Seakeeper produced gyrostabilizers for custom installs on large yachts and sportfishing boats. You can imagine how welcome this technology was for fishing charters trolling and rolling offshore at 3-knot trolling speeds.

Mark Lindsay, Doug, and I went for a demo ride with the system on a heavy Bertram 35 Sportfish with a top speed of only 16 knots. Idling abeam with waves in the Fort Lauderdale inlet, but the system did stop the roll. But how would it work in quartering seas for an MJM going 30–35 knots?

Several weeks later, Brook Stevens of Seakeeper arranged with Joe Brenna of Intrepid for me to experience the gyro in action in an Intrepid 40 on Tampa Bay. The Intrepid had similar speed and weight characteristics to our MJM 40z. It worked great. My thinking was, "This is a no-brainer. People complain about heeling on a sailboat, which is far more stable and comfortable than any powerboat in waves. A sailboat is stabilized by pressure on the sails and the weight of a keel. Powerboats may not heel, but all of them roll in waves. Wouldn't a powerboat stabilized by a gyro be the best of both worlds? No heel and no roll?"

Time to Get Creative. After we checked in at Tampa International, I said, "Brook, let's talk turkey. How many of these units are now installed worldwide? Is any builder offering one as standard equipment? If not, why not? And if we commit to installing them as standard equipment on the new MJM 50z being launched in May 2014, would you give us a better OEM discount in return for MJM putting the rest of the industry on the defensive?"

"Bob, we've installed over 1,500 units, sometimes two or three on large yachts. All are custom installs. Quite a few sportfish brands offer them as an option. Nobody offers them as standard equipment."

"So, Brook. With Shep's background at Hinckley, you'd think they'd have been the first. So how come they and others haven't offered the system standard?"

"Bob, it's like this. They and others say they worry that Seakeeper would send the wrong message about the stability of their boats…implying that they must be inherently unstable. But if MJM takes the lead by committing to be the first brand worldwide to install Seakeepers as standard equipment, we'll grant a greater OEM discount than at present to builders not doing so."

Learning that Burke Design, MJM's engineering resource, was also Seakeeper's primary go-to engineer for gyro custom refits, the decision was easy. "You've got a deal, Brook."

With that, MJM led the industry worldwide in establishing this major advance in boating comfort as a standard feature. SeaRay followed shortly thereafter with their new L-Series 650. They had initially offered Seakeeper as an option, but when the first dozen buyers in the spring of 2014 ordered it after sea trials, SeaRay also made it standard.

Part of the fun of being innovative is to watch attempts by competitors to rationalize why they weren't doing it. You guessed it! Hinckley pooh-poohed MJM's December 2013 announcement. "Those MJMs are so unstable they had to do something desperate to sell them." Of course, this overlooked that the MJM 40z and 50z were built to exceed ISO Category A Ocean specifications, the highest rating for seaworthiness and stability.

The MJM 50z received the AIM Magazine Group's Editor's Choice Award at the 2014 Fort Lauderdale Boat Show: "MJM Yachts 50z—Best Downeast Cruiser—50 Feet Plus." The panel included editors of *Passagemaker, Power & Motoryacht, Soundings, Soundings Trade Only, SAIL,* and *Yachts International.*

After the show in 2015, *Zing* did a Florida version of the AYC to AYC run: 195 miles around the tip of Florida from Fort Lauderdale to Naples in six hours, with a speed of 32.5 knots, burning 280 gallons of diesel, a little over half a tank, for an efficiency of 0.7 nmpg.

Ideal Loop Boats

MJM Yachts officially became a sponsor of America's Great Loop Cruisers' Association (AGLCA) in April 2015.

Having cruised parts of the Great Loop—Lake Michigan, the North Channel, the Gulf, Florida, and Maine, offshore and on the ICW—I was convinced MJM Yachts were ideally suited for powerboat owners' "bucket list" journey.

Cruising is about shared adventure, and to do the Great Loop, parts of it or any number of miniloops is a wonderful way to learn more about the country, see old friends, and meet new ones.

But the right boat makes a huge difference. I'll never forget one friend's Loop journey on their trawler. And he was a naval officer. It seemed each week's email report was of a boating nightmare or a narrow escape from disaster. That makes for a lifetime of storytelling but is not the type of experience to plan on when you have a choice. We circulated the following to explain why an MJM is a smart choice.

Seaworthiness Contrary to what some may think, the Great Loop is not just tranquil countryside canals like in France. There are 1600+ miles of what can be some very rough open water: 824 miles on the Great Lakes, 389 miles between Mobile and Clearwater, 209 miles on the Chesapeake and 130 miles of the Jersey coast. This doesn't count the Sounds in the Carolinas. MJM's are the most suitable express cruisers to deal with rough water on the Loop.

Managing Locks None of us are getting more agile. MJMs have either Volvo Penta or Mercury IPS joystick and DPS or Skyhook systems which automatically hold you on a constant heading and GPS position. You can go down the center of a lock. Stop. Use the joystick to go sideways until fenders are barely touching a wall. Then engage Skyhook to hover next to the wall while grabbing bow and stern lines. The Skyhook will keep the boat from slewing with the bathtub effect of water entering or leaving the lock. And, the flush deck from wheel to stern cleat makes it easy for the helmsperson to grab a stern line without having to go up and down a bunch of stairs or levels.

11–12 Foot Air Height. With radar and a Glomex HD TV antenna, MJMs can easily do the Erie Canal route. Between Fort Lauderdale and Palm Beach there are only two of 21 bridges an MJM has to wait for. On an MJM, the 37 miles can be done in less than four hours instead of six hours. You'd have to average 16 knots offshore via Lake Worth and Port Everglades inlets to equal that.

Flybridge Without Ladders Electric, fully-opening windshields, roll up Strataglass or sliding, tinted safety glass sides and back offer 360 degrees panoramic visibility and fresh air on the main bridge-deck. No need to be juggling food & drink or twisting ankles coming down or going up precarious ladders or flights of stairs to a flybridge in a rolling sea.

Seakeeper Gyro Stabilizers A Seakeeper is standard equipment on the 50z and 53z and an option just about everyone chooses on the 40z and 43z.

Speed There can be large distances between good marinas and anchorages. With 34–37 knot cruising speed, you can pick a weather window on the best day of the week to cover 275+ miles in daylight…the length of Lake Erie or Charlevoix to Chicago or Pensacola to Clearwater. No need to run overnight at 8 knots, be holed up for a week waiting for a break in a less-than-desirable anchorage.

Fuel Efficiency It's a myth that trawlers are fuel efficient. They are even less efficient than an MJM 43z with outboards. At 10.3 knots, a Grand Banks 43 burns 25.4 gallons of diesel per hour (0.4 nmpg) with a range of 219 miles. The gas-powered MJM 43z with triple Mercury Verado 400s at 10.2 knots burns 14.2 gph (0.7 nmpg) with a range of 340 miles. But you can't beat the diesel-powered MJM 40z for fuel efficiency: 6.8 gph (1.5 nmpg) at 10.1 knots with a range of 463 miles.

Trucking Should you want the flexibility to do the Loop in stages: the MJM 40z and 43z are within the 12' width and 13.5' height limits for trucking. No escort is needed. They can be readily shipped anywhere with a 'wide load' sign, drives in place, and antennas hinged down.

The 50z and 53z can be trucked after removing rooftop masts to fit under the height limit, but due to the 15' beam, require escort vehicles and are 2–3 times more expensive to move.

MJM 35z Outboard Express Cruiser

In the spring of 2016, three years after the 50z was designed, we became concerned about the lack of a smaller MJM "starter" model. All active MJM models were selling for over $1 million. Hinckley had sold 32 of its 34-footers in the $700,000 range, and Back Cove sold many of its smaller models down around $500,000.

To put some of these buyers on an MJM track, the company had to come up with a new design and a more appealing market positioning.

The 29z had become too expensive for a 29-footer. The 34z was replaced by the 36z, which, at over $800,000, was not selling. Introducing another Down East diesel model seemed like a nonstarter.

Time to Get Creative. OK, let's start with some analysis: Where would new buyers come from? What boats did they own now? And is there any way we could develop a design that would address the problems they had with those boats? At the same time, was there anything about our Downeast diesel designs that might be a turnoff to those boaters?

The most likely target was owners of outboard-powered center consoles—about 80 percent of the market. Thinking about it, outboards have the advantage of shallow-water operation, are beachable for family outings, and are easier to use than diesel inboards. The time-consuming and body-scrunching diesel precheck routine of crawling in the bilge is avoided. It's "push the button and *go!*" They were twice as fast as all boats in the Downeast category, 50 mph fast and sporty.

Innovation derives from solving problems people don't realize they had learned to live with. The center consoles they'd been living with had several drawbacks.

First, the only person comfortable, not being assaulted by noise, wind, and spray, was the driver—often the man in the family.

Secondly, it was the guys' boat for speed and fishing with buddies, not so much a boat for the wife and kids.

Thirdly, center consoles were not ideal for sociable, all-weather dock-and-dine evenings, nor were they suitable for venturing far from the local harbor or beach.

While the womenfolk and kids might appreciate a nice Downeast-style boat like an MJM, Back Cove, or Hinckley, more than likely the guys would look on these boats as a bit too precious and slow.

Courtesy of MJM Yachts

MJM designs already had a comfortable, all-weather layout, weekend-cruise capability, and offshore seaworthiness. What it was lacking was:

- Speed to keep guys happy
- Shallow-water operation
- Beachability for weekend family outings
- Turn-the-key-and-go outboard convenience

Was the solution so ridiculously simple as putting outboards on MJMs? We already knew from several outboard-equipped 29zs that Zurn hulls ran well with outboards. A 29z equipped with a pair of optional Yamaha 250s exceeded 50 mph.

The faster it went, the more stable it became, with no chine walking or wobbling from side to side at high speed, a nasty trait of several of America's more popular outboard-boat brands.

We heard from so many guys coming to us at boat shows after owning a center console for a couple of years, saying, "I've had to make a decision: either get one of your MJMs for all-weather family comfort and use or abandon them and go out with my buddies in all sorts of weather to fish. I've decided to spend more time with my wife and kids and get an MJM."

The answer was in plain sight: an outboard-powered MJM could appeal to that huge center-console market.

But small companies can have as much trouble adopting new ideas as ponderous Fortune 500s. The leadership of our licensed builder, Boston BoatWorks, and their advisor, a retired advertising agency principal, deemed outboards to be foreign to MJM's "classic" appeal.

They further objected to a profile with sloped transom to better allow outboard motors to flow into the boat's shape, rather than having a vertical transom with outboards standing quite proudly on a platform astern, similar to the Hunt 33.

Onne van der Wal photo

Time to Get Creative. The use of the online consumer research service, Survey Monkey, helped establish strong interest in outboards and that MJM owners, as well as prospective buyers, preferred the new sloped-transom look.

Then pencils had to be sharpened. The goal for an MJM 35z was a standard boat price of $595,000.

Options brought the sail-away price to about $730,000 at retail. But it was an instant success, exceeding initial sales of the Hinckley 34.

During press days and customer sea trials at Newport Shipyard in early July 2017, the initial response was, "It's a pocket super-yacht!"

We did the Fort Lauderdale-to-Naples trip after the 2017 show. The 195 miles around the tip of Florida took 6 hours and burned 195 gallons, with 53 gallons to spare, or 1 nmpg. Not bad for twin Mercury Verado 350s!

After launching the MJM 35z, we followed with a triple outboard MJM 43z. Hinckley didn't wait long to announce their Sport Boat 40, with outboards and "MJM" side-opening doors. Tiara followed with their outboard 38 and Back Cove with a 32O.

The race was on, with MJM Yachts initiating a new category of powerboats, "The Outboard Express Cruiser." The National Marine Manufacturers Association (NMMA) couldn't come up with a share of market statistics for us, because they said, "Sorry, there isn't any such market." How about that for proof of innovation?

MJM 43z Beach Cottage

Jim Raycroft photo

My son Peter, in Charleston, South Carolina, was the MJM dealer for most of the Southeast and was a strong advocate of extending MJM's outboard initiative by modifying the 40z to become a 43z with sloped transom.

He had several buyers, including a longtime friend, the owner of multiple J/Boats and MJMs and a member of MJM's advisory board of directors, Hank Bernbaum.

Another influential board member, who had MJM 43z #1 on order, is Michael Lamach, chairman of Ingersoll Rand and the National Association of Manufacturers, who is also on the President's Business Advisory Committee. He named his boat *Hail Mary* to honor both his wife and the Mary of MJM.

Mary and I had seen the north side of Napatree Point Beach, off Watch Hill, Rhode Island, on a Saturday afternoon with about 100 boats. We were convinced and excited to have come up with a new boat category

Imagine a large, outboard-powered MJM setting an anchor and backing onto the beach with outboards raised. One person would step off the swim platform with a light beach anchor to secure the boat, thus creating a veritable beach cottage. No longer was it necessary to have a 2nd outboard to transport family between the beach and a 40-foot cabin cruiser anchored a quarter of a mile out in the bay, nor to deal with logistics as to who stays on the mother ship and goes to the beach and when.

MJM 53z—
World's Largest Outboard Express

Onne van der Wal photo

Large, quad-outboard-powered center consoles appeared at the 2017 Miami International Boat Show. Our twin-outboard MJM 35z was about to be launched. The first triple-outboard MJM 43z was under-way. Why not a quad-outboard 53z? It could become the world's largest outboard express cruiser. At the time, it became the largest Mercury-powered outboard vessel ever.

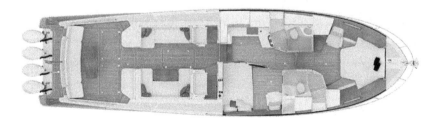

Time to Get Creative. An MJM 53z could match the 50-mph top speed of the new large center-console models. MJM 53z's dry weight of 28,000 lbs. with a cruising-yacht interior was comparable to the weight of conventionally molded center consoles. MJM's weight savings from high-tech construction is reinvested in luxury-yacht features.

Unique to Mary's and my 53z hull #1 was a dramatic upgrade of the "dual master suite" concept. Each would have a Stressless-type easy chair with a pouf as a footstool, a permanent double berth, a night table, a desk, and a picture window.

When introduced at the 2019 Newport International Boat Show, equipped with quad Mercury 400 HP outboards, the MJM 53z was awarded "Best New Powerboat over 35 Feet."

30+ Problems Solved by MJMs

I'd been creating boats to solve problems experienced with sail and powerboat designs of all sizes for over 50 years. Many were problems that boaters assumed went with the territory.

Jeff Bezos said, "The biggest needle movers will be things customers don't know to ask for. We have to tap into our inner imagination about what's possible."

We asked ourselves just how many boating problems MJM designs had solved or at least minimized. We came up with 30, most of which we've outlined, from hull side doors to Seakeeper gyros to electric opening windshields to all-weather pilothouses.

Then there's the less obvious until you've driven the boat four or more hours at 35 knots. It's not tiring but exhilarating. Cause? A length-to-beam ratio of 3.5:1 at the waterline creates a hull that slices through waves. Many powerboats are more barge-like in shape with a fatter, 2.7–3.0:1 ratio. Those hulls tend to collide with waves in a series of minijolts, which is exhausting.

MJM's flush deck from the helm to the transom, with only three steps below, avoids the hazard of guests accidentally being tripped up or losing their footing due to multilevels. And those side boarding doors at floating-dock height are greatly appreciated by all ages and pets.

2nd Generation Family Business

One challenge MJM took too long to resolve was the matter of succession. Corporate headquarters for MJM consisted of me, my desk, and several file cabinets. I was managing the dealer network, writing and placing all advertising, transmitting all boat orders with their numerous option issues to BBW, collecting all funds in payment for boats, wiring BBW a weekly work-in-process (WIP) advance, paying all the bills, developing new designs and their specs one-on-one with Doug Zurn, reviewing and developing the bill of materials on each boat, setting the pricing, and doing boat-show planning. Essentially, I was doing everything except actually building the boat.

I didn't regard this 12-hour, seven-day-per-week program as work so much as a creative endeavor, probably not unlike being an artist or a musician, totally wrapped up in what I enjoyed doing. Of course, constant contact with MJM owners and prospective owners was fun.

That was my routine since founding the company in 2002, not to mention during many of the early years with J/Boats, prior to renting 24 Mill Street from Trinity Church when our office staff grew to several people.

I wasn't getting any younger while the business was growing larger and more complex. At age 80 it was time to bring on a capable manager to relieve me of some of the work and eventually take over. That process lasted two years and culminated in bringing on Chris Hughes as a minority partner. Chris had been running BoatTest.com, the premier boat-review site with extensive video coverage of boats from all the major brands.

His video and digital marketing expertise complemented my 20th century-magazine print ad tendencies. The combination increased MJM sales by 50 percent to $25 million in 2016. MJM then got another boost.

The high cost of my son Peter's quality problems with the Chinese builder of his innovative Gunboat Catamaran business ultimately caused the filing of Chapter 11 in November 2015. While unfortunate for Gunboat, it was a blessing for MJM, making available arguably the most creative and persuasive selling talent in the marine business.

His desire to move to Charleston, South Carolina, fit well with the need for better sales representation in the Southeast, a market particularly well suited to the MJM brand. His experience in the Low Country and ICW would play a big part in MJMs leadership role in creating the outboard express market.

Peter became the MJM Southeast dealer, covering all but South Florida, as well as becoming a minority partner in MJM Yachts LLC.

At that point, Chris could see the handwriting on the wall. Peter was in place as the heir apparent. We both agreed that Chris's potential for long-term earnings from continued meaningful challenges was probably greater as a highly specialized consultant, leveraging his excellent track record with MJM. He remains a valuable member of the MJM Yachts marketing team but also has several nonconflicting consulting roles with other marine-industry clients.

After attending the Owner/President Management (OPM) Leadership Program at Harvard Business School (HBS) and recognizing the need for a succession plan not only at MJM Yachts but at J/Boats Inc., Peter persuaded our immediate five-member family to attend the HBS Families in Business weeklong course in the fall of 2018. This was just after we'd moved to Bishop Gadsden in Charleston. HBS put on a very stimulating and thought-provoking session.

Professor David Ager was particularly helpful and took a great interest in seeing an MJM succession program work, visiting Charleston for a "Family Board Meeting" and being available for countless back-and-forth emails between Peter and me, as well as MJM's accountant, Jeffrey Adams of Newport.

The net result was that Peter purchased my 75 percent of MJM Yachts to become the 100 percent owner on November 9, 2019 (Mom's birthday). Part of the deal is, Mary and I get to cruise around on MJM 43z *Breeze 2* until I've reached the age of 90. At that time, who knows? Maybe another negotiation will take place.

The above succession process left me with more time to make new friends as senior alumni advisor to the Princeton sailing team, act as commodore of the Bishop Gadsden Yacht Club, counsel other clubs forming DF95 fleets, take picnic cruises on *Breeze 2*, and work on this book.

CHAPTER 23

Back in the Racing Game

S ince October 2018, we've lived in a cottage on the magnificent con-
tinuing-care residential campus of Bishop Gadsden, on James Island, in Charleston, South Carolina. There were a couple of ponds and
an informal yacht club. A dozen or so members had a mixture of radio-controlled (RC) Lasers and Nirvanas.

When first arriving, I was told, "Bob, if you are serious about racing,
get a Soling 1M to race with the Charleston Model Yacht Club (CMYC)
five minutes away at James Island County Park." That sounded like a
good plan to pursue.

Not surprisingly in the small, interconnected world of sailing, the
builder of my Soling 1M was a longtime friend, Chuck Millican, who had
a boat immediately available thanks to Ned Nielsen. When Chuck was at
Harken in Pewaukee, Wisconsin, 48 years earlier, he had sold us two 470s.

My new, gold-colored RC Soling 1M with US-
549 on the sail brought back good memories of
Olympic aspirations in the full-sized version.

Charleston Model Yacht Club (CMYC) became my initiation to radio-control (RC) racing.
It's a talented, dedicated group with a well-orga-
nized, year-round schedule Their members are
enthusiastic RC devotees, most having several
models: Soling 1Ms, EC12s, DF95s, and a growing number of 10Ms.

2019 was a great year to get into the game. So much so, I even
caught the EC12 bug. "Bob, EC12s sail more like a real boat; you should
get one." What could be more elegant than a miniature America's Cup
12 Metre?

Six months earlier, our MJM 53z *Breeze* had been the Official Jury Boat for the 2019 12-Metre World Championship in Newport. I was smitten. My order went in for a brand-new, white, minimum-weight beauty with sail #24—my official US Sailing offshore sail number.

Onne van der Wal photo

This EC12 deep dive into RC Model Yachting involved more time rigging, tuning, and derigging each race day. The 25 lb., 5-foot long boat filled the back of my Jeep Cherokee with its custom carry cradle, a large canvas case for A & B rigs, and a folding setup table.

No matter. Having just sold MJM Yachts, there was lots of free time. However, I must admit to having moments of self-doubt.

Was I really ready to become such a dedicated hobbyist? My joy is the racing. On the plus side, the EC12 gave me an excuse to add Monday to racing a Soling on Wednesdays, then alternating boats on Sundays. What could be better?

Well, it wouldn't take long to get half the answer: all of two weeks. February 19, 2020, was a Wednesday "open" CMYC sailing day. Bring any boat to race on the same starting line...an RC version of PHRF handicap racing without the handicaps. That Wednesday didn't bode well for US-549: one Soling versus seven DF95s. I was not consoled by, "You did pretty well, Bob, for a Soling."

That woke up my hibernating one-design DNA as past chairman of US Sailing's One-Design Class Council and progenitor of countless J/Boat fleets. The handwriting was emphatically splashed on the water that day! I had to get a DF95 for my growing RC fleet.

DragonFlite 95—Pandemic Racing

I got on radiosailing.net that night to order a new DF95. The kit arrived the following Monday. Ten hours of novice assembly efforts later, tuned as directed in the kit's manual, the new #24 joined that Wednesday's DF95 fleet to win two races. What an amazing one-design product! Talk about instant gratification! Seven days from whim to win! And I thought we'd done such a good job with J/24s! *Wow!*

The DF95 had the convenient size of my Soling but half the weight, at 5 lbs. for easier handling. Pop the SUV back hatch, put the FlySky controller around your neck, grab the DF95 by the keel, push both switches "on," walk to the water, drop it in, race, lift it out, turn both switches "off," walk to the car, put it in, go home, repeat. What's more, it's fun and responsive, speedily planing in puffs and tracking true with little rudder action.

Then the pandemic hits! What could be worse? The county park shut down CMYC. Bishop Gadsden went into lockdown, Outdoor gatherings were limited to four people, socially distanced 6 feet apart, with masks.

Time to Get Creative. The DF95 is ideal for senior communities. It's small enough to race on a 1-acre (190-by-230-foot) pond, light for easy handling, holds its tune for weeks, and can be launched or pulled out by the top of its unstayed carbon mast without getting down on one's knees. So I invited 25 BG residents with sailing backgrounds to form a colorful new DF95 fleet. First-come, with $500, first-served, with choice of color and two-digit sail number. Yours truly would assemble and tune all equally to be "race-winning" craft. Why not? Worked selling J/24 Fleets 40+ years ago.

RC Pond Racing Rules

The first hurdle was, "What about my old Laser?" Thankfully, we found a home for those boats in nearby Wild Dunes. The Laser fleet captain there was looking for used Lasers at $150–$200 to expand his fleet of nine boats.

But a tougher challenge emerged to dampen progress. *Could it be endemic to RC racing elsewhere?* Several sailors, both experienced and novice, had tried RC racing and given it up as "not fun." The reason was either "I've been racing all my life according to the rules. RC racing is nothing but bumper cars out there. It's a joke!" Or "I thought RC sailing would be lots of fun and a way to make new friends. But a few know-it-all pros are always yelling 'Protest!' and throwing the rules at you, but then letting their friends off the hook and getting away with a future foul by saying, 'You owe me one.' That's no fun at all!"

Time to Get Creative. Sailboat racing is meant to be fun, not life and death. The Racing Rules of Sailing originated in the 1800s so large yachts could fix financial responsibility for collisions. This is not a problem with DF95 rubber bows and unstayed carbon masts. Being able to see contact and overlaps at distant marks is impossible. What can impair results is *boat contact* that causes loss of position in the race.

Solution? Come up with RC Pond Racing Rules, an adaptation of the Racing Rules of Sailing. Let boats bump other boats and marks, except start or finish marks. Who cares? If boat A causes boat B to lose place in the race, Boat A shall do a 360-degree turn. The word "enforce" as a responsibility in the RRS was deleted. Good sailors shall be role models by doing turns without being prompted. Instead of policemen, they are to encourage and instruct novices, explaining the rule while doing turns. Fun is now part of the DF95 phenomenon. Crowded mark roundings are cause for laughter and good-natured whining. BGYC's DF95 Fleet doubled to 18 boats overnight and now numbers 22.

Thankfully, BG management was persuaded to permit racing on its pond during the pandemic...as long as two groups, each with four seated sailors, were separated by 20 feet. That gave us eight boats on the starting line. To accommodate everyone, we doubled up the twice-weekly, hour-long sessions by including mornings and afternoons.

Running up and down the shore was not necessary, as is the case with longer course legs needed for larger RC models. No need for perfect W/L courses or squared starting lines...or racing in open water with steady winds.

The wilder the wind shifts and the closer the shore in a protected pond or cove, the more fun. Everyone gets a lucky break now and then. The DF95 sails with just air movement. With buildings and trees all around, you never know where the next puff of wind is coming from. Crazy fun!

DF95 Goes Viral

Word of our BGYC success with its socially distanced, masked, and seated-sailor format went viral and was celebrated as good news in the worldwide email newsletter *Sailing Scuttlebutt* (#5539) on April 1, and again on July 14 (#5611), under the title, "How to Sail in a Coronavirus Pandemic," describing in detail the "*fun*" pond rules.

Sail Newport adopted BGYC's colorful DF95 "fun" fleet program and pond rules to start their own fleet of 22 boats in July 2020. Under the leadership of Brad Read and Henry DiPietro this fleet has exploded in less than two years to over 80 boats, with frostbiting all winter. They are racing all three days of the 2023 New Year weekend.

I then worked with Carolyn Grant Zarella and Tom Darling to get Nantucket Community Sailing Center ready with a dozen DF95s for Race Week in August 2020—now 20 boats.

Clearly, RC racing is the most inclusive form of sailboat racing, whether it's age, gender, weight, or mobility. With everyone seated, a sailor with disabilities can win against a College Sailor of the Year. Ask Sail to Prevail's Paul Callahan. He's done it!

Intercollegiate Fleets

Princeton Sailing, restricted to campus like other college teams in the spring of 2021, races a new fleet of 10-DF95s on Lake Carnegie. Heavier team members can have fun competing level with dinghy lightweights.

The plan is to invite Harvard and Yale to a revival of the May Challenge Cup, the oldest trophy in intercollegiate sailing, dating back to 1928. "Coed Racing" can have new meaning. Each college has two boats, a male and a female, racing in A Division and two in B Division, instead of a mixed double-handed crew in one dinghy.

The US Coast Guard Academy cadets ordered a fleet of ten boats to be able to continue sailing even though their regular program and regatta travel was restricted during the spring of 2021.

Sailing Across America

Sailing Scuttlebutt No. 5539 of March 31, 2020, told of my excitement about what could stimulate major growth of sailboat racing in America. Here are excerpts:

> Radio-controlled sailing just happens to be the perfect option in these trying times, particularly if you are in a residential community with a 1+ acre pond. There's likely to be a ready group of lifetime boaters and sailboat racers among the emerging 77 million aging Baby Boomers. BGYC in Charleston could be setting a national trend.
>
> Radio-controlled sailboats could dramatically grow the sport of sailing... anywhere there's a pond.
>
> Think also of an elementary school curriculum. Skills of

assembling the DF95 kits, tying knots, learning the physics of sailing, the complexity of electronic controls, learning how to sail without having instructors on the boat or yelling with megaphones, and learning a lifetime sport of yacht racing. And, it's a sport that can involve parents participating with their kids in the same events. You know there's nothing more motivating to a kid than beating the old folks on the racecourse!

Sailing on these small ponds with winds coming from every direction, really teaches racing tactics. Must be how Buddy Melges got so good, being on Lake Zenda.

And in terms of helping a kid deal with life: Racing sailboats teaches decisiveness/judgement...acting without knowing all the facts...training the mind to assign probabilities to a number of possible outcomes like the Harvard Business School Decision Tree exercise.

It takes being immersed in each new phase of sailing to fully understand what its potential might be for the sport, and I am seeing the massive possibility here.

Time to Get Creative. The concept has been shared with US Sailing and Spike Lobdell, founder of the New England Science & Sailing Foundation (NESS) in Stonington, Connecticut. The hope is that those two organizations, with others, can put the elementary school program outlined above on the national map.

Afterword

Shared Family DNA

T his book wouldn't be complete without acknowledging the shared DNA and the passion for sailing on both the Johnstone and the Van Liew sides of the family.

All three of my sons have played a major part throughout this story. Stuart has volumes of stories of his own to tell about his early parallel business endeavors in digital company start-ups in the UK and the US, including Boats.com and Yachtworld.com, as well as attendance at just about every regatta, in exotic harbors around the world. Stuart and Peter were both Collegiate All-Americans, the former being College Sailor of the Year and the latter being inducted into the Connecticut College Athletic Hall of Fame.

Peter has had an eight-chapter marine-industry career, as touched upon in this story, from One-Design 14 to Sunfish-Laser to Escape to Johnson Worldwide to Gunboat Catamarans to J Boats to Alerion Yachts and now MJM Yachts.

Drake made a mark in the investment world with Davenport & Co. in Richmond, has been the sales manager of J/Boats, and earned an MBA at the University of Virginia's Darden School of Business. He is chairman of the J/Boats Inc. board of directors and has campaigned a J/70 out of the Fishing Bay Yacht Club.

My brother Rod's sons are all part of this story too. After Connecticut College, Jeff started out as president of J/World, then followed me as president of J/Boats Inc. Rod's son Alan took over his father's role as VP and chief designer to do an outstanding job, creating some of the best-performing boats in the world. A third brother, Phil, is a corporate attorney who has made an outstanding contribution toward keeping this family enterprise on the rails despite some ups and downs, as one can imagine, with half a dozen or so skippers all in the same boat. Rod's second wife, Lucia, played a key role right from the start in the 470 and 505 dinghy era, then all through the *Ragtime* building years and J/Boats. Rod's daughters, Pam and Becky, and his sons, formed part of the "family" crew for many years.

Jeff had some racing stories similar to my own. He lost the 2004 J/24 World Championship in Noroton to Jens Hookenson on a tie-breaker, was runner-up in a windy J/80 Worlds in Kiel with a pickup crew and a borrowed boat, and was helmsman on the winning 12 Metre *American Eagle* in the 2010 World Championship…on his 50th birthday!

We haven't talked much about my two other younger siblings. Next in line, my late sister, Bobette, sailed in the Women's National Championship Adams Cup at the helm as a teenager. The Wadawanuck team was doing so well that they were protested for having a teenage girl rather than a woman at the helm. "This is meant to be a women's championship," claimed a renowned female sailor Bobette was upstaging.

Bobette's son and my nephew, Clay Burkhalter, competed in the Mini-Transat with a boat designed by Rod. He could tell countless stories as a professional delivery captain. His sister, my niece Susan Burkhalter Green, will soon be able to write her own book. She is off this year on a new adventure, living aboard a cruising boat with her husband, Brian. I got an email from her while writing this segment. "In the Bahamas, a huge storm put us up on a sandbar in the middle of the night…but all is OK. A friend dragged us off at high tide…only a few scratches on the keel and rudder."

My youngest brother, John, worked outside J/Boats as an independent yacht broker. He had a heavy dose of the sailing DNA. He's won both ECYRA Midget and Junior Championships, as I have. He also helped win the Intercollegiate MacMillan Cup for Babson, along with capturing several Lightning and J/22 championships as a member of the Madison Beach Club. More recently, he's won the J/70 Fleet Championship of Fishers Island Sound. John's son (my nephew) Jimmy, who now resides in China, promoting and successfully racing J/80s, which are built there, won the 1989 Laser Radial World Championship in Denmark and is supplementing his income with prize money on the racing circuit in China. They reward race winners with hard renminbi instead of silver plate bowls.

Then there's a couple of first cousins who haven't escaped the pull of the sea. Doctor Holt Rose, my Sears Cup semifinal crew, lived in Southern California and eventually owned a J/120, which he sailed with his wife, Halaine, out of Marina del Rey. Cousin Fred Van Liew is a fellow Rhode Island sailor who has campaigned several boats named *Fiddler*: a Block Island 40 yawl, a 12 Metre, and one of the family's creations, a J/111.

Fred's nephew Brad Van Liew arguably has had the heaviest dose of sailing DNA in the family. He is the only American to have completed three solo-circumnavigation races around the world, placing 3rd in the Open 50 class in the Around Alone in 1998–1999, winning Class II of the Around Alone in 2002 with the Open 50 *Tommy Hilfiger Freedom America*, and winning the Vendee Globe in 2010–2011 in the Eco 60 *Le Pingouin*. He was involved with the restoration of the pilot schooner *Spirit of South Carolina* and has now retired, also in Charleston, to become a farmer, pilot, and real estate agent.

Déjà Vu All Over Again

Of course, for most grandparents, grandchildren are a special category. Some wag once quipped, "What makes that relationship so special is they have a common enemy." Amusing but not apropos when there's such a common-DNA sailing thread that's flowed through four generations, starting with my mom and dad.

While I didn't have much in common with my grandparents, that's not the case with my own grandchildren. It's like having fun living my life all over again for the third time. There were many similar stories to share, get excited about, and be proud of. Our own four kids never had a chance to do anything but sail. The oldest three got put on a Hinckley Sou'Wester 30 for two weeks of cruising in Maine when they were all age 3 or younger. Pictured below as "seasoned salts" standing watch on the schooner *White Wing* in 1965, they are ages 4, 7, and 6.

Our grandkids weren't given much of an option, either. They started aboard various boats practically out of the bassinet; then it was into Optimist dinghies, traveling to events like the Orange Bowl Regatta on Biscayne Bay and overseas.

Peter's oldest, Nick, won a race in the Optimist World Championships in Montevideo, became captain of the Tabor School team that won the ISSA National Team Race Championship, won Boat of the Week at Marblehead Race Week, was the winner of the Club 420 National Championship, and was a College of Charleston sailing team member. He is now the coach of the Citadel's sailing team. His newest love is a Sunfish. He sailed one for the first time in the first race of the 2021 North Americans and won, just like Grandma and Grandpa 55 years earlier! Talk about the family coming full circle! And along with his uncles Stuart and Drake, he has taken over his father, Peter's shares and become a board member of J/Boats Inc.—the first of the third generation to do so, with the gift of his father's shares.

His sister, India, has been a member of the United States National Optimist and Laser Radial teams competing in Uruguay, Slovenia,

Poland, France, and Norway. At the Easter Regatta in the Netherlands, she was the top American female. She was captain of the 2014 Tabor Sailing team, went on to sail in the ICSA Women's Nationals for George Washington, and was a successful racing coach at Conanicut and Noroton Yacht Clubs. She sails her own Herreshoff 12½ *Reverend* and is a member of the New York Yacht Club. She is a member of the MJM Yachts Advisory Board.

Billy Black photo

Son Stuart's oldest, Hunter, followed a similar Optimist path, winning the 12 and Under British Championship and the Midwest Championship and finishing 8th in the US Nationals. He was twice an Academic Collegiate All-American and captain of the Dartmouth sailing team. He's also a Sunfish owner and sails a DF95 as a member of the Texas Corinthian Yacht Club and the New York Yacht Club. His younger brother, Ford, was also initiated to racing in an Optimist but sized out rather quickly to excel in other sports, becoming a ranked squash and lacrosse player while being a great shipmate of his grandpa, watching whales on MJM offshore deliveries.

In Appreciation

This has been my story, with too narrow a focus to include many family tales worthy of further volumes. Nor have I given sufficient credit to the many coconspirators at all the places I've worked, or to all those friends among suppliers, advertisers, publications, and employees and management at Quaker Oats or their subsidiaries in Colombia and Venezuela, or to Gugler Lithographic, AMF Alcort, Tillotson-Pearson, and Boston BoatWorks, or to US Sailing staff and the volunteers and class officers worldwide who've managed countless regattas to keep the sport of yacht racing alive and well.

Writer Kevin Koenig has to be thanked for keeping my freestyle form of ad-copy prose reasonably within the bounds of proper English grammar and punctuation. Kevin has been executive editor of *Yachting* and senior editor at *Power & Motoryacht*, so he was thankfully familiar with the subject matter and a joy to work with between moments of caring for his newborn daughter.

Then there are the hundreds, if not thousands, of J/Boat and MJM owners who are like extended family and are fun to connect with when Mary and I are cruising New England, the ICW, and Florida. The overriding motivation for me in this business has been the opportunity to experience the joy of creating boats that positively contribute to the family life and shared adventure of others.

I've often said that when I left Quaker in 1973 at age 39, it was to pursue my God-given ministry of being involved with boats. This was more "mission" than "work." The people involved with boats are a pleasure to be around and do business with. My father told me I'd learn that 9 of 10 people are wonderful, and the 10th is a "stinker." My experience in boating has been closer to one in 100.

Like family are the fellow competitors and friends made over many years cruising and on the racecourse. It brings me immeasurable satisfaction to think that an event or a design I'd played a part in creating was a springboard to their joy or success.

Gary Jobson should be given great credit for founding the National Sailing Hall of Fame. There are more than 60 inductees and 20 nominees that are part of this book. Attending the annual induction ceremony is even more fun than a college reunion. Sailors from all over the country who've been sailing against or with each other most of their lives get together and share their stories. The National Sailing Hall of Fame abbreviation "NSHOF," in my book, stands for the "National Sailing Hall of Friends."

Image Credits

Special credit should go to photographers I've had the pleasure to work with at Naturescapes, AMF Alcort, J/Boats, and MJM Yachts.

In our Naturescapes years, getting a box of as many as a hundred 8x10 or 4x5 color transparencies to review from Philip Hyde or Ed Cooper was a thrill.

One of my most memorable moments in photography was a trip to Santa Fe, New Mexico, in 1975, to spend a day and evening with Eliot Porter reviewing his nature photography.

On the bus trip back to the airport in Albuquerque, there was only one other passenger. He was seated in the back. It was John Ehrlichman. He had just moved to Santa Fe, or was about to, before his stint in federal prison for conspiracy, obstruction of justice, and perjury in the Watergate scandal.

As a history major and recognizing him, this was too good a moment to pass up. So I rose from my seat, went to the back of the bus, introduced myself, and asked, "Mind if I join you?"

He responded, "Sure, please do."

We spent the rest of the 65-mile bus trip together talking about his Nixon White House experience. I remember him making one comment: "If the president doesn't get his agenda put forward in the first two years of his term, it's all over. The second two years are all 'politics,' and nothing gets done."

Another fantastic, photo-related adventure was a weeklong trip Mary, son Peter (age 9), and I took with *Sports Illustrated* photographer

Eric Schweikardt (esphoto8@gmail.com) to shoot *The Fun of Sailing*, AMF Alcort's full-line brochure. Mary, Peter, and I served as models. We went to a different restaurant each night and rated the key lime pies. The Holiday Inn in Marathon won.

Sailing has to be the most photographic of sports. To spend time with and work alongside Billy Black (billyblack.com), Onne van der Wal (vanderwal.com), Paul Todd (outside images.com), and Jim Raycroft (jimraycroft.com) has been a joy. I became an admirer of their talents and was privileged to work with their partner wives as well.

To the best of my knowledge, all the photos in this book other than family photos or the ones taken by me are appropriately credited or are courtesy of AMF Alcort, J/Boats Inc., MJM Yachts LLC, or their assignees, which are granted broad rights for their use in publications.

Should readers be interested in seeing the work of these photographers, they are encouraged to visit the websites indicated in the parentheses above. Please contact the author if, as a photographer, you have an issue with a specific photo or are credited for an image that is not yours. Thank you.

Appendix

Past Winners of the Laser (ILCA 7) Class

FOR THE

Robert L. Johnstone, III Trophy
In The United States Youth Sailing Championship

YEAR	NAME	FROM	YEAR	NAME	FROM
1973	Peter Commette	MIddletown NJ	1998	Charles Asper	Forestville CA
1974	Chris Maas	Seattle WA	1999	Andrew Lewis	Honolulu HI
1975	Carl Buchan*^	Seattle WA	2000	Andrew Campbell	San Diego CA
1976	Stewart Neff	Oyster Bay NY	2001	Andrew Campbell	San Diego CA
1977	Kelly Gough	Dallas TX	2002	Andrew Campbell*^	San Diego CA
1978	Andrew Menkardt*	Bethesda MD	2003	Emery Wager	Seattle WA
1979	Kevin Kempton	Ocean Gate NJ	2004	Michael Scott	Kaneohe HI
1980	Russ Silvestri	Tiburon CA	2005	Thomas Barrows^	St. Thomas VI
1981	Charlie McKee	Seattle WA	2006	Royce Weber	Surf City NJ
1982	Vince Kirby	Middletown RI	2007	Colin Smith	Fort Lauderdale FL
1983	Lou Verloop	Miami FL	2008	Cam Cullman	Rye NY
1984	Mark Eldred	Miami FL	2009	Zeke Horowitz	Sarasota FL
1985	Samuel Kerner	Honolulu HI	2010	John Wallace	St. Petersburg FL
1986	Keven Hall	Ventura CA	2011	Olin Paine	San Diego CA
1987	Andy Lovell	New Orleans LA	2012	Greg Martinez	Houston TX
1988	Peter Dreyfuss	Miami FL	2013	Mitchell Kiss^	Holland MI
1989	Alex Camet	San Diego CA	2014	Malcolm Lamphere	Lake Forest IL
1990	Jason Rucker	Bedford TX	2015	Richie Gordon	Ridgefield CT
1991	Brett Davis	Largo FL	2016	Ford Mcann	Coronado CA
1992	Brian Camet	San Diego CA	2017	Chase Burwell	Corpus Christie TX
1993	Bill Hardesty^	San Diego CA	2018	Joseph Hou	Charleston SC
1994	Bill Hardesty	San Diego CA	2019	Chase Carraway	Egg Harbor NJ
1995	Jonathan Baker	San Diego CA	2020	Not Sailed	
1996	Dalton Bergan^	Kirkland WA	2021	Daniel Escudero	Atlanta GA
1997	Brad Funk	Clearwater FL	2022	Benjamin Smith	Mission Bay CA
	* Won Youth Worlds			^ College Sailor of the Year	

1973
US Youth Sailing Championship
Laser Class

OFFICIAL RESULTS
1973 UNITED STATES YOUTH CHAMPIONSHIP

LASERS

Place	Name	From	Finishes	Points
1	Peter Commette	Middletown, N.J.	1-(10)-1-1-1	0
2	Augie Diaz	Miami, Fla.	2-(13)-2-3-3	17.4
3	Buzz Reynolds	Scotch Plains, N.J.	9-1-(15)-5-2	28
4	Carl Buchan	Mercer Island, WA	4-5-(8)-4-4	34
5	Dave Perry	Southport, Conn.	14-4-3-(18)-6	45.4
6	Tom Burton	Excelsior, Minn.	5-2-10-13-(16)	48
7	Carl Levinson	Indianapolis, IN	6-11-4-11-(d)	53.7
8	Lee Morrison	Brooklyn, N.Y.	8-(24)-20-2-17	66
9	Clark Thompson	Houston, Texas	12-12-(41)-10-8	66
10	Jack Bateman	San Diego, CA	10-20-6-8-(d)	67.7
11	Scooter Kinsey	Fort Myers, Fla.	11-3-13-24-(24)	71.7
12	Hugo Schmidt	Newport Beach, CA	16-19-(d)-7-7	73
13	Mark Reynolds	San Diego, CA	(27)-18-17-6-9	73.7
14	Charlie Hurd	Excelsior, Minn.	20-(34)-5-12-18	78
15	Peter Jones	Buffalo, N.Y.	7-9-(31)-16-25	81
16	Gary Knapp	Syosset, N.Y.	3-8-7-(d)-d	81.7
17	William Butz	West Bend, WI	13-(36)-9-25-12	83
18	Mark Makielski	South Bend, IN	(38)-26-18-9-10	87
19	Jamie McCreary	Larchmont, N.Y.	(37)-16-11-19-20	90
20	Todd Field	Manhasset, L.I.,N.Y.	22-14-12-20-(26)	92
21	Peter Rodin	Grosse Point, MI	30-(41)-21-15-5	94
22	Terry Kempton	Ocean Gate, N.J.	19-23-24-(29)-13	103
23	Craig Martin	San Diego, CA	(35)-29-25-14-11	103
24	Woody Stieffel	Bay St. Louis, MS	17-(d)-28-17-21	107
25	Marvin Duncan	Marblehead, MA	18-17-34-(34)-14	107
26	Mark Mueller	Miami Shores, Fla.	(34)-6-33-32-22	116.7
27	Peter Schwartzenbach	South Norwalk, CT	23-27-19-27-(d)	120
28	Bart Harris	Columbia, SC	26-31-14-(37)-27	122
29	James Bradley	Madison, WI	29-22-(38)-26-23	124
30	Gregg Griffin	Greenwich, CT	24-(35)-30-28-19	125
31	Gordon Curran	Honolulu, Hawaii	(42)-39-32-21-15	131
32	Barton Beek	Balboa, CA	(36)-21-36-22-28	131
33	Holland Hodges	Columbia, SC	33-15-29-31-(d)	132
34	Bruce Stevens	Williamsville, N.Y.	21-d-23-23-(d)	133
35	Gerald Stewart	San Diego, CA	25-7-42-40-(d)	138
36	Craig Haas	Coral Gables, Fla.	(39)-38-16-36-d	143
37	Tom Johnson	San Diego, CA	28-37-22-33-(d)	144
38	Mark Kastel	Glencoe, Ill.	43-29-27-30-(d)	153
39	Macy Nelson	Baltimore, MD	32-25-35-39-(d)	155
40	James Larimore	Miami, Fla.	15-33-40-(d)-d	155
41	Steve Steele	Littleton, CO	31-30-39-38-(d)	162
42	Marty Hublitz	Alexandria, VA	40-32-37-35-(d)	168
43	Nathaniel Philbrick	Pittsburgh, PA	41-40-26-(d)-d	174

1973
US Youth Sailing Championship
International 470 Class

OFFICIAL RESULTS
1973 UNITED STATES YOUTH CHAMPIONSHIP

470's

Place	Name	From	Finishes	Points
1	Terry Neff/Kevin Gaughan	Oyster Bay, N.Y.	1-13-(15)-1-4-1	27
2	Steve Hicks/Bill Langan	Greenwich, CT	(34)-9-1-5-3-3	36.4
3	Stu and Drake Johnstone	Wilmette, IL	6-2-(13)-2-7-7	43.7
4	John Hammel/Rocky Geyer	Noroton, CT	(29)-6-9-4-1-5	44.7
5	Bob and Dick Whitehurst	Pensacola, Fla.	9-7-(22)-8-2-4	53
6	John Aras/John Potter	Silver Springs, MD	2-3-2-15-(25)-19	57.7
7	Greg Fisher/Holley Petersilge	Columbus, OH	21-12-3-3-16-(23)	78.4
8	Griff Hall/Chip Jackson	Severna Park, MD	13-15-8-(17)-5-10	80
9	Kevin Downey/Keith Whittemore	Bellevue, WA	16-8-10-6-14-(dns)	83.7
10	Mike Morrisey/Mike Durkin	North Quincy, MA	(dnf)-1-19-10-22-22	97
11	Charlie Phelps/Mike Sivz	Severna Park, MD	26-25-12-(28)-9-2	99
12	Richie Stearns/Fred Albrecht	Northfield, IL	4-(31)-11-22-15-20	100
13	Peter Bowe/Peter Metzler	Annapolis, MD	31-5-(33)-12-6-18	100.7
14	John Thompson/Bruce Empey	Annapolis, MD	(30)-11-14-11-18-17	101
15	John and David Whittle	Long Branch, N.J.	14-4-26-20-(29)-12	104
16	Jim Adensam/Kelly Gough	Dallas, Texas	33-14-(dnf)-7-11-11	106
17	Tom Smith/Calvin Obara	College Park, GA	10-17-18-(dnf)-13-15	113
18	Tim and Mark Boucher	Columbus, Ohio	11-27-24-(dns)-8-13	113
19	Jeff Jones/Doug Cousino	Dearborn, MI	12-(dnf)-7-14-24-26	113
20	Allison Jolly/Rick Ericson	St. Petersburg, FL	(25)-16-20-23-10-16	115
21	Rod Glover/Peter Gruber	Cincinnati, OH	5-24-23-(33)-20-14	115
22	John Brodsky/Jon Harris	Rumson, N.J.	15-20-21-(26)-21-9	116
23	Peter Pierce/Patti Kirkpatrick	Wichita, KS	20-28-(32)-9-23-8	118
24	Rob Wilkins/Tom Whitemore	Lexington, SC	22-10-4-27-27-(27)	118
25	Bill Frissel/Blair Hamilton	Chagrin Falls, OH	7-22-5-25-32-(dns)	120
26	Gary Smith/Bob Holden	Arlington, VA	18-(30)-6-19-28-21	121.7
27	Charlie Scott/Carol Phelps	Annapolis, MD	24-26-30-13-(dnf)-13-25	128.7
28	Joe Balaconis/Jim Ansara	South Boston, MA	3-29-17-29-(dnf)-28	132.7
29	Art Rousmaniere/Wis Murray	Oyster Bay, N.Y.	19-19-28-16-(31)-24	136
30	Jud Smith/Campbell Seamans	Marblehead, MA	8-21-31-(dnf)-19-(dns)	144
31	Paul Duane/Jeff Schwarz	Vineyard Haven, MA	23-(32)-16-21-30-29	149
32	Wally Corwin/Lawson Fisher	Rye, N. Y.	28-(33)-27-24-26-15	150
33	Jane Sweeney/Tom Harrison	Indianapolis, IN	27-18-34-30-12-(dns)	151
34	Mike Rettig/Kurt Langford	Woodland Hills, CA	dnf-23-29-18-17-(dns)	151
35	Nina Nielson/Alice Cooney	Riverside, CA	17-35-25-32-33-(dns)	172
36	Tim Mooney/Russ Pearson	Bay Shore, N.Y.	32-34-(dnf)-31-dns-dns	199

J/Boats (1996–2022)

Model	LOA	PHRF*	Intro	Until	Yrs	Hulls	Major Awards
J/45	45.4	-3	2022	2023	1	10	SW BOTY - R/C. CW BOTY- Perf Crs
J/9	28.0	120	2020	2023	3	70	SAIL Best Boat -Daysailer
J/99	32.6	70	2019	2023	4	107	SW BOTY - ICRA BOTY
J/121	39.7	21	2017	2023	6	21	SW BOTY - R/C
J/112e	36.7	60	2015	2023	8	79	SW BOTY - R/C
J/97e	32	105	2014	2018	5	15	
J/88	28.9	84	2013	2023	10	110	SW BOTY - Best One Design
Intl J/70	22.7	117	2012	2023	11	1750	SW BOTY, Y&Y BOTY, Eur BOTY
J/122E	40	30	2012	2016	4	14	
J/11S	36.4	39	2011	2012	1	3	
Intl J/111	36.4	39	2010	2023	13	140	SW BOTY--Y&Y BOTY- VOILES BOTY
J/108	35.4	96	2010	2012	2	5	
J/97	32	102	2009	2014	5	65	SW BOTY - Club Racer
J/95	31	108	2009	2015	6	36	SW BOTY, CW BOTY, SAIL BestBs
J/122	40	30	2006	2012	6	90	RORC BOTY
J/124	41	36	2005	2007	2	35	
J/65		N/A	2005	2006	1	2	
J/100	32.8	90	2004	2014	10	168	SW BOTY - Overall
J/133	44	18	2003	2010	7	55	CW BOTY, SW BOTY - Overall
J/92s	30.2	99	2003	2012	9	170	
J/109	35.8	69	2002	2014	12	375	SAIL Top Ten
J/145	48	-18	1999	2006	7	18	SW BOTY - Racer/Cruiser
J/125	41	-3	1997	2003	6	16	SW BOTY - Racer
J/90	29.5	51	1997	1998	1	5	SW BOTY - Sportboat
J/32	32	126	1996	2003	7	85	
J/46	46	33	1996	2003	7	35	

* Performance Rating Example: A J/70 at 117 is 54 secs/mile faster than a J/24 at **171**

J/Boats (1977–1995)

Model	LOA	PHRF*	Intro	Until	Yrs	Hulls	Major Awards
J/160	53	3	1995	2004	9	35	SW BOTY - Offshore Cruiser
J/42	42	81	1995	2006	9	77	
J/110	36	93	1995	1997	2	16	
J/120	39	51	1994	2006	12	230	CW BOTY - Overall
Intl J/80	26	114	1993	2023	30	1680	
J/92	31	105	1992	2002	10	150	SW BOTY - Overall
J/130	43	21	1992	2002	10	43	CW BOTY - Overall
J/105	35	90	1991	2014	23	685	SW BOTY - Overall
J/39	39	51	1991	1993	2	21	
J/35C	35	96	1990	1994	4	36	SW BOTY -30-35'
J/44	44	36	1989	1995	6	68	SW BOTY - Overall
J/37C	37	81	1989	1991	2	6	
J/33	33	81	1988	1991	3	51	
J/37	37	69	1987	1989	2	46	
J/34C	34	114	1987	1990	3	36	SW BOTY - Overall
J/28	28	171	1986	1988	2	75	
J/34 IOR	34	114	1985	1987	2	25	
J/40	40	84	1984	1994	10	86	SW BOTY - Overall
J/27	28	120	1984	1992	8	189	MORC Intnls Winner
J/41 IOR	41	66	1984	1987	3	19	Won SORC & 1Ton NA's
Int J/22	22	183	1983	2018	35	1680	
J/35	35	72	1983	1992	9	330	Sailboat Hall of Fame
J/29	29	111	1982	1987	5	534	
J/36	36	81	1981	1984	3	55	
J/30	30	138	1979	1987	8	546	
Int J/24	24	171	1977	2018	41	5504	Sailboat Hall of Fame
				TOTAL		**15,702**	As of June 2023

MJM Yachts (2003–2022)

Model	LOD	Beam	Propulsn	MPH	Intro	Until	Yrs	No.	
34z	34' 0"	11' 0"	1 x 440	35	2003	2008	5	65	
29z	29' 0"	10' 2"	1 x 260	38	2006	2013	7	40	
40z	40' 0"	12' 0"	2 x 370	43	2009	2021	12	107	
36z	37' 0"	11' 0"	2 x 220	40	2011	2013	2	34	
50z	50' 0"	15' 0"	3 x 435	46	2015	2022	7	35	AIM Best DE Over 50'
35z	35' 8"	11' 0"	2 x 300	50	2017	Current	6	40	
43z	43' 0"	12' 0"	3 x 400	53	2017	2022	5	33	
53z	53' 0"	15' 0"	4 x 400	50+	2019	2022	3	15	NIBS - Best Over 35'
MJM - 3	35' 8"	11' 0"	2 x 300	50+	2020	Current	3	20	
MJM - 4	42' 7"	12' 0"	2 x 600	53	2022	Current	1	12	NIBS - Best New Pwrboat
MJM 42	42' 7"	12'	2 x 600	55	2022	Current	0	4	
						Total		405	

Bob's Boats (1947–1995)

Model	Hull #	Name	Years	Major Results
Long Island OD	43	*Prodigal II*	1947-9	4 - WYC. Junior Champs
				2x ECYRA Midget Champion
Lightning	4148	*Wassayek*	1949	Fleet #183 Champion
Lightning	4151	*Houqua*	1950-1	2x Fleet #183 Champion
				2x ECYRA Junior Champion
CC Mercury	16'	*Mussel*	1960	1st - LCYC Summer Series
Sunfish	V - 50	*Rabbit*	1964-6	2x Venezuelan Natl Champ
Rainbow	180	*C-Bird*	1967-8	2x National Champ
Penguin	8700	*Rabbit*	1969	1st Interntaionals
Soling	180	*Gull*	1969	9th NAmericans
Soling	430	*Houqua*	1970-1	7th Worlds
Soling	549	*Gold Rush*	1972	6th US Olympic Trials
470	616	*Rabbit*	1974	6th CORK
Windsurfer			1974	Chicago Area Dealer
Sunfish		*Rabbit*	1975-6	1st CT Down River
J/24	21	*Top of the World*	1977	1st - MORC BIRW
J/24	524	*Morning Sun*	1978	
J/24	653	*Top of the World*	1978-9	8th Worlds
J/30		*Sleighride*	1980	
J/24	2300	*Top of the World*	1980	10th Worlds
J/36	1	*Aja*	1981	
J/24	2424	*JJ*	1981	
J/29	19	*Merrimac*	1982	1st NEHF Ocean Race
J/24	3400	*Top of the World*	1982	11th NorthAmericans
J/35		*Merrimac*	1983	1st New England Solo-Twin
J/24	3700	*Rabbit*	1983	2nd Worlds
J/22	2	*Rabbit*	1983	
J/41	2	*Aja*	1984	Bermuda Race
J/27	2	*Rabbit*		
J/41	19	*Merrimac*	1985	1 Ton NorthAmericans
J/24	4151	*Houqua*	1985	5th J/24 NAs
J/28	1993	*Rabbit*	1986	
J/24	4300	*Tally Ho*	1986	13th - J/24 Worlds
J35		*Houqua*	1987	1st in Class - Block Island RW
J/40	21	*Shibui*	1988	
J/44	1	*Iona*	1989	1st NYYC Queen's Cup
J/105	1	*Sandpiper*	1992	
J/24	5000	*5000*		10th+ J/24 Worlds
J/105	73	*Tern*	1993	1st - Atlantic Coasts
J/120	15	*Tern*	1994	1st - NE Solo-Twin
J/22	2	*Rabbit*	1995	1st - BHYC Fleet Series
J/42	1	*Gannet*		1st NYYC Cruising 2nd DERW

Bob's Boats (1996–2022)

Model	Hull #	Name	Years	Major Results
J/42	15	*Gannet II*	1996	1st - NYYC Crusiing - 2nd DERW
Dyer 29	273?	*Grace*		Boothbay Harbor
J/120	70	*Gannet III*	1997	1st - FIGAWI & DERW Overall
J/105	224	*Camelia*	1998	1st Charleston Fleet
Dyer 29 DE	315?	*Grace*		Charleson SC
J/105	304	*Tern*	1999	1st - KW & CHS RW
J/105	500	*Tern*	2000	1st - KWRW & SORC
J/125	1	*Wings of the Wind*		1st - BI & DERW Weeks
J/42	61	*Iona*	2001	1st BI & DERW & MRetSR
J/120	9	*Gannet IV*	2002	1st - BI & DERW
MJM 34z	1	*Grace*	2003	Later to Friday Harbor WA
J/100	1	*Tern*	2004	1st- DERW
MJM 34z	3	*Grace*		Later to Blue Hill ME
J/100	50	*Tern*	2005	1st Maine Hospice Regatta
MJM 34z	11	*Grace*		Later to Eau Gallie FL
J/100	111	*Tern*	2006	1st DERW & Maine Ret Skip
MJM 34z Exp	33	*Glory*		Later to San Francisco
MJM 34z	36	*Grace*		Later to NE Harbor ME
J/100	132	*Tern*	2007	1st- DERW & Maine Ret. Skip
MJM 34z Exp	49	*Grace*		Later NE Harbor ME
MJM 34z	52	*Grace*		Later to Marblehead MA
MJM 34z	54	*Grateful*		Later to Jamestown RI
MJM 34z	61	*Grace*	2008	Later to Burnt Store FL
MJM 40z	6	*Grace*	2009	Later to Ft. Myers FL
MJM 34z	64	*Grace*	2010	Later to Vineyard Haven MA
MJM 36z	4	*MJM*	2011	Later to W Palm Beach FL
J/111	37	*Fleetwing*		Northeast Harbor & Newport
MJM 29z	36	*Zing*		Later to Marblehead MA
MJM 40z	21	*Zing*	2012	Later to Ft Myers FL
MJM 40z	25	*Zing*		Later to Charleston SC
MJM 40z	34	*Zing*	2013	Later to Vineyard Haven MA
MJM 40z	38	*Zing*	2014	Later to Naples FL
MJM 50z	1	*Zing*		Later to Nantucket MA
MJM 50z	4	*Zing*	2015	Later to Coral Gables FL
MJM 50z	12	*Zing*	2016	Later to Miami FL
MJM 50z	18	*Zing*	2017	Later to Rye NY
MJM 53z	1	*Breeze*	2018	Later to Sarasota FL
MJM 43z	7	*Breeze 2*	2019	City Marina Charleston
Soling 1M	549	*Gold Rush*		Cottage 5 - Charleston
DF95	24	Silver	2020	Quay Pond - Charleston
DF95	50	Gold		Quay Pond - Charleston
TOTALS	**81.**	**(56 Sail & 25 Power)**		

Author's Note

T hank you for reading this book. I always enjoy hearing from friends and sailors, many of whom are or have been J/Boat and MJM owners.

If you'd like to get in touch to say hello, or if you've found a typo or error, please feel free to contact me at any time at bobj@rjmail.us.

Motoring Back to Port After a Good Race

Photo by Dick Tillman^, Executive Director of the International J/24 Class Association during the 1983 J/24 World Championship in Malmo, Sweden.

CPSIA information can be obtained
at www.ICGtesting.com
Printed in the USA
LVHW050516030723
751386LV00009B/208

9 798822 9035